Design out Crime:
Creating Safe and Sustainable Communities

Frontispiece: Cherry Close, Caborn Road Tower Hamlets, London (1996):
good natural surveillance. Architects: Pollard Thomas and Edwards.

Design out Crime: Creating Safe and Sustainable Communities

Ian Colquhoun

AMSTERDAM • BOSTON • HEIDELBERG • LONDON • NEW YORK • OXFORD
PARIS • SAN DIEGO • SAN FRANCISCO • SINGAPORE • SYDNEY • TOKYO

Architectural Press is an imprint of Elsevier

ELSEVIER

Architectural
Press

Architectural Press
An imprint of Elsevier
Linacre House, Jordan Hill, Oxford OX2 8DP
200 Wheeler Road, Burlington, MA 01803

First published 2004

British Library Cataloguing in Publication Data
Colquhoun, Ian
    Design out crime: creating safe and sustainable communities
    1. Crime prevention and architectural design 2. Crime prevention and
    architectural design – case studies
    I. Title
    364.4'9

Library of Congress Cataloging-in-Publication Data
Colquhoun, Ian.
    Design out crime: creating safe and sustainable communities / Ian Colquhoun.
        p. cm.
    Includes bibliographical references and index.
    ISBN 0-7506-5492-9 (alk. paper)
    1. Crime in public housing – Great Britain. 2. Crime prevention and architectural
design – Great Britain. 3. Sustainable architecture – Great Britain. 4. Crime analysis –
Great Britain. 5. Crime prevention – Great Britain. 6. Crime – Environmental aspects –
Great Britain. I. Title.
HV6947.C53 2004
364.4'9–dc22

ISBN 0 7506 5492 9

For information on all Architectural Press publications visit our
website at: www.architecturalpress.com

Typeset by Keyword Typesetting Services Ltd
Printed and bound in Meppel, The Netherlands by Krips bv.

Contents

Foreword by Dr Tim Pascoe, Head of the Crime Prevention Research Unit, Building Research Establishment (BRE)   *xii*

List of Tables   *xiv*

Acknowledgements   *xv*

Introduction   *xviii*

Chapter 1: Housing and crime   **1**
    Nature of Crime   1
    Extent and Cost of Crime   2
        International Comparisons   2
        Crime Levels in Britain   3
        Regional Variations   4
        Household Variations   4
        Cost of Crime   4
        Crime Opportunity   5
        Displacement   6
    Fear of Crime   7
    Social/Economic Causes of Crime   8
        Decline of Inner Urban Areas   8
        Projected Changes in Society   11
    Housing Policy Background   13
        Social Exclusion   13
        Lack of Investment   15
        Housing Tenure   15
        Antisocial Behaviour and Neighbour Nuisance   16
    Youth and Crime   17
        Issues   17
        Engaging Young People   19
        Youthbuild   22

Contents

Rural Crime   24
Crime and Quality of Life   24
Design and Crime   26
    Aldgate Estate, Mansell Road, London   27
    Marquess Road Estate, Islington, London   27
    Byker Redevelopment, Newcastle upon Tyne 33

Chapter 2: Development of design principles   **37**
Introduction   37
Elizabeth Wood   38
Jane Jacobs   38
Oscar Newman   39
    Defensible Space   40
    Later Research   42
Patricia and Paul Brantingham   43
Alice Coleman   45
    Variable Design Features   45
    Design Principles   47
    DICE Projects   48
Situational Crime Prevention   51
    Rational and Routine Activity Theories   55
Crime Prevention Through Environmental
    Design – CPTED   55
    Definition of CPTED   55
    CPTED in an "Open Society"   56
    Sibeliusparken   57
Second Generation CPTED: Sustainable Development
    using CPTED Principles of Greg Saville and Gerry
    Cleveland   61
Christopher Alexander: A Pattern Language   64
    Pikku-Huopalahti, Helsinki   68
Bill Hillier: Space Syntax Theory   70

Chapter 3: Planning and design   **75**
Neighbourhood Planning and Housing Design   75
    The Brief   76
    Site Survey and Analysis   76
    Crime Pattern Analysis   77
    User Requirements   77
    Spatial Design   78
Density, Form and Tenure   94
    Density and Crime   98
    Child Density   110

Density and Culture   112
Housing for Elderly People   112
Roads and Footpaths   116
   Accessibility and Permeability   117
   Tracking   128
   Car Parking   129
   Poundbury   130
   Holly Street Regeneration   133
   Street Design, Woonerfs, Home Zones   139
   Stainer Street, Northmoor, Manchester   146
   The Methleys, Chapel Allerton, Leeds   148
   Old Royal Free Square, Islington, London   149
   Footpaths and Cycleways   152
Urban Villages, New Urbanism and Smart Growth   155
   Urban Villages   155
   Crown Street, Glasgow   155
   West Silvertown Urban Village, London   158
   New Urbanism and Smart Growth   158
   Crawford Square, Pittsburgh   162
   Middleton Hills, Madison, Wisconsin   165
Open Space   167
Children's Play   173
Landscaping   176
Schools   179
Local Shops and Facilities   183
Designing Out Vandalism and Graffiti   185
Street Lighting   186
   Benefits of Good Lighting   186
   Lighting requirements   186
   The Canadian experience   187
   Design Process   188
CCTV   189
Gating Alleys   192
The Alleygater's Guide   192
Dutch Experience in Haarlem   192

Chapter 4: Design guidance   **192**
Introduction   197
UK Government Guidance   198
   DOE Circular 5/94, "Planning Out Crime"   198
   Crime and Disorder Act 1998   198
   Planning Policy Guidance Notes (PPGs)   199
   Good Practice Guidance in Planning Out Crime   200

Contents

UK Police Guidance   202
   Secured by Design   202
   SBD Design Guidance   205
   West Yorkshire Survey of SBD Schemes   209
   The Royds Regeneration, Bradford   210
Dutch Police Labelling   212
   Principles   212
   Standards   214
   Success of Dutch Police Labelling   217
   De Paeral, Hoorn, The Netherlands   217
UK Local Authority Guidance   220
   Essex Design Guide, 2nd Edition   222
   Great Notley   227
   Nottingham City Council Design Guide:
     "Community Safety in Residential Areas"   227
Canada: Toronto Safer City Guidelines   230
Towards a European Standard   233
   Part 2: Urban Planning and Crime Reduction   234
   Part 3: Dwellings   235

Chapter 5: Creating safe and sustainable communities   **237**
Community and Sustainability   237
Balanced Communities   238
   Hulme, Manchester   242
   Selling Social Housing to Rebalance Communities   243
Density and Sustainability   247
   Sustainable Neighbourhoods   247
   Living Over Shops   247
   Sustainable Housing   248
   Urban Renewal, Copenhagen   249
   Egebjerggard, Copenhagen   249
   Bo01 Housing, Malmo, Sweden   253
Regeneration and Sustainability   255
   Neighbourhood Renewal in the UK   255
   Slade Green Regeneration, Bexley, London:
     Community Safety Action Zones (CASZs)   258
Participation   260
   Principles   260
   Stages of Participation   262
Participation in Practice   265
   Tudor Road Renewal, Belfast   265
   Regeneration in Turin and Milan   270
Gated Communities in the USA and Britain   279

Brightlands: The Gated Society   281
Gated Community: Cromer Street, London   284
Neighbourhood Management and Maintenance   291
Neighbourhood Management   291
Neighbourhood Wardens   293
Neighbourhood Watch   293
Conclusion: The Need for Joined-up Action   294

Appendix   **296**
CEN(2002) Committee for European Standardisation.
Prevention of Crime – Urban Planning and Design,
Part 2: Urban Design and Crime Reduction; Part 3:
Dwellings. CEN/TC325 (in progress)

Bibliography/References   **304**
Index   **316**

Foreword

Dr Tim Pascoe, Head of the Crime Research Unit, Building Research Establishment (BRE)

Crime, fear of crime and antisocial behaviour are major concerns for society today – but these are battles we can win and are winning. For example, the British Crime Survey[1] reports that since 1995 there has been a fall in crime at every survey. Indeed, they state that there has been a 22 per cent decrease over the last five years, following a period of crime expansion where crimes rose steadily between 1981 and 1991. This success in stopping and reversing the crime "climb" has been down to a number of themes including innovative policies such as the Crime and Disorder Act 1998, sustainability in housing, better and more policing and new positions such as neighbourhood wardens.

Included amongst these proactive initiatives has been a focus on and the development of crime prevention through environmental design (CPTED). Over the last few years I have had the pleasure of playing a small part in that development. I now lead the Crime Risk Management team at the Building Research Establishment. We are a team of researchers who have helped and continue to develop CPTED research and solutions. I am also the current chair of the Design Out Crime Association, the independent organisation representing leading UK CPTED professionals. As such I recognise that Designing Out Crime is still a developing area that bridges the gap between design and management of the urban environment. It is a relatively young "school" and in vital need of some standard references, and Ian Colquhoun's book ideally fills that gap.

Ian Colquhoun recognises that the public's concern about crime is highest when they are talking about their own neighbourhood and residential areas. His book therefore focuses on those areas. He approaches the subject as an architect and town planner with experience of the practice of housing design. He has also taught the subject in Schools of Architecture and written a number of earlier books on housing design.

---

[1] Considered by most to be the best measure of overall crime in England and Wales.

His book pulls upon a variety of opinions from different sources and brings together strands of thought, both historic and new. He then shows how these have been applied in numerous good practice examples that could be used anywhere.

This book is, therefore, primarily a practical guide, which should assist architects, planners and other designers. Its account of the broad principles of housing design will help people such as police crime prevention design advisers (architectural liaison officers) understand the complexities that have to be considered in the design process.

It can be used as learning manual for those new to CPTED and, equally, be dipped into by seasoned professionals looking for practical exemplars.

Finally and perhaps most significantly, Ian Colquhoun places the subject in its social and economic background, which is important to understand if developments built today are to have long-term sustainable futures.

List of Tables

1.1. Crime rates per 100,000 people (1998) from police records for selected "comparator" countries   3

1.2. Blackburn: Bank Top audit of crime and its perception   9

1.3. Crime problems in residential areas   16

1.4. What makes somewhere in the UK a good place in which to live   25

4.1. The Royds, Bradford: burglary statistics   211

5.1. Sherry Arnstein's ladder of participation   261

Acknowledgements

Writing this book has opened up a new world for me. My professional architectural and university teaching career has revolved largely around housing design and I was aware of the need to design to reduce the possibility of crime, but I knew little in depth. What has surprised me was to find a world of people specialising in the subject – police, architects, planners, criminologists, academics and others. There are communities of interest in many countries who come together through the international CPTED Association. I am indebted to DOCA – the UK Designing Out Crime Association – for helping me to liaise with these people.

The Dutch contacts have been particularly helpful. Paul van Soomeren provided information on the European Prestandard documents and a copy of his excellent research for a book on the subject, which regrettably he was never able to publish. He and Architectural Liaison Officer, Armando Jongejan, took me to look at Dutch Police Labelled housing in Hoorn. Inspector Theo Hesselman provided details of Police Labelling, of which he quite rightly speaks with such pride for its success in reducing crime in The Netherlands. Dr Massimo Bricocoli assisted with research in Italy and Dr Bo Gronlund in Denmark and Sweden. I was fortunate to attend conferences of E-DOCA (European Chapter of the International CPTED Association) at the Escola de Policia de Catalunya in Barcelona. Their hospitality, which was given entirely free, enabled me to participate.

Terry Cox, Camden Crime Prevention Design Advisor, and Dr Tim Pascoe, Head of the Crime Prevention Research Unit at the Building Research Establishment (BRE), both read and commented on the text during its preparation. I really appreciate the time they spent doing this. David Levitt of Levitt Bernstein Associates and Ben Castell of Llwellyn Davies freely gave information and plans (Ben is heading the study for new government guidance on the subject). Mary McKeown, who once worked with Alice Coleman, provided a substantial amount of information on Alice's work. I am also grateful to Gary Hughes of the Tudor Road Renewal Project in Belfast for his help. Others I wish to thank for providing information are David Taylor of Alan Baxter Associates, Caroline Davey of Salford University, Rachel Armitage of the Applied Criminology Group at Huddersfield University, Brian Spencer, AIA, for details of New Urbanism and Middleton Hills, Robert Stephens of the Toronto City Council, Canada, for his city's policies on CPTED, Barry Munday for information on Marquess Road and PRP's recent housing study in Europe. Les Webb of Webb Seeger Moorhouse showed me the Royds in

Bradford and David Crease and his former practice, Crease Strickland Parkins, helped me research their schemes and those of the former York University Design Unit. Information on housing in Japan is thanks to Professor Mineki Hattori, of Chiba University. Dr Amy Tseng provided much useful information on resident participation.

Everyone I met in the police went out of their way to be helpful, particularly a number of police architectural liaison officers (crime prevention design advisers): Steve Everson, Peter Woodhouse, Roger Kelly, Derek Harrison, Jim Brown, Martin Stokes, Steve Town, Bill Cass, Dave Orr, to name but a few; also Martin Millburn at the Home Office Crime Reduction College. Calvin Beckford's work on Gating Alleys and Heather Alston's thoughtful feedback on the Essex Design Guide in practice have made important contributions to the book.

The Architectural Liaison Officers as a body have a wide knowledge and understanding of planning and design in the built environment, as well as of crime prevention. This is a remarkable resource that must be used to the full if we are to tackle the huge crime problem and fear of crime that currently faces society. I must apologise to individual officers whose contributions could not be included due to lack of space.

Authors need support from their publishers and I must thank Neil Warnock-Smith, Alison Yates and Liz Whiting and their colleagues at the Architectural Press for all their patience and continual encouragement.

I am particularly grateful to Dr Tim Pascoe for writing his thoughtful foreword, which provides an excellent starting point for the book. Tim has an outstanding national and international reputation for his work on the subject. His own books and publications, and those of his colleagues at BRE, have helped develop policy and principles of crime reduction through environmental design. I have been extremely fortunate to have his support.

My thanks go to Liz Cagney who kindly helped with typing and sorting out the bibliography and captions for illustrations; also to Martha Maguire who gave much encouragement at the beginning of the research, and to Environmental Assistance in Immingham, North-East Lincolnshire, with whom I now work.

Finally, the book would not have happened without the support of my wife, Christine, who, throughout the research and writing, helped with so many aspects of the work – photography filings, etc. – and all the normal things of life which I had little time to do.

I am grateful to the BRE and DOCA for endorsing the book, but it is an independent piece of work and they hold no responsibility for the views and opinions expressed therein.

Professor Ian Colquhoun
August 2003

Introduction

"We need stronger local communities and an improved quality of life. Streets where parents feel safe to let their children walk to school. Where people want to use the parks. Where graffiti, vandalism, litter and dereliction is not tolerated. Where the environment in which we live fosters rather than alienates a sense of local community and mutual responsibility." (Tony Blair, UK Prime Minister, Croydon, 2001)

This book is about the design of communities and housing in which people can enjoy a good quality of life, free from crime and fear of crime. Its aim is to offer a practical overview of the issues and guidelines that can be used by planners, architects and others in their everyday work. The book reflects a common recognition that crime, vandalism and antisocial behaviour are issues of high public concern. Dirty and dangerous places encourage fear, which undermines public confidence in an area and discourages investment, both individual and corporate. Crime and fear of crime are key driving forces that determine the choice of where people wish to live and work and to send their children to school. They affect everyday activities such as going out for a walk after dark. Burglary, theft of and from cars, drug trafficking, nuisance generation and general antisocial behaviour are all perceived as the downside of urban living. Women, children and older people, despite being least at risk, often feel inhibited from walking alone to school or to the shops. Many women are afraid to go outside the home after dark and therefore have limited freedom of movement. These problems have great impact on the social, economic and physical viability of urban areas throughout the world, as reflected by the interests of the membership of the International CPTED Association (ICA).

Crime costs the UK economy up to £50 billion per year (Foresight Crime Prevention Panel, 2002, p. 3). In the USA the figure is $450 billion. In Canada it is 46 billion Canadian dollars and in Australia 18 billion dollars a year, which represents more than 4 per cent of the gross domestic product

(Schneider and Kitchen, 2002, p. 20). Criminal offenders in residential areas range from the opportunist to the career criminal, but they are more likely to be young people between the ages of 13 and 24. The driving forces behind crime are numerous and include social exclusion, poverty, drug abuse, psychological problems, family breakdown, economic trends, and wickedness and greed. They also include poorly designed housing and environment.

Good design can help tackle these issues and add value both commercially and in terms of user enjoyment of the housing (see Frontispiece). Understanding these issues is important for planners, architects, builders and other people who create and manage housing, so that they realise the social, economic and cultural context within which they are working. This book makes the case that, through integrating simple crime prevention principles into the design process, it is possible, almost without notice, to make residential environments much safer. This must be an integral and inherent part of the process and not an add-on feature at the end. It may involve trade-off between different and sometimes opposing design demands. Through dealing with crime in the context of neighbourhood planning and housing design as a whole, it is hoped that this book will provide the essential information for these kinds of decisions to be constructively made.

Design Out Crime is aimed at planners, architects and developers who, at times, have difficulty with the issues surrounding crime prevention. There is a genuine fear of creating a "fortress environment" (Fig. 1.1). There is also a belief amongst architects that "good design", whatever this may mean, is all that is needed. Some developers worry that any mention of crime will scare away the purchaser and affect their investment. Yet crime is now such an important issue in public opinion that it is one of the key issues that a purchaser considers when buying a house. Therefore, if housing is to meet people's needs, the design must address these essential issues – and not merely be subject to those concerns considered important by designers and developers.

It is also aimed at others involved in the creation of housing:

- The police (as crime advisers). It is hoped that they will gain much from this book and see their important role within the broad context of housing design.
- People responsible for briefing, management and maintenance of housing in local authorities and housing associations.
- Communities, particularly those participating in regeneration.
- Community Safety Partnerships now set up in the area of every local authority in the UK and similar organisations in other countries that link the police with planners, architects and local communities.

The book is written from the perspective of an architect and town planner with experience of housing design and urban regeneration. It is not intended to be an academic study of crime prevention and environmental psychology but rather a practical guide for planning and design purposes. It is hoped that the coverage of social and economic issues is sufficient for making planning and design decisions within an informed background. Throughout the book are plans and photographs of projects from Britain, the USA, The Netherlands, and Scandinavia, and other countries that illustrate the themes under consideration. It can be seen that, while housing design has a common language, designs solutions must reflect local characteristics. This is as true for reducing the possibility of crime as it is for any other aspect of housing design.

How a society houses its people is a mark of its civilisation. The legacy of one generation is passed on to others to enjoy or contend with. The clear lesson from the past in so many countries is to create not merely housing, but communities that are sustainable. This means designing a living environment in which people feel they belong, in which issues of crime and fear of crime are dealt with in harmony with all the other requirements of a civilised life. This requires "joined-up" thinking, which is a theme addressed throughout the book.

It has proved very difficult to collect crime data on individual schemes that also illustrate the best practice in design terms, but reference has been made where this is available.

The book is divided into 5 chapters.

Chapter 1 gives an overview of the causes of crime in residential areas. It considers the nature, extent and cost of crime and fear of crime in the community. It outlines the common causes including social/economic deprivation and exclusion, the effect of poor environment, youth crime and rural crime. It relates crime to the effects of poor design, which has a significant bearing on quality of life.

Chapter 2 looks at the origins of crime prevention in residential areas through the design of the built environment. This includes the theories of Jane Jacobs, Oscar Newman, Alice Coleman and others. It refers to the design principles set out in Christopher Alexander's book *A Pattern Language: Towns, Buildings, Construction* (1977). This is a reminder of a timeless approach to good design – it was reflected in the Dutch Police Labelling scheme. The chapter concludes with the development of CPTED (Crime Prevention Through Environmental Design) principles and Space Syntax theory.

Chapter 3 covers the process of neighbourhood and housing design. It emphasises the importance of a good brief, which includes the preparation of a Crime Pattern Analysis. There is a section on spatial design – streets, squares, footpaths, etc. – with the intention of raising awareness of the broad range of design principles that have to be considered. The design of residential roads and footpaths including Home Zones is written with the view that streets should come under the "stewardship" of the residents they serve as an effective way of reducing crime in the environment. It is important to understand the relationship between density, crime and design. The provision of open spaces and children's play areas are important elements of the built environment but, unless carefully located and designed, can be misused and become a focus for antisocial behaviour. The role of good street lighting, closing of alleyways and installing CCTV in reducing crime is also considered.

Chapter 4 considers current design guidance including current UK government and local government advice and Secured by Design standards. It considers the Dutch Police Labelling Standards, and the Prestandards of the European Union. However, it should be understood that guides must be merely tools for good practice and not dictates. Neighbourhood planning and design must be site specific, and this means that flexible, localised, preventative design considerations will always be preferable to ready-made solutions.

Chapter 5 discusses the concept that creating communities is the most effective means of designing out crime. Design alone will not solve the problems. People should participate in the design, management and maintenance of their communities. Now, more than ever before, we need to think of neighbourhood and housing design in holistic terms that includes social, economic and cultural considerations as well as physical.

Successful housing renewal at Tent City, Boston, USA has created a safe living environment.

CHAPTER 1

Housing and crime

Nature of crime

Crime in housing takes on many forms: vandalism, i.e., the wilful destruction of objects and materials; burglary, i.e., theft carried out by breaking and entering into property; thefts of and from cars; racial crime; drug misuse; nuisance and antisocial behaviour against people in public and semi-public areas; domestic violence; sexual violence (particularly indecent assault and rape) in public and semi-public spaces. Patterns of crime in many housing areas show that the problems are frequently caused by a small number of persistent offenders who live nearby. In many instances, people have given up all hope that anything can be done. They do not even report crimes, such is their lack of confidence in a successful outcome.

It is important to understand the following principles:

- There is a dynamic interplay between the physical environment and the behaviour of offenders.
- The majority of offenders are basically ordinary people who think rationally and make conscious choices – even when they are committing an offence.
- Crime takes on many forms: different crimes involve different types of offenders, motives and opportunity structures.
- There is no single theory that explains the nature of crime. It is very varied and usually opportunistic.

Figure 1.1 "Fortress environment". (Reproduced by courtesy of City of Haarlem Urban Safety Department.)

- There is a strong relationship between crime, social and economic deprivation and the state of the local environment. Places that are dirty, poorly maintained and strewn with litter affect the physical health of communities.
- Most offenders are not specialists and they will as readily steal from a car as burgle a house.
- Most offenders (discounting white-collar crime) live in poor areas and commit crime near their homes.
- Most crimes in residential areas are undertaken within a mile of the offender's home.

Extent and cost of crime

International comparisons

Comparisons between countries are most alarming. England and Wales top the international table for domestic burglary. Both countries have a higher burglary rate than the USA and over four times the rate of Germany (Table 1.1).

Table 1.1. Crime rates per 100,000 people, 1998, from police records for selected "comparator" countries

Country	Total number of crimes	Domestic burglary	Theft of a motor vehicle
England and Wales	8545	902	745
Germany	7682	198	193
France	6085	330	710
USA	4617	862	459
Canada	8094	728	547
Australia	6979	1580	703
Japan	1612	188	559

Schneider and Kitchen, p. 57. (Developed from Barclay G.C., and Taverns, C. (2000), and International Comparisons of Criminal Justice Statistics (1998), London, Tables 1, 1.1, 1.3–1.5.)

Of particular notice is the low level of domestic crime in Japan which is considered in Chapter 3 (p. 112).

Crime levels in Britain

The magnitude of the current crime problem can be seen by looking at the 2001/02 statistics for England and Wales in the British Crime Survey (BCS). The survey refers to two types of figure – crimes reported to the police and estimates, based on interviews, that include crimes not actually reported. Based on interviews taking place in 2001/02, crimes against adults living in private households were just over 13 million. This represents a decrease of 2 per cent compared with the estimate for 2000 and a fall of 14 per cent between 1999 and 2001/02. However, these figures are still high. The total number of crimes recorded by the police in 2001/02 was 5,527,082, an increase of 7 per cent compared to 2000/01. Of the crimes recorded by the police, 16 per cent related to burglary, 18 per cent to theft of or from vehicles, 2 per cent to drug offences, 19 per cent to other property offences, 15 per cent to violent crime, and 30 per cent to other thefts and offences (Simmons et al., 2002, pp. 5–7).

The BCS estimates from its 2001/02 interviews indicate that there were 1,119,000 offences of arson and criminal damage (vandalism) in England and Wales, not including offences against vehicles. In terms of recorded crime, there was an 11 per cent rise in total criminal damage offences from 2000/01 to 2001/02. Excluding arson, 42 per cent (422,000) were to a vehicle and 27 per cent were to a dwelling (271,000). Many criminal damage offences were relatively minor. The number of arson offences recorded by the police rose by 14 per cent in the same period to 60,472 offences. Levels have risen by over 70 per cent since the mid-1990s (Simmons et al., 2002, p. 37).

Regional variations

Domestic burglary rates vary widely from region to region and within each region. In 2001/02 the highest was in the North-East region (454 per 10,000 population), Yorkshire and Humberside (364), the North-West (310) and London (308). All of these were around double those of Wales (159) and the South-East (149), which were the lowest (Simmons, 2002, p. 35). Generally speaking, the highest rates of burglary are in metropolitan areas with the lowest in the commuter belt. The most commonly stolen items were cash, jewellery, CDs, tapes, videos and video recorders.

Household variations

The British Crime Survey has consistently shown that the risk of burglary varies considerably across households with different characteristics and situated in different localities. The national average for households perceiving they are at risk of burglary from interviews in 2001/02 was 3.5 per cent. The percentage increased with type of accommodation: flats/maisonettes and council estate housing in general, 4.7 per cent; private renters, 5.7 per cent; houses with a high level of physical disorder, 6.8 per cent; head of household within the age 16–24, 9 per cent; and single parent, 9.3 per cent (Simmons et al., 2002, pp. 32–33).

Cost of crime

Estimates place the cost of each domestic burglary in Britain at between £1,411 and £1,999 without consequential costs such as police, courts, probation, etc. If this kind of figure were applied to the number of domestic burglaries the total cost is in the order of £12 billion per year (Knights et al., 2002, p. 7). These costs are critical. They demonstrate beyond all doubt the significance of the impact of crime in housing and the benefits that could come from its prevention through design. The costs of designing to Secured by Design standards could be minimal in comparison (see p. 209). It is therefore important for everyone involved in the planning, design, management and maintenance of housing, especially at policy decision level, to understand this principle.

Crime opportunity

Most crimes are committed because the offender can see the opportunity. This can be one or a combination of opportunities, such as easy access, places to hide, an absence of a clear definition between public and private space, poor lighting and landscape planting that can conceal someone's presence. The more that offenders feel unsafe and vulnerable, the less they are likely to commit an offence. There are three basic criminological theories relating to crime opportunity:

1. **Rational choice** that assumes that potential offenders will undertake their own risk assessment before deciding to commit a crime. They will consider the chances of being seen, ease of entry and the chances of escape without detection.
2. **Routine activities theory** that assumes that for an offence to take place there needs to be three factors present: a motivated offender, a suitable target or victim and a lack of capable guardians. To prevent a crime it is necessary to alter the influence of one of these factors. For example, an offender can be demotivated by increasing the level of surveillance or by making access more difficult. A target can also be made less attractive by increasing security or removing escape routes. Creating a sense of neighbourliness, blending socio-economic groups and creating a lively street layout can be a deterrent.
3. **The defensible space theory** applies to the different levels of acceptance that exist in order for people to be in different kinds of space. Offenders normally have no reason for being in private or semi-private spaces, so by distinguishing the spaces between public and private it is possible to exert a measure of social control in order to reduce the potential for crime and antisocial behaviour (CEN (2002), Part 3: Dwellings, p. 5).

In their paper *Opportunity Makes the Thief* (1998), Marcus Felson and Ronald V. Clarke set out ten principles of crime opportunity:

- Opportunities play a role in causing all crime – design and management play an important role in generating crime and preventing it.
- Crime opportunities are highly specific – theft of cars for joy-riding has an entirely different pattern of opportunity than theft of cars for their parts.
- Crime opportunities are concentrated in time and space – dramatic differences are found from one address to another within a high crime area. Crime shifts greatly by hour of day and day of week, reflecting the opportunities to carry it out.
- Crime opportunities depend upon everyday movements of activity. Offenders and their targets shift according to the trips to work, school, leisure activity,

etc. Burglaries frequently occur in the afternoons when residents are at work or school.

- One crime produces opportunity for another – a successful break-in may encourage the offender to return at a later date.
- Some products offer more tempting crime opportunities – these opportunities reflect particularly the value, inertia, visibility of, and access to potential crime targets.
- Social and technological changes produce new crime opportunities – products that are highly marketable, e.g., laptops, are prime targets.
- Crime can be prevented by reducing opportunities – the opportunity-reducing methods of situational crime prevention fit systematic patterns and rules which cut across every walk of life. Prevention methods must be tailored to each situation.
- Reducing crime does not usually displace crime but each effort to reduce crime can accomplish some real gain. Even crime that is displaced can be directed away from the worst targets, times or places.
- Focused opportunity reduction can produce wider declines in crime. Prevention measures in one location can lead to a "diffusion of benefits" to nearby times and places because offenders seem to overestimate the reach of the measures. Moreover, there is good reason to believe that reductions in crime opportunity can drive down larger crime rates for community and society.

Displacement

There is a widely held view that a crime prevented in one location will simply move to another area or be reflected in another form of crime, e.g., a move from burglary to street crime/antisocial behaviour (Fig. 1.2). However, there has been a large body of research into displacement (Barr and Pease, 1990; Hesseling, 1994; Clarke, 1997; Chenery, Holt and Pease, 2000; Hill and Pease, 2001), which in overall terms is very positive. In 1994, in research for the Ministry of Justice in The Netherlands, Professor Rene B.P. Hesseling categorically proved that displacement is not always the serious issue people imagined it to be. He systematically reviewed 55 published articles on crime prevention measures in which researchers specifically looked for evidence of displacement. 20 of these were British studies and 16 were from the USA. 22 of these studies found no displacement, and 6 of these crime prevention measures had produced beneficial measures in adjacent areas. 33 studies found some form of displacement, mostly quite limited, and no study found complete displacement of crime. The summary states "displacement is a possible, but not inevitable consequence of crime prevention. Further, if displacement

Displacement?

Figure 1.2 "Displacement". (Reproduced by courtesy of City of Haarlem Urban Safety Department.)

does occur, it will be limited in size and scope." (Town, 2001; Schneider and Kitchen, 2002, pp. 113–114.)

Fear of crime

Fear of crime is a very real and powerful force that can shape people's lives. The British Crime Survey 2001/02 claimed that people's perceptions of crime are associated with actual levels of risk. The survey found that there was a notable increase in the proportion of people believing that crime had risen a lot in the first quarter of 2002, rising to 35 per cent from 27 per cent in the final three months of 2001 (Simmons et al., 2002, p. 79). Women, the elderly and disabled people are more likely to fear crime. They are frightened for their personal safety and frightened of street violence. In the case of women, there is also the possibility of sexual assault. Young men have a sense of fear mostly below the average, even though they are at a much higher risk of being a victim of a violent incident. Elderly people, particularly those aged 60 or over, are frequently concerned about walking alone in their area after dark, even though levels of risk for elderly households tend to be lower than average, especially with respect to personal crime. Ethnic minorities living in low income areas particularly perceive high levels of disorder (British Crime Survey 2001/02, Table 9.12).

People living in areas where the risk of victimisation is high are more likely to consider that they would be victimised. Residents in inner-city areas or council estates often feel very vulnerable. Respondents living in areas with high levels of physical disorder are much more likely to believe they would be victimised. It is a serious matter affecting the quality of their lives. Other groups who are more likely to believe that they would be victimised are those with low household incomes, those living in social rented accommodation and those living in neighbourhoods where people "go their own way" (low neighbourhood cohesion). Results from the British Crime Survey (2001/02) indicate that private renters, along with owner-occupiers, had lower perceptions of risk than social renters (Simmons et al., 2002, p. 82).

The extent of the problem is illustrated by an audit undertaken in 2000 to assess levels of crime and its perception in the Bank Top area of Blackburn (Fig. 1.3) (see p. 202). The results are shown in Table 1.2.

Common places that people avoid during the day, according to a Crime Audit undertaken by Bradford Metropolitan District Council in 2000, are quiet/secluded streets, subways, parks and woods. After dark, people avoid poorly lit areas, secluded/quiet streets, parks and woods; in addition, town and city centres, where young people enjoy the public houses, clubs and discos, can be frightening places for others, particularly middle-aged and elderly people (Schneider and Kitchen, 2002, p. 18).

Fear of crime can be heightened in people's minds by adverse media coverage in the newspapers, radio and TV. There is, therefore, a need for the media to accept responsibility for giving a balanced viewpoint.

Social/economic causes of crime

Decline of inner urban areas

The past prosperity of inner urban areas in most Western industrial cities was based on centralised structures, mass production, stable work relationships and strong state intervention in the economy. Globalisation and monetary

Figure 1.3 Bank Top Terraces: Blackburn.

Table 1.2. Blackburn: Bank Top audit of crime and its perception

■ 35% of residents reported not feeling safe where they lived in the last year.
■ Only 17% feel safe walking alone in the area after dark, with 14% saying they would never go out alone after dark.
■ 52% were dissatisfied with the way the area is policed, but the same proportion feel that the police understand the problems of the area.
■ The area's main problems were judged as (in order): litter and rubbish; young people hanging around in groups; drugs; speeding cars; personal safety after dark.

Source: Levitt Bernstein Architects and Llewellyn Davies.

policies of recent decades brought about the decentralisation of industrial production, the differentiation of products aiming at profitable market niches, high manpower turnover and lower state influence on the economy. This has resulted in the dispersal of business and commerce to more attractive out-of-town locations close to the intersections of motorways and main roads, and to countries overseas where labour costs are lower, leaving vast areas of vacant industrial land in the inner cities.

The overriding consequences of this are as follows:

- **Outward migration** – particularly among the younger and more skilled, who migrate in search of work elsewhere, leaving a largely unskilled workforce in the inner urban areas. They seek not only a suburban lifestyle, but also new out-of-town forms of employment, shopping and entertainment. Traders and small businesses also move out to where they can secure a greater turnover and avoid theft and vandalism to their properties. This has been matched with the development of segregated single land uses communities, tied together by a public realm seemingly more orientated to the car than to the person. New communities are less dense than the cities and each is separated from the other by more space. The local beat policeman has disappeared and patrolling communities in police cars is the norm. Furthermore, police forces have gained responsibility for larger geographical areas, and solving community problems has become less apparent.

  Added to this in Britain is migration from the peripheral and overspill public sector housing estates. Huge numbers of houses and flats have become boarded up or semi-derelict as no one wishes to accept the stigma of living in such a neighbourhood, far removed from the urban centre, with expensive public transport costs to work. Boarded-up properties create fear of crime and a consequential downward spiral of estates.

  In the USA, rising crime rates are a major cause of the depopulation of large cities, especially from the central cores, by the more affluent and families with children. Americans are so sensitive to the problems that "each additional crime is associated with a one-person decline in city residents" (Schneider and Kitchen, 2002, p. 18).

- **Concentrated poverty** in the inner urban areas arising primarily from an absence of job opportunities. Added to this in many cities is the concentration of immigrant workers and ethnic minorities who find it even more difficult to gain long-term employment.

- **Declining services** – fewer buses following privatisation of public transport; schools and clinics have closed down or have been amalgamated with others at a distance from the community; parks and open spaces have deteriorated; local shops have gone out of business. Housing has decayed, as both public and private landlords could no longer afford adequate maintenance, particularly of the environment. All of this has discouraged investment.

- **Increased crime rates**. People who remained became bitter and frustrated and some resorted to crime, vandalism, drug misuse and antisocial behaviour. Others took on a fortress mentality and withdrew behind their front doors.
- The outward migration resulted in a **lower tax base** for city and local authorities already struggling to meet the need for increased social services, policing, health care and housing repair.

Projected changes in society

Together these paint the picture of a spiral of decline. On top of this, the UK government's think-tank, "Foresight" identified a number of other drivers that are likely to have a growing prominence in Britain (and other countries) towards 2020. They are:

- demographics
- Individuality and independence
- 24-hour culture/information communication technology usage
- Globalisation
- Decline of civic pride

(Foresight, 2002)

Demographics

The last few decades have witnessed a rapid expansion in the proportion of elderly people in British society, particularly those living to over 75 years of age. This increase is expected to continue in the years to come, and by 2020 some 40 per cent of the population in the UK is expected to be over 50 years of age. In the USA, this has led to the development of huge retirement villages of low density housing. These have not taken off in Britain to the same extent but small schemes of gated housing and sheltered housing for sale and rent are popular, particularly with people who have a fear of crime. The majority of elderly people, however, prefer to remain in their family homes for as long as possible, which has implications for their long-term care.

At the same time there are rapid changes in youth culture resulting in a greater disparity in attitudes between young and old. The National Population projections from the Government's Actuary Department indicate that the number of young men between the ages of 15 and 20 who are likely to commit crime will rise during the next decade (Foresight, 2002).

These rapid demographic changes are best illustrated by experience in the USA where only one in ten households is a standard family type with mother, father and children under 18. The majority of couples are having fewer or no children at all. Single people constitute a quarter of households, and single parent families another 12 per cent. New groupings of people have appeared: young adults who would previously have lived at home for a longer period now prefer to share housing with other young people. This makes for new kinds of community (Colquhoun, 1995, p. 33).

Individuality and independence

In the new society traditional family forms will no longer be the foundation of community. Crime could increase if social values become eroded. Traditional communities may be replaced by ones that come together around shared beliefs/interests, based on social and economic ideals. "Gated estates" may become the physical symbol of this social change, and such groups may reinforce rather than challenge antisocial views.

24-hour culture

This is already with us. 24-hour supermarkets claim that their busiest hour is between 2.00 and 3.00 am. This culture will lead to different work and leisure patterns. The current regulation of the day, when and how people live and work, may disappear as a result of a mixture of electronic networks and globalisation.

Globalisation

The global reliance upon interconnected computer systems will increase. Consumerism, rather than communitarianism, is expected to be the predominant social philosophy. Already, crimes on the internet, drug dealing and smuggling show the power of global crime and the difficulties it poses for local level law enforcement. The result is that highly localised crime may be complemented/replaced by something more global.

Decline of civic pride

Added to these problems is a general decline in the level of civic pride. Suburbanisation, two-career families, TV, and other forms of electronic entertainment have led to a steady replacement of the old "civic" generation by their less involved children and grandchildren. This decline in traditional civic pride needs addressing with a new kind of civic awareness. Schools have become aware of this and courses in "Citizenship" are now general practice.

Housing policy background

Tackling crime and fear of crime has to be seen in the broader picture of housing policy. In the case of the UK, the housing factors that need understanding are:

- Social exclusion.
- The lack of investment in housing and community development.
- Change in housing tenure
- Neighbourhood nuisance.

Social exclusion

Economic decline over the last 20 to 30 years has resulted in many poor neighbourhoods witnessing their basic quality of life become increasingly detached from the rest of society. There is a polarisation of social and economic deprivation in urban areas where people are unemployed or low-paid. In some areas there are three generations of people who have no experience of work and three generations of single parent families. People living just streets apart have become separated by a gulf of prosperity, opportunity and attitude. In the UK these are places where more than two in five people rely on means-tested benefits, where three-quarters of young people fail to get five good GCSEs, and where houses are empty or hard to fill. They exist right across the country, north and south, rural and urban. They may be cut off on the edge of cities, or close to city centres and wealthy suburbs. They may be high-rise or low-rise council estates (Fig. 1.4), or streets of private rented or even owner-occupied homes. People are stuck in a spiral of decline. At the same time, there has been family breakdown, a decline in the popularity of social housing and ever-greater concentration of vulnerable people in poor neighbourhoods. As people move out, high turnover and empty homes create more opportunities for crime, vandalism and drug dealing.

In the past, government policies were insufficient to tackle the extent of the problems. Too much reliance was put on short-term regeneration initiatives in a handful of areas and too little was done about the failure of mainstream public services in many neighbourhoods. There was too little attention given to the problems of unemployment, crime, and poor education and health services. The Government failed to harness the knowledge and energy of local people, or empower them to develop their own solutions. There was a lack of leadership, and a failure to spread what works and encourage innovation. UK Government programmes such as New Deal for Communities and Neigbourhood Renewal, the introduction of Local Strategic Partnerships and other measures based on a "joined-up" approach are tackling these issues.

Figure 1.4 1970s deck access housing in Tower Hamlets, London.

In the USA the regeneration of inner-city residential neighbourhoods has shown that there is a viable alternative to living in suburbia, and there have been significant achievements in neighbourhood renewal. More could have been done if housing were higher on the political agenda. However, the overriding problem in American inner cities is the lack of work.

Unemployment among black people is higher than white people but, according to Professor John Julius of Chicago University, "The trauma of persistent urban poverty is not automatically linked to racial issues . . . nothing will go right for an inner city, whether black or white, until the disease of joblessness is overcome. A job, at whatever level, links your family to the rest of society in a way that nothing else can" (Barker, 1993, p. 25). The alternative in so many American cities is involvement in youth gangs and drug dealing. The American ideology of work is not absent but there is simply no work available in inner-city areas.

Lack of investment

In 2000 and 2001, Britain built just 162,000 new homes, which is the lowest level of activity since 1927, except for the war years. This compares with over a million in Japan for twice the size of population. The Government grant of £2.1 billion to the Housing Corporation to help build new homes in 2002–3 remains lower as a proportion of national income than in almost every other industrialised nation. A consequence of this is a squeeze on design standards, and housing associations frequently seek to build new housing on cheaper land in less popular areas in which to live. They are required to adopt "Secured by Design" standards, but providing fencing and locks alone, without creating an image of high quality, is a false economy.

At the same time, housing regeneration is not keeping up with need. Some 750,000 homes are unoccupied, but these are not in locations where people want to live, i.e., predominantly in the South-East of England. Many areas of pre-1919 houses have become abandoned, producing areas of ghost housing as people move away from consequential high levels of crime and antisocial behaviour. Whilst there are government programmes to tackle these issues, the level of investment is inadequate (Summerskill, 2001, p. 1).

Housing tenure

For most of the 20th century there was a high demand in the UK for social rented housing and local authorities were central to its provision. From the early 1980s the right-to-buy legislation allowed people to purchase their council homes. The better housing in the more desirable estates sold most easily, leaving councils with the remaining, poorer stock. Housing associations have now taken over the role of building social housing and many are, through stock transfer, taking over the management and maintenance of council housing. The demand for council housing has significantly declined in recent years and there is a surplus of housing resulting in many void properties with accompanying problems of crime and vandalism.

Over 70 per cent of the population now lives in owner-occupied housing but the price of purchasing an average home has exceeded £100,000. This may be far beyond reach of the average wage earners on £23,600 a year. On the other hand, for people whose incomes have risen in real terms there is a rise in expectations and a demand for greater choice. There is also a resurgence of the private rented market. To many former supporters of social housing it would be inconceivable for people to prefer to pay higher rents in the private sector but such is the demise of social housing, its stigma and its image. This also works to concentrate the more deprived households in social housing.

There is also a change in the housing demands of single people on low incomes. Previously they would be content with social housing where they would live for most of their lives. Now social housing is more and more considered to be a short-term choice. Single people want to live closer to urban centres where they are less reliant upon public transport. They also prefer smaller, more intimate developments in mixed-use areas.

Antisocial behaviour and neighbourhood nuisance

Antisocial behaviour is a huge issue and can include a whole range of problems. The British Crime Survey for 2001/2002 reported percentages of adults who said it was a significant problem in their area (Table 1.3).

Fear is frequently generated by neighbour nuisance, which can come from a range of annoying actions such as playing music too loudly, shouting and banging frequently, harassment (perhaps because of a person's race or sex), or threats of violence, verbal abuse and stalking. The police have powers to deal with this under the Protection from Harassment Act 1997 and can issue antisocial behaviour orders in certain cases. Some local authorities have established mediation services, which are funded from a variety of sources including the local authorities themselves, the Home Office and the National

Table 1.3. Crime problems in residential areas

Vandalism, graffiti and other deliberate damage to property	34%
Teenagers hanging around on streets	32%
Rubbish or litter lying around	32%
People using or dealing drugs	31%
People being drunk or rowdy in public places	22%
Noisy neighbours or loud parties	10%
People being attacked/harassed because of their race or colour	9%

Home Office Crime Reduction College, 2003, p. 5.

Lottery. They employ trained mediators to act as an impartial third party in assisting neighbours resolve their conflicts.

Youth and crime

Issues

Crime and antisocial behaviour by young people features high in people's perception of fear of crime and it is inevitable that young people in deprived areas get labelled as troublemakers. Youth has been targeted by adults as a social problem for at least 100 years, but enough time and money has never been devoted to hearing the other side of the story and acting upon what really needs to be addressed. In many locations the situation has reached such a level that the whole approach to the design of the built environment is dominated by the issue of youth, the consequence of which is that the quality of life of the majority is determined by the actions of a small number of disengaged young people.

The problem for many young people is that their antisocial action is part of the process of growing up. They are often not aware of the significance of what they are doing when engaged in vandalism and antisocial behaviour – they are merely "having a laugh". During this period of their lives, their values are different to the rest of society, which must be recognised and not rejected out-of-hand. The American crime prevention expert, Al Zelinka, summed up the importance of the situation when he wrote:

> "The bottom line to long-term public safety must be focused on youth. We know that youth who are not provided with adequate nurturing, support and structure, run greater risks of becoming involved in the criminal justice system. We know that the physical structure of communities contributes to the challenges facing youth ... but we know that youth, when provided with opportunities to engage in productive activities, will do so. When they aren't, they are more vulnerable to take another route ... if we do not give youth an alternative to destructive, or counter-productive behaviour, who has failed whom?" (Zelinka, 2002b)

The problem is that, from an early age, young people hang about outside shops, on street corners, in car parks, and so on, drinking large amounts of cheap alcohol. This age group cannot frequent the pubs, and youth clubs are often only open on specific nights for specific groups. Other options such as the cinema are too expensive. Drinking alcohol is the only exciting option, and many choose it. The result is vandalism in the local environment and displays of antisocial behaviour.

Young people frequently commit crime from as early as 10–12 years old. By the age of 12 or 13 the people concerned have disengaged from school and have participated with their peers in street drinking, drug use and petty crime. They particularly lose any interest they might have had in the environment in which they live.

The major causes of youth crime are frequently put to:

- Low income and poor housing
- Living in deteriorating inner city areas
- A high degree of impulsiveness and hyperactivity
- Low intelligence and low school attainment
- Poor parental supervision and harsh erratic discipline
- Parental conflict and broken families

A survey carried out by the Joseph Rowntree Foundation, published in April 2002, based on a sample of 14,000 pupils, revealed some new and startling facts about youth crime in the UK:

- Almost half Britain's secondary school children admitted breaking the law at some time.
- A third of 14–15 year olds admitted committing criminal damage and a quarter admitted shoplifting in the past year.
- One in five 15–16-year-old boys admitted attacking someone intending serious harm.
- One in 10 boys aged 11 and 12 said they had carried a knife or other weapon in the past year and 8 per cent said they had attacked someone intending serious harm.
- One in 10 boys aged 15 and 16 said they had broken into a building to steal during the previous year including 4 per cent who said they had done so three or more times.
- A quarter of 13 to 14 year olds indulged in binge drinking, consuming five or more alcoholic drinks in one session.
- Also identified were serious drug problems.

This situation is serious and demands attention. Problems existed amongst the young people surveyed, despite their saying they were generally well supervised and supported by parents who had positive expectations about behaviour. A large majority of those interviewed agreed that there were clear rules at home and that their parents would think it wrong of them to steal, or use illegal drugs. Most schools enforced their rules against lateness, absenteeism and bullying.

The survey identified high risk factors linking criminal behaviour and drug and alcohol misuse to family, school and community characteristics. Protective factors included strong bonds with families, friends and teachers, opportunities for involvement and praise for positive behaviour. Most young people said they liked their neighbourhood, but a fifth felt no attachment and reported significant levels of crime, drug dealing and other antisocial behaviour. A fifth said they felt unsafe going out after dark – girls more than boys.

Despite these statistics, the survey found that most young people were law-abiding most of the time: "to brand young people in general as a problem could run counter to the evidence and make it harder to respond effectively to the minority whose behaviour does cause problems. Indeed to do this would mean that society as a whole has failed to set the scene in which young people can develop in harmony with it" (Beinhart et al., 2002; Carvel, 2002, pp. 1 and 15).

Engaging young people

Clearly, what is needed are ways of getting young people into stimulating and positive activities that will bring about change. They need to be given a chance to become the builders of their own future. Young people are becoming adults at a much earlier age than before and they have heightened levels of awareness, enthusiasm and energy. They have valuable ideas, which need to be utilised to give them a sense of ownership. As they feel little physical stimulation when they step outside of their homes, they get bored easily and therefore create their own entertainment. With a little encouragement, young people can come up with ideas for activities that have positive outcomes. They should be given responsibility for taking their ideas from start to finish with adults giving them guidance and support. The key is to get them involved and to allow them ownership of what they do – let them even have their own graffiti walls and educate them by taking them on trips to see more pleasant places. Most important is that the action is continuous and that young people are involved in activities all the way through.

One problem with young people is inherent in the participation process. Some young people find that their main conflict is not with the external agencies such as the police or the local authority or housing association officials, but with the residents' groups. Whilst these are set up to represent residents, and to foster community spirit in the neighbourhood, they may limit their discussion to issues of interest to adults. In these situations, the young people, who make up the majority of the residents, may not be heard at all.

In particular, young people simply need places that are clearly theirs to "hang around" within the environment, as well as facilities that reflect their real and full needs. They must be engaged in the planning of these facilities and be responsible for their management. Youth shelters, after-school clubs and local cafés (Figs. 1.5 and 1.6) are all important for this purpose, but to be successful they require the interest and support of the local community, the resources to run activities, and skilled personnel. For their part, schools can

Figure 1.5 Young people meet in the community café at Preston Road, Hull: funded by New Deal for Communities.

seek funding for "extension hours" to pay for out-of-school activities. There is clearly an overwhelming need but, regrettably, in some areas community buildings and club areas are underused, which leads to abuse by the very people who need them.

Education in the built environment

Many primary and secondary schools are now taking a much greater interest in education in the built environment as a means of engaging young people in the issues affecting their neighbourhood. Built environment education can be taught through discrete subject disciplines, through multi-disciplinary

Figure 1.6 After School Club, Preston Road, Hull.

approaches, with subjects working in parallel, and through interdisciplinary study, where subjects work together in an interactive and interdependent way. Each subject offers different ways of investigating and examining the environment. Art, design, history, geography and verbal language skills all have particular importance. Science, technology and social sciences also have key contributions to make. Citizenship is now part of the National Curriculum in the UK, which, with the Healthy Schools Standard, means there is an increasing opportunity for children to learn about the built environment. At the heart of this must be the development of an understanding by young people of the relationship between people and place (Adams and Kinoshita, 2000).

These educational ambitions are being stimulated by the development of centres for architecture and the built environment around Britain supported by CABE (the Commission for Architecture and the Built Environment) and by Creative Partnerships, a new scheme in schools launched by the Arts Council. It is to be hoped that this educational approach could stimulate sufficient interest in the built environment amongst young people to have some influence on their behaviour when out of school.

Youthbuild

Young people can be socially disengaged well into their late teens and beyond. One way of engaging those between 16 and 25 years of age, in a means that helps them feel they belong, is through Youthbuild. This enables young people to contribute directly to the regeneration of their community and in some cases build housing in which they themselves can eventually live. It is a way in which to raise the self-esteem of young people by enabling them to take up apprenticeship training and work towards self-employment in the building industry. They work on site with an established employer and attend college on a regular basis. They receive weekly payment, personal support and development, confidence building and an opportunity to gain up to NVQ Level 3 in the building trade of their choice. Experts in the various trades work with the young people on the site. One most successful scheme is at Grimsby, in the north of England, where Doorstep has, over the past few years, successfully built a number of new houses and refurbished properties within the inner urban area. In a location where youth unemployment is nearly twice the national average, the project has proven the value of economic investment in such a locally based activity. The main partners are the young people themselves, who are addressing community issues in a positive way (Fig. 1.7).

Figure 1.7 Young people building new homes through a Youthbuild programme initiated by Grimsby Doorstep.

Rural crime

Just over 25 per cent of Britain's population live in rural areas. In the past 20 years, the countryside's population has increased by more than one million people due to the greater mobility of the affluent commuter. While rural crime is less of a problem than urban crime, fear of crime in the countryside is exacerbated by the isolation that many rural dwellers feel, particularly elderly people. Jack Straw, as Home Secretary, summed up the situation in 2001 when he wrote: "The problem is that, although the chances of being a victim (of crime) are fewer than in urban areas, people nevertheless feel more vulnerable because they have fewer neighbours and police response times are likely to be longer in rural areas." (Straw, 2001, p. 8). While people living in rural areas fall victim to the same types of crime as people living in urban areas, these are compounded by other aspects of rural life, such as limited access to services, physical isolation and social exclusion. And of course, those living in rural communities also suffer crimes that are peculiar to the countryside, like the theft of livestock and farm equipment, and trespassing. However, on the positive side, rural communities tend to be small-scale, close-knit communities, where there are traditions of mutual help and self-reliance. Local information is rapidly shared and criminality is more difficult to hide.

Much has been written about the merits or otherwise of building new housing in rural areas, particularly affordable houses for rent or sale. The need for affordable housing for people who already live and work in rural areas, especially for elderly people and the young, is immense. These are the people who would help make a rural settlement a community and help it to be safe from crime, but they are caught between rich commuters who push prices up and conservation lobbyists who object to any form of development taking place. Nevertheless, some excellent affordable housing has been built in the last few years despite the difficulties within the current funding regime for housing association development (Fig. 1.8).

Crime and quality of life

The Crime and Disorder Act, 1998, now requires all local authorities in the UK, through their Community Safety Partnerships, to conduct audits, which reveal the impact of crime on quality of life. These audits are important in helping the newly established Local Strategic Partnerships determine best value from future expenditure.

Reducing crime and fear of crime frequently comes at the top of the list of what makes a place good to live in (Table 1.4).

Figure 1.8 New rural housing at Broadwindsor, Dorset (1995–6): ensures a balanced community in the village.

Table 1.4. What makes somewhere in the UK a good place to in which to live

Preference	% rating
Low crime	56
Health services	39
Affordable decent housing	37
Good shops	28
Public transport	27
Good schools	25
Good job prospects	25
Clean streets	24
Activities for teenagers	23
Facilities for children	22

Base 2031 GB adults aged 15+, 18–22 October 2001. Information provided by Communities Count (North Lincolnshire/North-east Lincolnshire).

When asked what were the worst things about living where they do, top of the list for many people was young people hanging around, vandalism and graffiti, crime and litter. Things most identified for improvement were local policing, activities for young people, cleaner streets, better public transport, less dog fouling, better roads, less drugs.

Improvements to quality of life can be measured by expressing how good a place is to live in through statistics that indicate:

- Outward migration has been halted
- More visitors have been attracted to the area
- Average salaries have increased
- People have spent more money in the shops

Design and crime

Crime problems in many countries are synonymous with their history of housing from 1945: large development programmes and projects built to meet urgent need, untried construction systems, large numbers of high-rise housing in the 1960s and a concentration of high density/low rise in urban areas in the later 1970s and early 1980s. Overall there was an acute lack of experience on the part of all involved, not solely amongst architects.

Oscar Newman summed up the relationship between design and crime by saying that high-rise housing with a resident janitor and security staff worked well for upper middle-income families with few children but this "cannot be simplistically transplanted, minus the accompanying staff and accoutrements, for the use of large, low-income families" (Newman, 1973a, p. 7). He considered that there was no reason for building high-rise housing save the "narrow dictates of investment economics. Once built, they proved dangerous to live in and costly to maintain. The economic argument that led to their initial construction is reversed exactly. Their cost of operation is surpassed only by the social costs borne by the inhabitants." In their design there was no reference to previous traditions and no attempt at understanding the range of need to be answered in human habitat. Newman's concern was high-rise housing in New York. Experience in Britain since 1945 suggests that similar problems can occur in other much lower density forms of housing. These lessons must be heeded to avoid mistakes in the future.

Feedback is an important part of the design process, but all too often it is sought only a short time after the residents have moved in. The real test is to undertake research much later. The examples that follow were all built in Britain during the heyday of public sector housing. Their designs were based on sound social considerations at the time. The question to ask is, what is the extent to which design contributed to their deterioration, or are the problems all due to social and economic decline? What are the lessons to be learned and how can the problems be avoided through design in the future?

Aldgate Estate, Mansell Road, London

A typical example of a lack of awareness of crime potential at the detailed design stage is shown in Fig. 1.9. The Aldgate Estate, Mansell Street, was built by the City of London in the 1980s as housing for "city workers", and it is now managed by the Guinness Trust. It was designed in the form of 6- to 8-storey deck access blocks, loosely arranged around a green with a large separate parking area at the far end of the site. Fear of crime amongst elderly people is very high and drugs are a major issue. There are particular problems at the eastern end of the estate where steps go down from the road above to a sunken footpath level leading to the entrance of the flats. The view of this path from the road above is totally blocked by high walls, which are designed in a manner that creates recesses and places where a potential attacker could hide. The police crime prevention design adviser for the City of London, Roger Kelly, recommends the installation of CCTV cameras and the replacement of walls with railings. The Guinness Trust may even consider the possibility of a small community centre at one end to make the space more active.

Marquess Road Estate, Islington, London

The Marquess Road Estate was designed in the early 1970s by the award winning architectural partnership of Darbourne and Darke. It was widely hailed as the antidote to concrete high-rises and deck-access slabs. "At last", it was said, "designers and builders had combined inner-city densities with large amounts of open space" (Kelly, 1999) (Figs. 1.10 and 1.11). Problems occurred from the beginning. The estate became a no-go area and there was a "regime of terror" about which no one would give evidence in court. Measures to rectify the problems experienced in the estate included entry phones, road-ways, fencing and improved security on staircases and at entrances. These failed to rectify the problems and the estate is being largely rebuilt.

Looking back in hindsight, Geoffrey Darke commented on the original design in *Building Homes*, May 1998: "We applied the lessons of Lillington Gardens in Pimlico (a similar scheme built earlier) where flats now change hands for huge sums ... you have to remember that there were social problems, like mugging, of which we had no experience then. Everybody said they wanted enclosed gardens, but they proved to be places where people could get mugged."

Figure 1.9 Walls built to accommodate ground level change are the cause of fear of crime in this social housing at the Aldgate Estate, London.

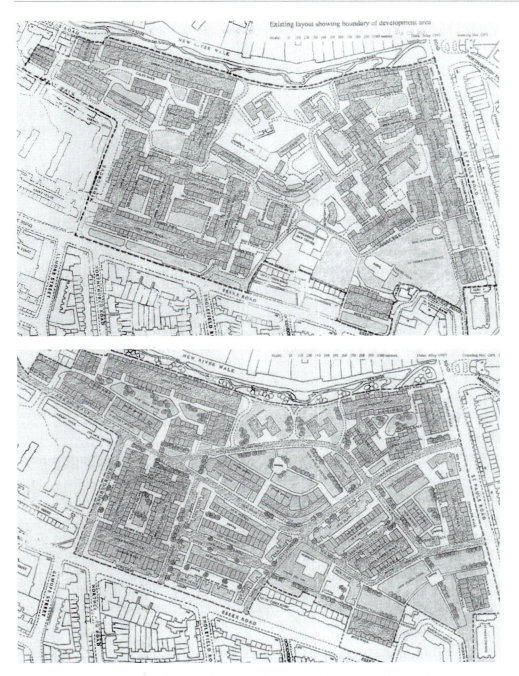

Figure 1.10 Marquess Road Estate as designed by Darbourne and Darke in the 1970s (above). And as redesigned by PRP Architects (below).

Figure 1.11 Marquess Road Estate: existing housing after refurbishment.

Commenting on the scheme by Darbourne and Darke, Barry Munday of PRP Architects, the architects for the new scheme, said: "In the 1960s Darbourne and Darke was, like us, looking for more humane ways of housing people in cities than system-built high rises. D&B's Lillington Gardens in Westminster was inspirational and, as far as I know, still works well. Does this say something about allocation and management being factors rather than design?"

The following problems were key to the Marquess Estate's problems:

■ Underground garages did not work without supervision and day-to-day management, which a local authority could not afford. It is all too easy to see such a concept working elsewhere, particularly in other countries, but account must be taken of the local situation.

Figure 1.12 Marquess Road: new corner housing.

Figure 1.13 Marquess Road Estate: new housing and shops fronting Essex Road.

- Complicated cross-sections imposed demands on workmanship and detail that were probably beyond what was achievable within the budget constraints of social housing. Hence, they leaked and the leaks were difficult to rectify.
- Complicated layout tends to be difficult to "read". Visitors experience difficulty finding their way around, and the streets were not overlooked, so there is no natural surveillance. The estate was not seen as part of "normal" society.

The new scheme by Southern Housing Group and PRP Architects creates traditional street patterns and provides simple terraced homes with gardens, or flats in small groupings. Houses are entered from the street with secure entrances and natural surveillance; cars are parked on the streets or in small open courtyards (Figs. 1.12 and 1.13). Barry Munday's view of the new proposals is, "this is how most homes in Islington are laid out and if it doesn't work it is unlikely to be the buildings that are the problem" (Kelly, 1998, pp. 13–15).

Byker redevelopment, Newcastle upon Tyne

When the first stages of the Byker redevelopment were completed in the 1970s the scheme was hailed at home and abroad as a new beginning for social housing after years of grim, bureaucratic housing (Figs. 1.14 and 1.15). Peter Buchanan of the *Architectural Review* wrote in 1981 that he was delighted to find it was "not only designed *for* a community but *as* a community" (Buchanan, 1981). At that time, the tenants were enthusiastically

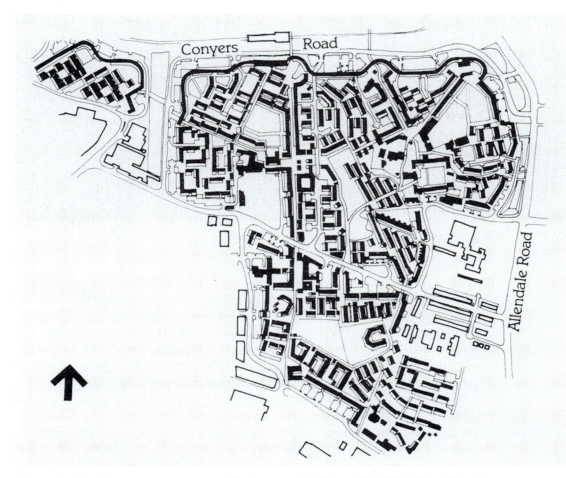

Figure 1.14 Byker redevelopment: Site Layout. Architect: Ralph Erskine, Vernon Gracie & Associates. From RIBA Northern Region, *Housing North*, p. 25 (1987).

Figure 1.15   The Byker Wall.

tending their gardens and there was a strong sense of community, which had been kept together in the move from the old terraced streets to the new development. Tenants were involved in the original planning and a network of nine tenants' associations continues to the present day. In addition, social and community rooms, down to small hobby rooms shared by groups of neighbours, were built into the estate; community spirit was high.

Problems of social and economic deprivation took over from the 1980s and today a large proportion of Byker's population is out of work. Houses and shops became boarded up. "At one time Byker was great. Everyone helped each other. Now the area has deteriorated, and people are frightened to let anyone in their house" (Spring, 1998). There are problems of antisocial behaviour. The layout and planting foster crime. "Like other estates in the city, we suffer from youths causing disorder and damage ... in parts of the estate, a lot of undesirable people have moved in. The area has become stigmatised. People move out and others don't want to move in."

When asked to comment, Vernon Gracie said that he would take participation much further today to provide a more holistic approach linking physical regeneration with social and economic. He cites the triangular block of sheltered housing for elderly people as particularly successful. The shape of the block produced a variety of dwelling types and internal spaces. He claims it has always been a popular place in which to live for many reasons including the strong sense of community within it.

Unfortunately, the richness and complexity of Erskine's design meant maintenance was always a problem. The local authority struggles to maintain the planting, although a large number of trees and bushes have been removed to increase surveillance.

But there is hope for Byker. It has been listed for its architectural/historical significance. The buildings are well maintained, including preserving the original colours to the timber, and are popular internally. It is nevertheless illustrative of housing that is perhaps too sophisticated in its design to be adequately managed and maintained, the result of which is that its sustainability as a complete entity may continue to be severely under threat. (*Architectural Review*, 1997, p. 213).

Figure 2.1 Refurbished 18th century terraced housing in Baltimore, USA, much admired by Jane Jacobs.

CHAPTER 2

Development of design principles

Introduction

> *"The time has come to go back to first principles, to re-examine human habitiat as it evolved, to become attuned again to all the subtle devices invented over time and forgotten in our need and haste to house the many. For even within the widespread chaos of our cities, it is still possible to find isolated examples of working living environments, which are crime free, although at times located in the highest crime precincts of cities"* (Newman, 1973a, p. 2).

There are three schools of thought that determine much of today's practice in designing out crime from the environment:

1. **Defensible Space** – including the idea that access points to an area should be restricted so that only those with a legitimate reason to be in a place would be there.
2. **Crime prevention through environmental design (CPTED)** – developing defensible space through the belief that the physical environment can be manipulated to influence behaviour to reduce crime. This is the basis of Secured by Design.

3. **Situational Crime Prevention/2nd Generation CPTED** – extending defensible space and CPTED ideas to consider both management and design interventions that reduce the opportunities for crime; also by developing social and economic strategies with physical development to produce sustainable communities.

These principles have evolved through the work of a number of specialist researchers in crime prevention in the USA and Britain.

Elizabeth Wood

In the early 1960s the American sociologist, Elizabeth Wood, focused on the micro-environment of blocks of public housing in the United States (Wood, 1961). Her starting point was the concept that housing projects can never employ enough police officers, caretakers, service engineers, etc., to prevent crime from occurring. She emphasised the need for managers to work closely with residents and concentrated her thoughts on physical improvements to the redesign of public and semi-public spaces that should become places of leisure, thereby improving visibility. For example:

- Place children's playgrounds and seating areas for adults (chatting places) so that they are visible from the surrounding houses.
- The entrances to large blocks of flats should function as lobbies, reception areas or meeting places (with seating, refreshment areas, etc.). Such a meeting place must be easily visible from outside and should be well lit in the evenings.

Much ahead of her time, Wood focused on teenagers. She based her ideas about them on the assumption that, because of the lack of good recreational areas, they are more or less forced to "hang around" and wreck property and the environment. Her solution was to provide more facilities which must be vandal-proof. She also proposed appointing one of the tenants of a block of flats as caretaker. This person would then be responsible for forming a link between housing management and the residents and initiating and coordinating the activities of the residents.

Jane Jacobs

Jane Jacobs' *The Death and Life of Great American Cities*, first published in 1961, was the first real indictment of the new urban architecture that had developed after the end of the Second World War. She wrote:

"Deep and complicated social ills must lie behind delinquency and crime, in suburbs and towns as well as in the great cities ... if we are to maintain a city society that can diagnose and keep abreast of deeper social problems, the starting point must be to strengthen whatever workable forces for maintaining safety and civilisation do exist ... To build city districts that are custom made for easy crime is idiotic. Yet that is what we do" (Jacobs, 1961 p. 31).

She criticised the rigid separation in the USA of land uses into different parts of the city and the concentration of similar uses into exclusive centres, such as civic, cultural, shopping, etc. She argued against new residential developments, which arranged housing around green spaces away from streets. She considered that new housing would only be successful if it followed traditional street patterns with mixed uses (Fig. 2.1), rather than following the utopian theories of Le Corbusier and other twentieth-century planners.

To demonstrate how new housing developments were a failure, she drew attention to the higher incidence of crime and observed:

- There must be a clear demarcation between public and private space. Clarity about the function of a particular space is one of the conditions for "territoriality", i.e., when residents feel that a particular space is "theirs" (under their control).
- There must be eyes on the street on the part of the people who are the natural proprietors of the street. It must be possible to look onto the street from inside the buildings, which must be orientated onto the street.
- Where public spaces like streets and parks lack intensive use and surveillance there is a high incidence of street crime. The sidewalks must have users on them fairly continuously to add to the number of effective eyes looking onto the street. This should result from a substantial quantity of shops, pubs, restaurants and other publicly used buildings.
- Residential neighbourhoods should comprise a mixture of people and housing – old people, young people, housing for rich and poor, rental housing and properties for private ownership.

The first two requirements can sufficiently be accommodated by design, but the last two are much more difficult to achieve. Jacobs herself asked: how do we get people in the street to whom it is second nature to keep an eye on what is happening? The problem is that few streets in residential neighbourhoods will ever have the mixture of uses required to make them lively.

Oscar Newman

In his book *Defensible Space: Crime Prevention through Urban Design* (1973a) Oscar Newman set out his theories based on access to detailed statistics on the physical form of housing in New York, including a profile of the residents and recorded incidents of crime in housing owned by the New York Housing Authority, ranging from 2-storey terraces to 36-storey tower blocks. His study produced some significant findings:

■ The lowest recorded crime rates occurred in the 3-storey buildings, whereas buildings higher than 6 storeys and developments larger than 1,000 dwellings suffered significantly higher crime rates.
■ In high-rise buildings, a higher proportion of crime takes place inside the interior public spaces than in similar areas in low-rise housing. He pointed out that whilst high-rise can be successful for higher income households with few children, and when protected by permanent security devices and concierge staff, it does not work for general use.

Defensible space

Newman's central concept was Defensible Space (Fig. 2.2), which has four main design elements. These contribute both individually and together in the concept of Defensible Space. They are:

■ Territoriality
■ Surveillance
■ Building image
■ Juxtaposition of residential with other facilities.

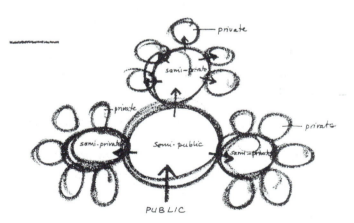

Figure 2.2 Defensible Space: sketches of main principles by Oscar Newman (Newman, 1973, p. 9). Reproduced by courtesy of Macmillan Publishing Ltd.

Territoriality

With the use of real or symbolic barriers, residential environments can be subdivided into zones that are manageable for the residents through their adopting the attitude that "this is my territory". The transition from private (easily manageable) to public space (difficult to manage) is important. To achieve this:

- All spaces both outside and inside buildings should as far as possible be under the control of or under the influence of the residents.
- External spaces should be seen to be clearly private or semi-private when viewed from public streets and footpaths. Walls, fences and gates clearly define territoriality, but symbolic devices may also be used, such as changes of level, steps, gateways, portals, etc.
- In higher density developments, common staircases should serve as small a number of residential units as possible so that residents recognise each other, but more importantly, they recognise intruders.
- External communal areas – such as play areas, drying greens, parking – should, where possible, be accessible from and in close proximity to the entrances of buildings, or should be entered from the private domain.

Surveillance

Residents must be able to survey what is happening in and around public spaces inside and outside the buildings. To achieve this:

- Windows should also be positioned not just to suit the internal plan of a house, but to survey public spaces, both external and internal, within the scheme.
- Gable ends of terraced housing should have windows to overlook adjoining streets or open space.
- Front entrances to buildings should face onto streets so that passing pedestrians and motorists can notice anything strange happening.
- It is preferable if all common areas within buildings – staircases, lift lobbies, landings, etc. – are visible from the street outside the building and, where regulations permit, should also be overlooked by windows from the dwelling units.
- Fire-escape stairs should be glazed, be located on the outside of buildings, and able to discharge any users to the front of the buildings.

Building image

Proper use of materials and good architectural design can prevent residents from feeling stigmatised, which can lead to a feeling of isolation. This can be achieved by:

- Avoiding building forms and layout that stand out as completely different, since they draw specific attention to the project.
- In very large redevelopment projects where there is an existing grid of streets, retaining the streets rather than closing them off. This will help the scheme from appearing totally different and will maintain street surveillance.
- Not letting high-rise/high-density housing blocks to low-income people as they are particularly vulnerable to crime.
- Ensuring that finishes and furnishings in interior spaces are robust, but attractive to residents. Institutional hard materials may encourage an urge to test their destructiveness and could be vandalised.

Juxtaposition of residential areas with other facilities

The security of adjoining areas is partly determined by the "strategic geographical location of intensively used communal facilities", but:

- Housing should be mixed with commercial and social facilities as this helps improve security in an area (Fig. 2.3).
- Parks and playgrounds should be overlooked by housing to afford natural surveillance.

Newman proved his theory by analysing 133 public housing complexes in New York City. He carried out an analysis of crime in these complexes using figures obtained from the New York City Housing Authority Police Department. He proved that approximately two-thirds of the offences occurred inside the complexes and one-third outside. The insides of lifts were the most dangerous feature, followed (at some distance) by the hall, lobby and staircase. Despite criticism of a lack of consideration of social and demographic factors in his methodology, his ideas became immediately popular in the US and in Britain. He was to have an enormous impact on housing design in many parts of the world.

Later research

In his later research he attached more importance to social factors and people became the centre of his attention. In his book *Community of Interest* (1981) he advocated segregation according to "age" and "lifestyle". Similar people should live together in groups (micro-environments). This would have a positive effect on contact between people: they would have more in common, bringing about what Newman calls a "Community of Interest". Such a community would naturally keep the environment around its houses under surveillance.

Figure 2.3 Mixed use development at Temple Bar, Dublin: overlooking helps improve security in the area.

Patricia and Paul Brantingham

At the same time as Jacobs, Newman and others were developing their Defensible Space principles, Patricia and Paul Brantingham were exploring other theories in the city of Tallahassee, Florida. Through their research they made some very important discoveries.

They demonstrated that average crime figures for a large area, such as a region, a city or a district, sometimes concealed more than they revealed. They found that there were considerable differences between neighbourhoods as far as the numbers of burglaries were concerned, but also that there were differences in distribution within neighbourhoods. They examined where burglaries took place in neighbourhoods and made a distinction between apartment blocks at the periphery of each homogeneous neighbourhood and the blocks near the centre. They found that the border blocks – "the skin" of a neighbourhood – had relatively more burglaries than the inner blocks. To explain this phenomenon they researched the behaviour of offenders, who, they claimed, did not want to enter the inner part of the neighbourhood because it was unknown territory. There they would be more noticeable, particularly because the residents in the middle of the neighbourhood would be more aware of who does and does not belong. From this study, the Brantinghams indicated that the planning layout of a neighbourhood had obvious consequences for the number and distribution of the burglaries committed in that neighbourhood. In addition, the relationship between the skin and the centre of a neighbourhood can be influenced by the layout. Thus, a small, elongated neighbourhood has relatively more skin (and a higher risk of burglary) than a compact neighbourhood – a square, for example.

The Brantinghams based a comprehensive theory on the results of their study. Firstly they assumed that offenders have different motivations for committing crimes. The most important difference is between emotional/impulsive offences, such as vandalism, assault and certain types of sexual offences, and instrumental offences such as burglaries and robbery. Their second assumption was that, given the motivation of the offender, the actual offence is the result of a selection process where the offender chooses the most suitable victim. In the case of an emotional/impulsive offence, this search is generally more limited than with more planned offences. They then examined the search process in depth, under the assumption that offenders pick up signals or cues from the environment, i.e., this is a good target, that is a bad target. This brought them to the following two questions:

1. Which environments are the offenders familiar with (within which area does the offender operate)?
2. Which cues (signals) does the offender notice during the search process?

These questions have subsequently been the subject of much investigation. Some researchers have focused on the offenders' homes while others have concentrated on the places where crimes are committed. Their conclusions have suggested that the likelihood of offenders choosing their own direct neighbours in their own housing locality is small because the chance of being recognised is high. However, the further from home the offenders are, the less chance they will strike due to distance and the lack of familiarity with the area. Consequently the majority of crime committed (by young people) – assault, theft/burglary, vandalism – takes place within a mile from home (van Dijk and van Soomeren, 1980, p. 137).

Alice Coleman

Alice Coleman of the Land Use Research Unit at King's College, London, features strongly in the early development of the principles of designing out crime. Her book, *Utopia on Trial: Vision and Reality in Planned Housing* (1985) proved highly controversial but perhaps more significant was the high-profile support her ideas received from the Prime Minister at that time, Margaret Thatcher. Her greatest weakness was that she claimed design alone determined, rather than influenced, behaviour. She criticised architects and planners by claiming that the real grounds for building blocks of flats were neither financial nor spatial, but due to their ideologies. In return, architects much maligned her ideas. They saw a gap in her understanding of the broader aspects of housing design. Nevertheless her work made a contribution towards the debate and is worthy of deeper investigation.

The book reported on a study of all 4099 blocks of flats and maisonettes in the London Boroughs of Southwark and Tower Hamlets. It showed that 16 design features created problems for residents and management staff alike. Litter, graffiti, vandalism and excrement as well as burglary, theft, arson, criminal damage, vehicle crime, violence and sexual assaults plagued poorly designed housing. The book showed that the more numerous the defective designs in any given block, the commoner were these types of social breakdown.

Variable design features

Her 16 variable design features were:

Size: 1: Dwellings per block; 2: Dwellings per entrance; 3: Number of storeys; 4: Flats or maisonettes

These are concerned with the number of people sharing the block. The more there are, the harder it is for the people to know each other, and the more anonymous is the general atmosphere. The threshold number is 12. The threshold number of dwellings per entrance is 6 and the number of storeys is three. Flats are better than maisonettes as the latter are intended for larger families. It is not good for children to be brought up above ground level without the benefit of a private garden to play in under parental supervision. The presence of maisonettes increases the number of children living above the ground and increases the child/adult ratio of the block and the estate.

Circulation: 5: Overhead walkways; 6: Connecting exits; 7: Connecting lifts and stairs; 8: Dwellings per corridor

The easier it is for people to circulate within and between blocks, the more criminals can find penetration points and escape routes. Overhead walkways, interconnected lifts and staircases (vertical routes) and long corridors make crime and antisocial behaviour much easier.

Entrance variables: 9: Entrance type; 10: Entrance position; 11: Doors or apertures; 12: Stilts, garages, facilities

The entrance to a block is the key point through which everyone must pass, and should be designed in ways that welcome residents but deter intruders. A good arrangement is for the communal entrance to serve only the upper floors, and for each ground-floor flat to have a separate individual entrance fronted by its own wall and gated front garden. Front private gardens act as a buffer zone to would-be criminals. Waist-high walls facilitate residents' surveillance of the road in front of the blocks and the persons entering, which deters criminal activity and reduces the fear of crime.

Whilst shops offer valuable facilities, they need careful location to avoid bringing the public into areas that should be private residential space. They can also offer congregating points for youngsters.

Grounds: 13: Blocks per site; 14: Access points per site; 15: Play areas; 16: Spatial organisation

Coleman considered that the layout of the grounds has a very powerful effect upon the degree of social breakdown. If the residents of different blocks as well as outsiders have free access to all the grounds, the site acquires the anonymity of public space, with multiple escape routes for criminals. In such circumstances, defence of individual blocks by surveillance of those approaching and leaving is much more difficult, owing to the need to look in many directions instead of only towards the street. She therefore considered the threshold level of blocks per site to be one. Where there is more than one block on an open site, each block would be more secure and defensible if it had its own individual site facing a public road, with high side and rear walls, but lower front walls (allowing surveillance), and a single front gate (signifying private space).

The research found that play areas were often associated with environmental degradation, crime, hassle and conflict. Toddlers' play is better restricted to the homes and private gardens of their parents, while older children use public parks. Both of these offer adult supervision of play and the presence of more mature people can be a restraining influence upon a child's behaviour.

Spatial organisation is the final and most powerful of all 16 design variables in respect of the volume of crime, and is also a strong influence upon other forms of social breakdown. There are three types of space:

- Semi-private – individual front and back gardens belonging to a single household.
- Semi-public – shared by residents of a single multi-dwelling block
- Confused communal – open to more than one block and/or people from outside the estate.

Semi-private and semi-public were considered acceptable, but confused communal space is highly undesirable. The creation of single-block sites can often remove all confused communal space by organising ownership of the grounds to either individual dwellings or blocks. The flow of pedestrians and vehicles within and through the estate is then restricted to the roads. Each block becomes an individual unit and the concept and ethos of "the estate" is dissolved. This "privatisation" of space assigns responsibility and control for each area to individual households or groups of residents, and creates a more defensible residential environment.

Design principles

The book added principles relating to the design of space immediately round the house:

- There should be waist-high walls or fences between front gardens and along the street frontages. Gates are also essential. Low step-over fences that do not deter dogs, high fences, hedges or walls that impede surveillance, and flimsy fencing materials should be avoided.
- Front gardens should be of around 3m in depth, but not more, if there is to be proper surveillance of the street.
- Rear gardens should be back to back and all entrances should be from the front, via tunnels between pairs of houses in the case of terraces. Tunnel access should begin inside the front gardens and not be an alleyway from the street.
- Houses should be arranged in traditional streets with all open space allocated to individual front and back gardens.
- There should also be only one way into each housing group. Main footpaths are best located so as not to pass through individual housing groups in order to reduce possibilities of disturbance.

The design of dwelling facades can aid or hinder surveillance of the dwelling from the street and vice versa. Window visibility is maximised where the front ground-floor room has clear glass windows set at a height that gives a clear view of the garden and road to occupants sitting, standing or moving about inside. Oriel windows afford a wider view, and walk-in bays are best of all. Projecting features such as porches and garages should not obstruct the sightlines from the windows. The front route should be a public road with two footpaths. End-of-terrace houses should be corner houses with front gardens facing both front and side roads. Back garden access should not be seen from the front of the dwelling (Fig. 2.4).

Parking provision

The best provision for residents' cars is for each individual household to have its own garage or hard-standing within its own grounds. Failing this, street parking immediately in front of the house allows residents and neighbours to both see and hear their vehicles and this deters vehicle crime.

DICE projects

Coleman was commissioned by the Department of the Environment to put these views into practice in a number of estates: in London, the Ranwell Road Estate, Tower Hamlets (Figs. 2.5 and 2.6), and the Mozart Estate, Westminster (Fig. 2.7), and in Manchester, the Bennett Street Estate (Figs. 2.8 and 2.9) The Design Improvement Controlled Experiment (DICE) carried out systematic trials of design improvement as an approach to remedying some of the social problems of inner urban housing estates. By removing the bad features from blocks and grounds, the project endeavoured to show that problem estates could become pleasant places in which to live.

Coleman included a large number of social and socio-demographic variables in the study, such as poverty, deprivation, child density, management, maintenance, etc., but concluded that these factors did not explain – or did not sufficiently explain – the social malaise. The final outcome of the project was considered to be inconclusive. For example, at the Mozart Estate (Westminster), following the removal of the overhead walkways, the injection of new roads to make the estate more accessible and permeable, and other design changes, residents were divided over whether the change had been worthwhile. Research in 1993 found the changes had not brought about reductions in burglaries, and the need for additional improvements, including social and economic regeneration, was highlighted (Osborne and Shaftoe, 1995). At Bennett Street, residents felt much safer (and still do) after the changes. They much prefer the traditional street layout and welcome the creation of more defensible space. However, the scheme failed to achieve sufficient quality of improvement in overall terms to ensure the estate's long-term sustainability as suggested by the many boarded-up flats.

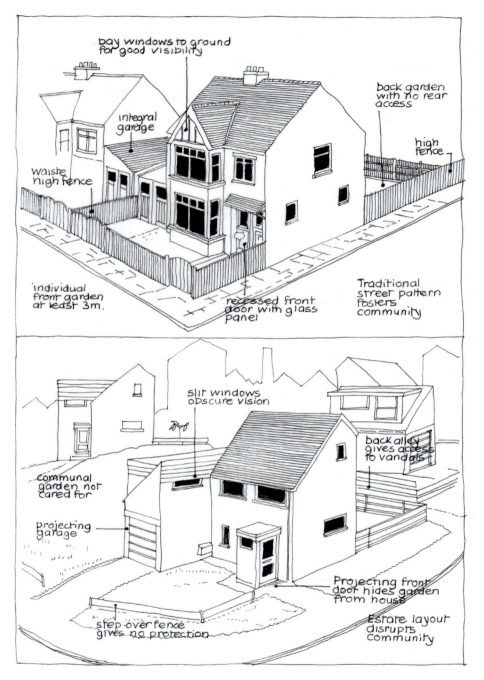

Figure 2.4 "Suburban Utopia Rules": diagram of Alice Coleman's concept as it appeared in an article by Deyan Sudjik in the *Sunday Times*, 5 May, 1985, p.13. (Original drawing by Gordon Beckett.)

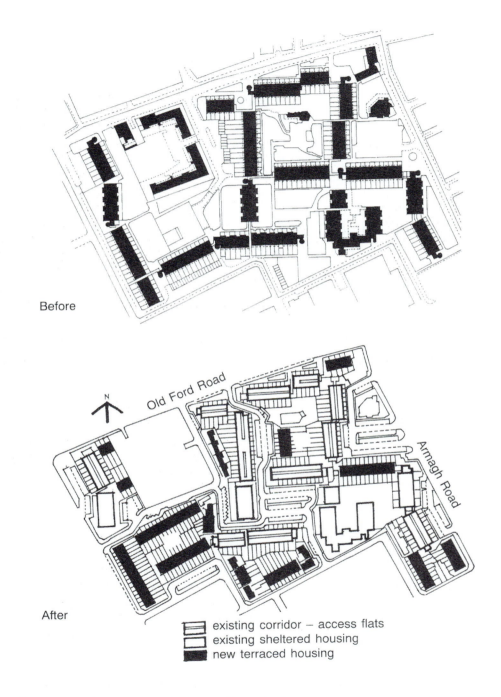

Before

After

existing corridor – access flats
existing sheltered housing
new terraced housing

Figure 2.5 Alice Coleman: Ranwell Road Estate, Tower Hamlets, London, before and after the DICE interventions (*Building*, November 1997, p. 48.)

Figure 2.6   Alice Coleman: new housing in the Ranwell Road Estate, Tower Hamlets, London.

Nevertheless, many of Alice Coleman's principles, particularly "permeable" housing layouts, are now widely accepted. The essence of her message was that "small is beautiful": not large-scale buildings, but small, preferably detached or semi-detached, houses (1920s/1930s-type houses).

Situational crime prevention

Since the mid-1970s, the UK government, through the Home Office, has initiated many studies into how particular types of crime can be prevented. Much of this has extended beyond practical advice about buildings and the built environment to incorporate management and use issues. This has raised many important questions about the nature of crime and its relationship with the built environment. Situational crime prevention operates at micro level and focuses on place and specific crime. It establishes a link with the offender.

The principles were formulated by Ron Clarke and Patricia Mayhew in their book *Designing out Crime* (1980). This included seven preventative strategies:

Figure 2.7 Alice Coleman: new roads in the Mozart Estate to increase the level of permeability, with pitched roofs to change the image.

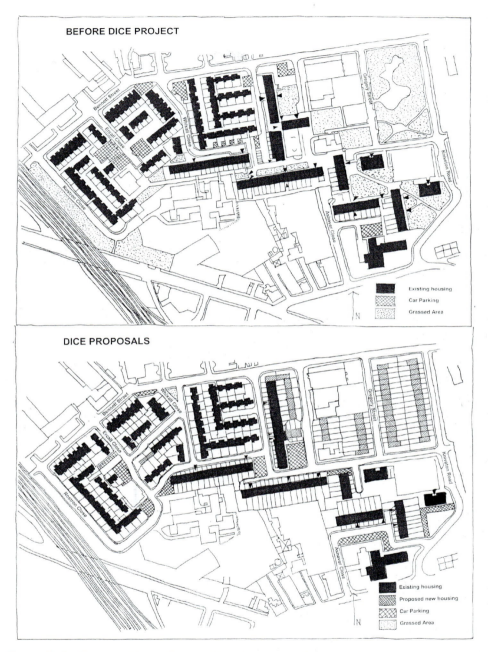

Figure 2.8 Bennett Street Estate, Manchester: before and after improvement.

Figure 2.9   New bungalows at Bennett Street Estate, Manchester.

- Target hardening: sturdier locks, doors and windows to prevent burglary and sturdier materials against vandalism.
- Target removal: for example, a bank transfer replaces the monthly pay packet in cash; the much-vandalised telephone box is simply taken away.
- Removing the means to crime: for example, the removal of loose stones on the ground near a glazed public building; or the removal of the ladder in the garden. The modern wheely-bin can be an aid for climbing – it is often too large to lock away.
- Reducing the pay-off for the offender: for example, marking valuable goods with an engraved postcode and house number so the stolen item is more difficult for the offender to dispose of.
- Formal surveillance: by the police and private security firms – and now Neighbourhood Watch.
- Surveillance by employees (semi-formal surveillance): an immediate measure that does not involve the police or local residents, but an official or employee who is present somewhere with a clearly defined objective – as long as it is not solely to prevent or act against crime. This could be the doorman in an apartment building, shop personnel, the conductor in a bus, etc.
- Environmental management: housing measures such as avoiding housing a high percentage of young people in a complex; public transport not running when the pubs close, resulting in some customers who have had too much to drink being stranded – this is a recipe for vandalism, the theft of cars and bicycles, etc.

In his later book, *Situational Crime Prevention: Successful Case Studies* (2nd edition, 1997) Ron Clarke adds further opportunity-reducing techniques to this list. These include natural surveillance – exercised by passers-by and residents – and measures to increase the perceived effort and the perceived risks on the part of offenders, reducing their anticipated rewards, and removing excuses for crime to happen.

Many of the measures recommended involve the use of space and the management of people and the environment, which are beyond the scope of planning and design. They are important, however, in looking at crime issues holistically. The list recommends measures that can diminish a particular type of crime and it may be found that solving the problem through management is simpler, cheaper and more acceptable than creating a fortress environment.

Rational and routine activity theories

Rational choice is a vital supporting element of situational crime prevention. With very few exceptions, crimes do not happen at random, because offenders choose one target in preference to another. They make what is known as a "Rational Choice". The decision to commit an offence is based on the offender making a calculation that acknowledges the costs (including personal effort), benefits (the potential rewards) and the risks. Therefore, measures to increase the risk and the effort by the offender and reduce the likely reward are beneficial. Also complementing situational crime prevention, the "Routine Activity Theory" suggests that offenders, like everyone else, have day-to-day schedules such as going to work, visiting friends, shopping, etc. Whilst doing this, they search out likely targets. These are often associated with the offenders' idiosyncrasies, meaning that they look for targets that relate to themselves, e.g., a drug addict would look for targets close to drug markets. This makes it possible to make informed speculations about search patterns of offenders in certain circumstances and the likely places where offences could be committed.

Crime prevention through environmental design – CPTED

Definition of CPTED

The term "Crime Prevention Through Environmental Design" was first used by the American criminologist, Professor C. Ray Jeffrey, in his book of the same name written in 1971.

The concept is based on one simple idea that crime results partly from the opportunities presented by the physical environment. This being the case, it should be possible to alter the physical environment so that crime is less likely to occur.

This principle is at the centre of the books by Jane Jacobs and Oscar Newman, and by Ronald Clarke and Patricia Mayhew, Patricia and Paul Brantingham, Timothy D. Crowe, Barry Poyner, Richard H. Schneider and Ted Kitchen, Tim Pascoe (BRE) and others. Interest in CPTED has continued to grow to the present day in many countries around the world as expressed in the International Crime Prevention Through Environmental Design Association (ICA), the European Designing Out Crime Association (E-DOCA) and the British Designing Out Crime Association (DOCA), which comprises police officers, architects, planners, criminologists, security professionals and others concerned with the built environment. The Building Research Establishment (BRE) has developed a research programme, under Dr Tim Pascoe, on designing crime out of the environment. This and a number of universities that specialise in the subject are contributing significantly to the development of the concept.

CPTED in an "Open Society"

Bo Gronlund of the Royal Danish Institute of Fine Art School of Architecture has recently undertaken valuable research on CPTED. One of the most important issues that this has raised is the relationship of CPTED to the "Open Society", which is important to the culture of many western countries, particularly in Scandinavia. The issue is the extent to which society is prepared to accept crime in the environment in relationship to the barriers that it can create for quality of life. There is often a large difference between experienced and imagined safety on the one hand and actual, real safety on the other. The image of crime reported through the mass media often gives a very different impression of risk compared to real statistical crime rates. There are different risks for different groups of the population, in different places and at different times. The feeling of safety or lack of safety is also to some extent age and gender dependent – sometimes proportional in reverse to the real risks. With this in mind, Bo Grunland asks, "what level of risk is acceptable as the starting point for this?" This lies at the heart of planning out crime from the environment and creating the humane contemporary city (Gronlund, 2000).

He draws attention to a number of key issues for CPTED.

■ There are social differences that influence the approach to designing crime out of the environment.

- Should CPTED be related to the real or the perceived fear of crime? Should the emphasis be on reliance on policing and social efforts, or on physical design?

- There are question of rights and freedom of use and the degree to which CPTED should be enforced by law or be voluntary.

- There is a lack of interest from central and local governments (lack of guidelines), a lack of skilled people, and a lack of appropriate organisational framework related to the issue.

- Insurance companies frequently have little interest in crime prevention as they, although indirectly, profit from crime (insurance companies are mostly interested in technical matters in relation to insurance rates, not in reduction of crime basically).

- There is a lot of money to be made on technical security gadgets and on guard services, which makes their promotion profitable.

- The spatial "gated communities" in the US are being taken on in many other parts of the world. They have frequently proved more profitable for developers than other kinds of development. The possibility of CPTED certification for new housing could therefore have significance in marketing crime prevention by design in a profitable way.

- There are implementation problems, such as resistance from architects (ideological, economic) and resistance from builders (economic and/or lack of knowledge and experience).

These issues may appear negative, and could be used as excuses for doing nothing, but they are nevertheless matters that will need to be addressed if CPTED is to develop in Britain beyond Secured by Design. The last point about the views of architects is particularly important. The effect of Danish CPTED guidelines has been to point towards designing more traditional development forms. CPTED in Denmark, in Bo Gronlund's viewpoint, has "turned out to be an architectural anti-modernist approach". This appears also to be mainly the case with New Urbanism and Smart Growth in the USA.

Sibeliusparken

Sibeliusparken was the first project in Denmark chosen for special consideration for safety and security through urban design (Fig. 2.10). It is unique because, according to Gronlund, no better design has been carried out in Denmark since then, although a few cases are almost as good, e.g., Egebjergaard built at Ballerup in 1996 (p. 249). Sibeliusparken received special grants for the development of the design from the Danish Development Council. The Danish Crime Prevention Council also took part but it needed the special interest of architect, John Malpass, without whom crime preven-

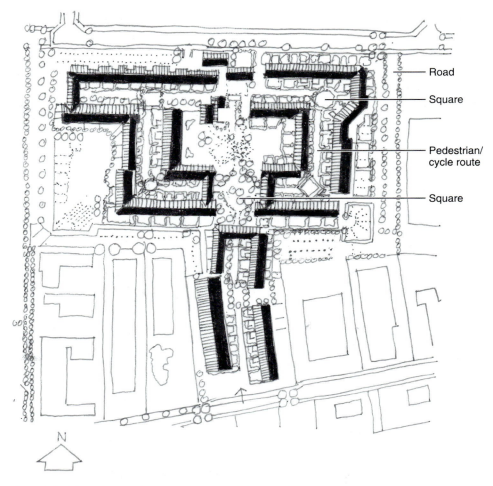

Figure 2.10 Layout of Sibeliusparken, Copenhagen.

tion through urban design in Denmark would be less developed. Could such support ever be possible in Britain?

Sibeliusparken is a scheme of social housing in Rodovre, situated some 8 km from the centre of Copenhagen. The site was previously a run-down industrial area, and the scheme was built with the purpose of stimulating the establishment of a more mixed urban environment. Constructed in two stages, the first one in 1986 and the second southern one in 1994, the total number of dwellings is 265. 20 per cent of the women inhabitants and 12 per cent of the men are over 67 years old. There are more 20–30 year olds than normal for such housing in Denmark and 67 per cent of the households are single or single parents. Unemployment is high – 21 per cent live on social security. The annual turnover of property is in the region of 20 per cent annually. The average income is only 63 per cent of the common average for Denmark. This demographic and social composition would normally present problems, but this does not appear to be the case here.

The clear structuring of the whole area into public, semi-private and private zones is important. Also significant is the pedestrian/cycle route running through the development, and the way in which the housing is grouped on either side to form streets and squares. Figure 2.11 shows the small

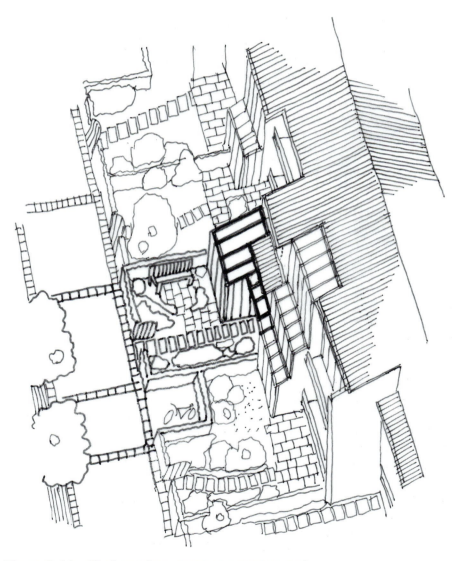

Figure 2.11 Sibeliusparken: common entrance yard.

common entrance yard or garden supporting a bench and other common facilities. On each side are small private gardens. The detail design of gates, walls, railings, and hedges, parking storage, bicycle parking, green areas, pavement surfaces and common rooms creates a lively street scene. The importance of visibility is stressed – low walls define private spaces and entrances are often marked with symbolic gates (Fig. 2.12). Children are supposed to play in or close to the street, and they do. From the street and the glazed balconies it is easy to view the outside spaces (Fig. 2.13). Each stairwell has a common room in the form of a greenhouse; from this it is possible to see the street. In parts of the development there are no stairwells but outdoor stairs instead. Most often these stairs serve two apartments thereby stimulating the personalisation of each space on either side of the top of the staircase (Fig. 2.14). Ground-floor apartments have private gardens, preferably both front and back.

Research has shown that crime in the scheme is very low, around 50 per cent of the rate experienced in other areas. Analysis showed that most burglaries took place in places with fewer opportunities for overlooking and fewer passers-by. Car theft is extraordinarily low and burglaries about one-fifth of the normal. The evaluation indicated that crime prevention through physical

Figure 2.12 Sibeliusparken: details of the entrances and gates are well worked out.

Figure 2.13 Sibeliusparken: glazed common room and staircase leading off the pedestrian/cycle route.

planning and design measures had been effective. Investigation confirmed that well arranged external spaces and a good overview close to entrances and gardens prevents burglaries and vandalism to a very high extent.

Second generation CPTED: sustainable development using CPTED principles of Greg Saville and Gerry Cleveland

A new and most important direction is emerging for CPTED, which is reflected in this book. Second generation CPTED views the design of the

Figure 2.14 Sibeliusparken: staircase serving two apartments on the first floor.

built environment as only the first step to creating healthy, sustainable communities. What really counts is creating a sense of community through a holistic approach to physical, social and economic development.

In their paper *Second Generation CPTED: An Antidote to the Social Y2K Virus of Urban Design*, Greg Saville and Gerry Cleveland refer to how the Dutch Labelling Standards incorporate the pattern language of Christopher Alexander and apply it to safe urban design. They draw attention to five categories embedded in the Dutch standards that link the physical environment with how people live:

- Size of the district, density and differentiation of dwellings – human scale
- The importance of urban meeting places without which urban spaces can be empty and dangerous
- The provision of facilities for young people – particularly youth clubs
- Residents' participation
- Residents' responsibility

However, they go further than this by introducing a new form of "ecological, sustainable development that uses traditional CPTED design principles". They consider it necessary to expand efforts into the realm of residents' responsibility, residents' participation, youth activities, urban meeting places and human scale neighbourhoods. This means living in smaller, locally based, neighbourhoods; living near to work, school and where people socialise. It means developing ways of encouraging more local contacts for social, economic and political interaction. There should be more opportunities for friendships and family in neighbourhood context without sacrificing the important needs for personal space and privacy. Just as physical spaces are planned, so too must effective social zones of community be planned.

They advocate small systems for survival – "we have relied . . . on large economies of scale, massive schools, empirically-based scientific and tertiary academic institutions, large organisations, big government and large scale places of employment. These are no longer viable in our turbulent social environment. They are too slow, too inflexible and too unresponsive" (Saville and Cleveland). Instead, they suggest small, sustainable systems, small business and locally based sustainable economies. What is needed are holistic and open-minded programmes, non-governmental agencies, not-for-profit ventures, local organisations and flexible companies based on personal networks.

In their prescription for the future they say we must cultivate skills in neighbourhood building at a small, local scale. These skills must include values based on ecological principles, and on the values of a healthy community. Such a place should be able to heal itself if it gets sick. This means having local opportunities for play and work. It means respecting personal choice and privacy, while still creating common places and events of social interaction that allow people to celebrate their diversity. It also means that these factors are structured in such a way as to create an effective community environment, whether this is a workplace, a school, a market, or a residential neighbourhood, which has the capacity to resolve its own problems on its own terms.

They say this will not happen in a day, but when CPTED solutions finally include both the physical and the social to become truly ecological, they will have enhanced the quality of the day for society and its children, and for the communities in which they live.

Christopher Alexander: A Pattern Language

The link referred to in the previous section between CPTED and the writings of Christopher Alexander is significant. Whilst his book, *A Pattern Language*, published in 1978, does not focus on crime, there are design elements that could have crime preventive and fear-reducing effects. To compile the Dutch Police Labelling Guidelines, these "patterns" were taken from Alexander's work and moulded into a set of standards and procedures (van Soomeren, 2001).

Alexander's book contains 253 archetypal patterns (55 were used by the Dutch) consisting of problem statements, discussions, illustrations and solutions to provide laypersons with a framework for engaging in architectural design. At the core is the idea that people should design for themselves their own houses, streets and communities. The idea was highly innovative for the time and implied "a radical transformation of the architectural profession", but "it comes simply from the observation that most of the wonderful places of the world were not made by architects but by the people" (Alexander, 1977).

A Pattern Language is based on the principle that there is a "language" for the design of the environment, which allows people to articulate and communicate an infinite variety of design within a formal system that gives them coherence. "Patterns", the element of this language, are answers to design problems (How high should a windowsill be? How many storeys should a building have? How much space in a neighbourhood should be devoted to grass and trees?). The book contains more than 250 patterns. Each pattern consists of a problem statement, a discussion of the problem with an illustration, and a solution. He advises that many of the patterns are "archetypal"– so deeply rooted in the nature of things that it seems likely that they will be part of human nature and human action for all time.

Key principles of a pattern language are:

- **Size of community (12):** Communities and small towns should have a population of between 5,000 and 10,000 people. Beyond this, individual people have no effective voice.
- **Identifiable neighbourhoods (14):** These should contain between 500 and 1000 people. A neighbourhood has a maximum diameter of 300 yards (0.914 m). Neighbourhoods should have clear boundaries and be marked symbolically at the entrances.
- **House clusters (37):** People associate closely with a small number of households on either side and across the street, on average 6 to 8. Above 10 the balance is strained. Use this pattern for housing up to a density of 15 houses per acre (50 houses per hectare). At higher density, the cluster could be modified with additional structure given by Row Housing (38) or a Housing Hill (39).

- **The family (75):** People need to have at least a dozen people round them so that "they can find the comfort and relationships they need to sustain them during their ups and downs". Since the old extended family, based on blood ties, seems to be gone, this can only happen if small families, couples, and single people join together in voluntary families of ten or so.
- **Life cycle (26):** Essential to creating a community is to plan for this to have a "balanced life cycle". "This means that each community includes a balance of people at every stage of the life cycle from infants to the very old to include the full state of settings needed for every stage of life. Each building project . . . can be viewed as either helping or hindering the right balance for local communities" (p. 143). Instead we have "retirement villages, bedrooms, suburbs, teenage culture (i.e., too high child density which can be a cause of high levels of crime, vandalism and antisocial behaviour), ghettos for the unemployed, college towns and industrial parks (add to this out-of-town shopping centres)".
- **Four-storey height (21):** In recommending a maximum storey height of four, Christopher Alexander draws attention to the human need for contact with the ground. "It seems as if the ground, the common ground between houses, is the medium through which people are able to make contact with one another and with themselves. Living on the ground, the yards around houses join those of the neighbours, and, in the best arrangements, they also adjoin neighbourhood byways. Under these conditions it is easy and natural to meet with people. Children playing in the yard, the flowers in the garden, or just the weather outside provide endless topics for conversation. This kind of contact is impossible to maintain in high rise apartments" (Alexander, 197, p. 211) (Fig. 2.15).
- **Private gardens (39):** The need for a small garden with sunlight and privacy, or with some kind of private outdoor space is fundamental. It is equivalent, at the family scale, to the biological need that society has to be integrated with the countryside.
- **Housing Hill (39):** Alexander's solution to building higher density housing of more than 30 dwellings per hectare, or to build housing three or four storeys high, is to build a "hill of housing . . . to form stepped terraces, sloping towards the south, served by a great central open stair which also faces south and leads towards a common garden". His solution to the problem of lack of identity in high density housing is to let each family build and rebuild its own home on the terraced superstructure. If the floors of this structure are capable of supporting a house and some earth, each unit is free to take its own character and develop its own tiny garden.
- **Local facilities:** Alexander advocates a **local town hall (44)** for every community of 7,000 people with shops and a **necklace of community projects (45)** close by: "Make each shop small, compact and easily accessible." He prefers to see **individually owned shops (87)** rather than large shops con-

Figure 2.15 Dwellings at all levels have contact with the ground. Elm Village, Camden, London. Architects: Peter Mishcon and Associates.

trolled by absentee owners: "shops run as a way of life" rather than for money alone.

- **Open space:** He recommends building small public spaces at focal points for people to loiter – **public outdoor room (69)**. Use shops and other public buildings to form an edge to public open spaces – **building fronts (122)**, **building edge (160)** – and keep buildings and public spaces open to the street – **opening to the street (165)**.

- **Roads and parking**: He recommends **looped local roads (49)** "serving less than 50 cars – at one and a half cars per house, such a loop serves 30 houses; at one car per house, 50 houses; at one-half car per house, 100 cars". He does not favour culs-de-sacs: "Culs-de-sac are very bad from a social standpoint – they force interaction and they feel claustrophobic, because there is only one entrance" (p. 262). He considers there is "too much hard asphalt in the world" and favours "green streets" comprising a rough surface of grass and gravel with paving stones for wheels of cars – **green streets (51)** – with parking off the road in driveways or small spaces serving not more than 5 to 7 cars – **small parking lots (103)** and **car connection (113)**. He positively supports cycling – **bike paths and racks (56)**.

- **Your own home (79):** Alexander advises on the value of owning your own home. "People cannot be genuinely comfortable and healthy in a house which is not theirs. All forms of rental – whether from private landlords or public housing agencies – work against the natural processes which allow people to form stable, self-healing communities." Partnerships, shared equity and tenant management are all part of this ethos and are important to creating sustainable communities.

- **Teenage society: (84)** His comments on this are highly relevant to the current problems of youth crime. "Teen-age is the time of passage between childhood and adulthood. In traditional societies, this passage is accompanied by rites which suit the psychological demands of the transition." This does not exist in modern society, but planning for teenage society (now 8 to 18 or more) is a core element and not merely an add-on to planning communities. This includes youth clubs, after-school clubs and anything to which young people will respond (in joined-up thinking the cost could be met by savings in crime and vandalism).

- **Shopfront schools (85):** Alexander placed his faith in a new kind of school, which also houses social functions, opportunities for sports and games, and a library. For the school to play this role, it must suit the convenience of the neighbourhood rather than merely the efficiency of the education service and be physically joined to the community rather than placed in the centre of its grounds with high walls and fences around to keep people out for most of the day except during school hours.

He recommends that apartments are built in such a way that each individual apartment has a garden, or a terrace where vegetables will grow, and that even in this situation each family can build, change, and add to their house as they wish" (p. 395–6). This creates a particular challenge for the design of apartments. Flexible/adaptable forms are possible, such as the Open Building in Japan (Fig. 3.6). Wide balconies and and winter gardens can be built on the sunny side of apartments to compensate for people living above ground level (Figs. 2.18, 3.24 and 3.34–3.36). There is a cost involved, but perhaps it is the price for sustainable housing at a higher density.

Pikku-Huopalahti, Helsinki

It is rare to find a model community that meets the rigorous principles set down by Christopher Alexander but Pikku-Huopalahti comes closer than many schemes. Completed in 2000, it is situated approximately two miles from the centre of Helsinki. It accommodates 8,500 people in mixed tenure housing on a site that was undeveloped previously due to poor ground conditions. The site is set in woodland and it contains a large lake which, with the adjacent open space, forms a District Park overlooked by the new housing (Fig. 2.16).

At the head of the lake the development forms a town square (Fig. 2.17), where there is a lively centre of shops, cafés, banks, workshops and other community buildings. Nearby is the primary school. The town square is also the terminating point for a new tramway system into the city centre. Building heights follow the form of the landscape in such a way that the taller buildings are located towards the boundaries of the site and in the centre of the development. There is plenty of diversity of housing form to avoid an "estate" image. Instead, Pikku-Huopalahti is a small off-shoot with its own identity that is part of Helsinki. Close to the town square is a pyramid of housing (similar in concept to Alexander's "Hill of Housing"), which rises to 12 storeys, forming a landmark that can be seen from all parts of the site and beyond (Fig. 2.18).

Housing investment is considered important in Finland for social and economic reasons. A sound housebuilding industry is essential to the national economy and there has therefore been an acceptance that government subsidy is necessary to achieve the high standard of design. In particular, the investment ensures the essential ingredients for creating sustainable communities, a subject which is dealt with in the last chapter of this book.

Figure 2.16 Sustainable community at Pikku–Huopalahti, Helsinki. Architects: Karii Piimies, Markku Lahti and Erkki Kantola.

Figure 2.17   Pikku–Huopalahti: the Town Square comprising higher density, mixed-use development.

Bill Hillier: Space Syntax Theory

In the UK, space syntax has pioneered new techniques for the regeneration of urban areas through urban design. The techniques focus specifically on making physical connections between the way people use places and the design of the places themselves. Professor Bill Hillier of University College, London, has developed the concept from 1984, since when he has published a wealth of books, papers and other publications.

Space syntax is a means for explaining from a sociological point of view relations between human behaviour and spatial use. It asserts that spaces are

Figure 2.18 Pikku–Huopalahti: the hill of housing provides a focal point at the centre of the development.

extended fields of our everyday lives and can be analysed. The more important element in the architectural experience is not visual characteristics, but the way in which the sequence of spaces is used, e.g., how these will affect patterns of pedestrian movement, economic vitality and safety. The techniques allow the effects of design to be measured together, so that design can be informed and objectively assessed.

The process uses computer-based technologies, which produce graphic representations of factors such as spatial networks, pedestrian movement rates, land use, patterns of reported crime, etc. These are used in three ways:

- For analysis, to better understand the urban context and identify regeneration opportunities.
- For design, to make sure that new proposals respond to the spatial potentials of their new context.
- For consultation, to explain the reasoning behind proposals, discuss the implications of these and test new ideas emerging from this process.

Hillier has researched different forms of housing and found a number of typical characteristics. On the one hand, housing predating 1900 had outward facing dwellings and a clear distinction between private and public space. It was designed on a regular grid in which streets were easily accessible and there was a mixed age-group community. The design of public housing, on the other hand, particularly after 1950, was based on other principles – particularly aspect, solar orientation, open planning, pedestrian/vehicular segregation, etc. – which resulted in blurred boundaries between public and private spaces. Pedestrian route networks were complicated and in some cases became labyrinthine. Pedestrian and vehicular segregated layouts made this even worse. This and the proliferation of spaces weakened the link between children and adults as children explored isolated areas without adult supervision. This separation is heightened as few non-residents walk through the estates. The consequence is acute fear of crime amongst vulnerable elderly people who feel threatened when they encounter groups of young people. "In this way, many housing estates which were originally recognised for their design qualities – such as Maiden Lane in Camden and the Marquess Road Estate in Islington (Fig. 1.10) – soon became some of the least desirable places to live" (Davis, 1988, pp. 74–78).

Through computer modelling of housing estates such as these, Hillier showed that:

- Crime is most likely to occur where places are quieter and less connected. Many places that suffer higher crime rates are often isolated and clinically zoned. The built form, movement and use of these places increase opportunity for crime, particularly where there are unclear definitions between private and public spaces and poor natural surveillance of the street environment.
- The pattern of adult pedestrian movement is directly related to the degree of spatial accessibility with more accessible streets carrying more pedestrian movement.

- It is the downscaling of urban space which creates the conditions for children to explore the less accessible parts of the estates that adults normally avoid.
- There is a direct relationship between the lack of outward-facing dwellings and fear amongst pedestrian movement, as well as an actual pattern of crime and antisocial behaviour.

One of the main conclusions is that a clear effective pattern of movement is itself one of the most effective ways to control crime in housing estates. Hillier's research has had a strong influence on the development of the concept of permeability.

Figure 3.1 Mixed-use, high density housing creates a sense of place around the Saint Martin Church, Cologne. Architect: Joachim Schurmann.

CHAPTER 3

Planning and design

Neighbourhood planning and housing design

"The success of cities depends upon successful neighbourhoods – physical areas within which people organise their lives.... Neighbourhoods have three inter-locking aspects; the home and its immediate surroundings; services such as shops and schools ... the environment, which gives a powerful sign of who we are and how we should behave. They offer a sense of familiarity and security, countering fear of the unknown even when the neighbourhood is poor, run down or unpopular ... if these elements are disrupted then security disintegrates and the neighbourhood breaks down." (Power, 2000, pp. 46–51).

This chapter outlines the principles of neighbourhood planning and housing design, which must be understood by all members of the procurement team. For crime prevention design advisers, it provides a design context in which they can make their contribution to the process.

The planning and design process involves a number of activities:

- Preparation of a good brief including a site analysis and crime pattern analysis
- Spatial design
- Integrating vehicular and pedestrian movement into the spatial design

The brief

The brief is a most important document and it is at this stage that the potential for designing out crime begins. The brief should be based on:

- An assessment of the natural environmental and physical characteristics of the site
- An analysis of the users and their requirements
- The relationship between the user requirements and the site characteristics

The interaction between the physical characteristics and user needs is the key to the process and enables the development of a number of alternative design solutions, which can be tested against social (including crime possibilities), natural, environmental and visual objectives. Seen in this way, layout planning is no longer merely to do with subjective judgement but is a well-reasoned process, which can be followed and understood. The brief will inevitably involve compromise (including aspects relating to crime prevention), which is best resolved where possible at this stage.

Site survey and analysis

Common features of a site survey include:

- Physical features, levels, ground conditions, geological information, land form and ecology. The location of existing trees and other vegetation.
- How the site relates to the local neighbourhood and local planning policies.
- Status of roads around and within the site, traffic intensity, existing services, noise from traffic, surrounding buildings.
- Major pedestrian movements, particularly to shops, schools, bus stops, play areas, open space, or other communal facilities. This information could be particularly relevant to designing out crime.
- Views of the site from surrounding streets, buildings or other locations, together with views looking out from the site.
- In urban areas the "urban grain" within which the development is taking place. This can be obtained from a survey of old maps illustrating the changing pattern of buildings from the earliest times through to the current layout of buildings.
- Urban design analysis – architectural character of the area including heights of existing buildings, landmark buildings and important landscape features, door and window patterns and detailing of buildings.
- Materials analysis – photographs and/or drawings indicating the range of materials that are used for walls and roofs of buildings, on the streets and pavements and on walls, fences, etc.

- The hopes and fears of the wider community within which the development will take place.

Crime Pattern Analysis

At this stage a Crime Pattern Analysis should be undertaken to inform the design by analysis of criminal activity in an area. This will help assess the level of risk that can be taken in the design. A diagnostic survey of crime in the immediate area should be carried out to identify the type of crimes reported, when the incidents occurred and who the victims were. If the site is not within an existing built-up area, then it is advisable to look for similar precedents to research. Existing environments can be examined by reference to registered crime statistics, surveys, carrying out safety audits, and interviewing and recording opinions of local residents and others visiting/using the area, such as shopkeepers.

When the area has been examined, the possibility of crime and fear of crime should be carefully considered. An effective means of doing this is to adopt a "what if" approach as used by Essex Police (p. 226), and proposed for the European Standard (p. 296) Areas that could require special consideration are those characterised by fear-generated features (such as gangs of young people) or areas of poor maintenance, lack of visibility, poor orientation, etc. The next step is to determine what action might be required.

Dr John Parker of Greater London Consultants recommends asking the following questions:

- Are pedestrian areas and routes subjected to good natural surveillance?
- Is there an absence of venues that attract large numbers of adolescents?
- Are there good definitions between the public and private ownership of spaces?
- Is artificial lighting adequate at night?
- Are the public spaces busy with people passing throughout the day and evening?
- Is there a good public transport service?
- Are acceptable standards of maintenance and cleanliness in evidence?

If the answer to all these questions is yes, then the locality is probably safe and secure (*DOCA Journal*, 2001, p. 14).

User requirements

Very few future occupants of housing schemes in the UK contribute to the formation of the brief for the housing they may purchase or rent, let alone the design of the housing scheme. Housing agencies or developers, land values and availability, economic factors, professional consultants, building techniques, and central and local government policies have all generally had more influence on the quality of housing than the eventual occupant. It is these people who determine the location of the development, the dwelling types and internal planning arrangements, and, with the approval of the planning bodies, the density and layout form.

User surveys and feedback studies of similar projects in similar locations can help get the brief right but these need to be undertaken, not just after occupation, but several years afterwards when people have settled for a few years and problems have become identified. Questionnaires have limited use. The major problem is that the ways in which the questions are asked can influence the responses. A much better approach is to involve the future residents in the design process, the techniques of which are dealt with in Chapter 5.

Spatial design

"A home is not just an apartment or house but also the place it occupies. The way in which homes/houses are situated along streets and around yards, thus creating a gradual transititon from private to public, is of utmost importance to feeling secure and at home" (Bjorklund, 1995, p. 19).

The home is the focus of everyday personal life but the space outside is where people come into contact with the outside world. The need for a variety of spaces in the built environment is vital to quality of life. The essential spatial design principles to be followed in the design of residential neighbourhoods are (DETR, 2001):

- Character: a place with its own identity (Figs. 3.1 and 3.2).
- Continuity and enclosure: a place where public and private places are clearly distinguished (Fig. 3.3).
- Quality of the Public Realm: a place with attractive and successful outdoor areas (Fig 3.4).
- Ease of movement: a place that is easy to get to and move through (Fig. 3.5).
- Legibility: a place that has a clear image and is easy to understand (Fig. 3.5).
- Adaptability: a place that can change easily (Fig. 3.6).
- Diversity: a place with variety and choice (Fig. 3.7).

The basis for successful housing design is the organisation of clear, well-defined spaces. These are made up of the organisation of streets, squares, and other groupings, walls, trees, hedges and soft landscaping. Spaces can be consciously designed to produce specific feelings within the user, which is particularly pertinent to their perception of crime (Figs. 3.8a and 3.8b). Large spaces can cause a person to feel small and

Figure 3.2 A place with its own identity: Bristol Docklands regeneration. Architects: Fielden Clegg.

insignificant – "in awe of the space" (Colquhoun and Fauset, 1991, p. 240). Very narrow spaces between high buildings can be almost completely in shadow and may therefore be considered dangerous. "Restricted" spaces should only be planned if there are also "open" ones in the immediate neighbourhood. Too many large spaces cause a sense of anonymity. They become a kind of "no man's-land" provoking vandalism. Smaller, limited spaces, unequivocally belonging to a certain group of dwellings, will on the other hand promote the feeling of identification among their residents. They also create a feeling of intimacy, protection and security – spaces

Figure 3.3 Streets, squares and other public places are clearly distinguished from private areas: Hulme, Manchester.

that are scaled to people are most successful in residential areas. The exact number of dwellings in which people can relate with one another depends upon the location, but normally 12 to 15 dwellings is considered the maximum.

Scale and proportion

This is one of the most exacting parts of housing design. A number of design guides prescribe appropriate distances between buildings in relationship to their height. The general consensus is that to achieve the successful

Figure 3.4 A place with attractive and successful outdoor areas; Pasture View, Rothwell, Leeds. Architects: York University Design Unit (David Strickland).

containment of streets, a ratio of between 1:1 and 1:2.5 is required (Colquhoun and Fauset, 1991a, p. 242). The recommended proportion for squares is around 1:4 (Fig. 3.9). It is extremely difficult to achieve these proportions because of the low storey heights of modern housing in comparison with older housing. The minimum planning distances between windows usually results in the houses being too far apart and the street feeling too wide. The need to accommodate car parking often makes this even worse. However, distances can be reduced by careful location of housing and windows and separating long- and short-term parking.

Figure 3.5 A place that has a clear image, is easy to understand and move through. Regeneration of George Street and Queen Street: Whitehaven, Cumbria. Architects: Barnett Winskell.

Poundbury in Dorset is particularly successful in this respect. Distances can be reduced by the careful location of housing and windows along the street: Poundbury in Dorset (Fig. 3.54) is particularly successful in this respect.

The extent to which space is enclosed depends upon how far the views from it are controlled. A space is most complete in a cloister or courtyard

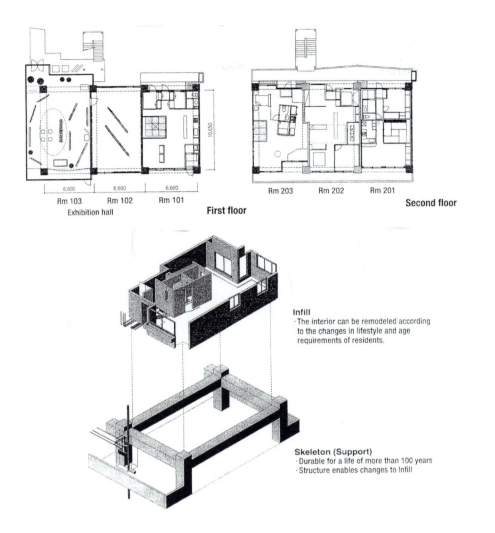

6,600 6,600 6,600

Rm 103 Rm 102 Rm 101

Exhibition hall **First floor**

Rm 203 Rm 202 Rm 201

Second floor

Infill
· The interior can be remodeled according to the changes in lifestyle and age requirements of residents.

Skeleton (Support)
· Durable for a life of more than 100 years
· Structure enables changes to Infill

Figure 3.6 A place that can easily change: "open building", frame and infill construction in Japan offers adaptability of use (by courtesy of the Urban Development Corporation, Japan).

form (Fig. 3.10) and is least complete when the buildings are separated by wide gaps and when the buildings that form the space bear little formal relationship to each other. There are distinct advantages in creating a feeling of strong enclosure: it provides a sense of identity and privacy to the group of dwellings. However, a variety of spaces are essential to avoid uniformity and monotony (Figs. 3.11 to 3.13).

Figure 3.7 BoO1 housing: Malmo, Sweden, a place with variety and choice.

Movement

In all but very small schemes there will be a need to balance the sense of space with the need for vehicles and pedestrians to move through spaces. Here, spaces will be formed through the relationship between buildings and roads. Buildings can be arranged to emphasize a change of direction of the road or can be arranged to cut off a view – whether the layout is formal or informal. In his book *Townscape*, Gordon Cullen described the process as the "art of relationship". "Townscape is seen here not as decoration, not as a style or a device for filling up empty spaces with cobbles; it is seen as the art of using raw materials – housing, trees, roads – to create a lively and attractive environment" (Colquhoun and Fauset, 1991a, p. 242).

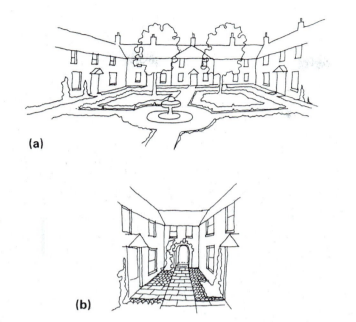

Figure 3.8 Enclosure. (a) Large open space. (b) Restricted space. Size of space can affect how people feel in it. (Colquhoun and Fauset, 1991, p. 240.)

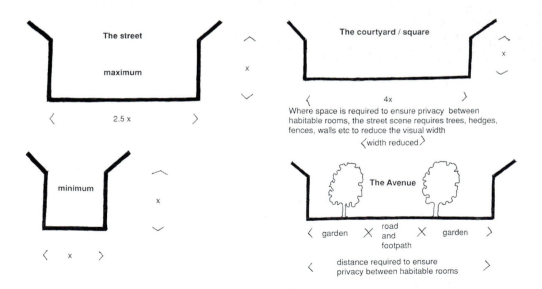

Figure 3.9 Scale and proportion: ratios of width of space to height of building. (Colquhoun and Fauset, 1991, p. 242.)

85

Figure 3.10 Cloistered housing: Nunthorpe Avenue, York. Architects: York University Design Unit (Lionel Curtis).

Structure

The structure of housing, open space and other uses should blend new housing naturally into the surrounding neighbourhood (DTLR/CABE, 2001, p. 40–41) or into the natural characteristics of the site. Housing should be planned in simple street blocks with dwellings facing the street and back gardens enclosed at the back. There should be a variety of different block sizes and forms to add richness to a neighbourhood. Visual quality should come, not from the layout form as such, but from a mix of activities and from the quality of detailing of the buildings, the landscaping

Figure 3.11 Larger courtyard space contrasts with smaller, tighter space in Figure 3.12: St Andrew Street, Beverley. Architects: David Crease and Partners (David Strickland).

and the interface between these elements. Good corner buildings (Figs. 3.14 and 3.15) are important in creating landmarks. The set-back of dwellings from the street can vary from nothing (as at Poundbury, Fig. 3.54) to 3–5 m or more depending upon the local design situation. The decision on whether a front garden is required, its size, and the need to provide defensible space, should be determined locally.

Orientation

Getting good daylight and sunshine into main habitable rooms can add considerably to their special quality, but lining all dwellings on a site in parallel

Figure 3.12   Lurk Lane, St Andrew Street, Beverley.

lines with gardens on the south side can undermine the relationship between the fronts and the backs of dwellings and reduce natural surveillance of the street. It is therefore important for orientation to be carefully balanced with other layout design requirements.

Layout design

It is important to form clear groupings of buildings to create positive public and private spaces, and avoid leftover space. It is preferable to

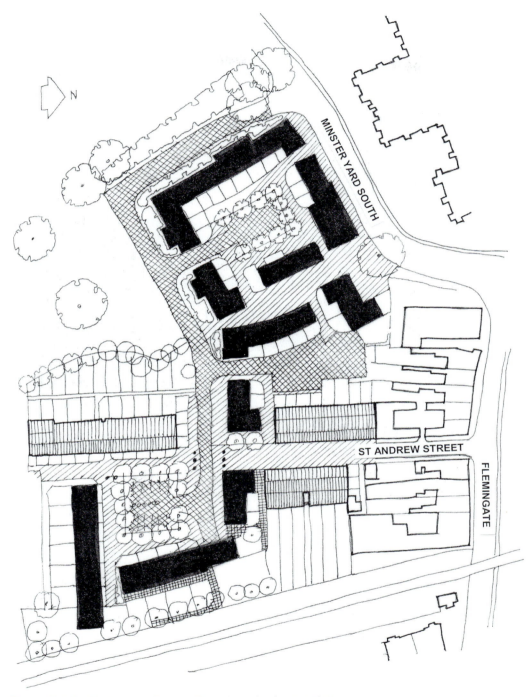

Figure 3.13 St Andrew Street, Beverley: site layout plan.

Figure 3.14 Corner buildings creating landmarks: Hulme, Manchester. Architects: North British Housing Association.

link dwellings with walls and fences to minimise obvious gaps in the street frontage. A disciplined building line with a limited use of projections and set-backs is preferable to avoid creating hiding places. The windows of principal rooms and front entrances should be positioned to maximise casual overlooking of public spaces and front entrances should be clearly visible from the street. Windowless gables and façades fronting either public or vulnerable private spaces should be avoided. Parking places, boundary walls and fences should not impede the overlooking of public places.

Figure 3.15 Good corner design in private housing at Martlesham Village, near Ipswich, Suffolk. Architects: Fielden & Mawson.

Entrance to housing areas

Symbolic gating at the entrances to a development, a street or a court, is a well-established design principle. It gives the sense that the space beyond is not quite public and that it belongs to the people who live there. The feeling of entrance can be created by a change of road surface or by a feature that signifies entrance (Figs. 3.16 to 3.20).

Walls and fences

Information on designing out crime will usually advise that walls and fences to front gardens are essential, although there are situations in areas of low

Figure 3.16 Entrance "gate" marked with the name of the development. Woolloomooloo, Sydney, Australia. Architects: Allen Jack & Cottier, Phillip Cox & Partners & others.

vulnerability where open fronts would be most appropriate. Each scheme must be considered on its individual merits. Good screening is, however, usually necessary around private rear gardens.

The following guidelines for walls, fences, hedges, etc., are suggested:

■ For gardens facing on to public areas, a high brick wall (1.8 metres minimum) or close boarded fencing to screen rear gardens is usually necessary. To make walls or close boarded fences appear less solid, a trellis could be provided on top to soften the impact.

■ Front boundary walls close to windows should be designed to discourage people from sitting on them. In the case of a brick wall this can be achieved

Figure 3.17 Entrance defined with solid brick piers: The German Hospital, Dalston Lane. Architects: Hunt Thompson Associates.

by using a suitably shaped coping, by ensuring that the walls are not at a comfortable sitting height or by putting railings on top of the wall (Fig. 3.22).

■ Where privacy is less important, but there is need to delineate a semi public/ private space, a simple low wall, fence or hedge may be sufficient.

■ Hedges should be of a quick-growing species that can be easily maintained. Some form of temporary fencing may be required to provide a barrier until the hedge has grown sufficiently (Fig. 3.28).

Figures 3.21 to 3.31 show a whole variety of options from very minimal treatment through to more secure options.

Figure 3.18 Entrance "gates" to private sheltered housing for elderly people: Northumberland Village, Monkseaton, North Tyneside. Architects: Jane Darbyshire & David Kendall Ltd.

Density, form and tenure

The recent demand for higher densities in the UK was the outcome of the report *Towards an Urban Renaissance*, produced by the Urban Task Force chaired by Lord Richard Rogers (Urban Task Force, 1999). The density agenda is important for London and the South East of England where there is both a demand for new housing and pressure to avoid green-field development. In addition, the market in the South East is more receptive than elsewhere to a high-density product. Typical housing densities in London are:

■ Outer London suburb – 30 dwellings per hectare (12/acre).

Figure 3.19 Entrance defined by simple timber arch and fencing: Gothenburg, Sweden.

Figure 3.20 Symbolic "gateway" in residential area in Tokyo, Japan.

Figure 3.21 Good combination of walls and railings: high wall screening the side of private gardens and light railings protecting front space. Woolloomooloo, Sydney, Australia. Architects: Allen Jack & Cottier.

- Inner London housing association scheme – 70 dwellings per hectare (30/acre).
- Victorian Street in Islington – 100 dwellings per hectare (40/acre).
- Street in Kensington and Chelsea – 200 dwellings per hectare (80/acre) (PRP Architects, 2002, p. 13).

The UK government's policy on density is given in Planning Policy Guidance Note No. 3, *Housing* (PPG3). It advises that housing developments should be designed to at least 12 or more dwellings per acre (30 per hectare) while 16 (40) is preferred and 20 (50) the minimum for all

Figure 3.22 Front walls with railings and gates designed to discourage sitting: North Hull Housing Action Trust. Architects: Hull City Council Architects.

urban locations. Higher densities than this are to be encouraged in locations near to good public transport. The need to design housing to higher densities means that schemes are more complex and that developers are at long last employing architects. It also strengthens the planner's hand in creating a product that is chosen for its design rather than merely its price.

Density and crime

Past design mistakes have created a common belief and fear amongst people in many countries that high-density housing in itself is a cause of crime and

Figure 3.23 Lions on brick piers defend the front parking and gardens in an East New York housing development.

vandalism, drug taking, etc., yet this has never been proven. Where high-rise has been improved and made secure from crime with door entry systems and other design features, it has proved very popular (Fig. 4.5). Many blocks that were once difficult to let have been successfully converted into sheltered housing for elderly people. Flats in other blocks have been successfully sold on the open market. In the USA, Al Zelinka, writing on crime and the environment, comments on the issue by saying that "not one study has shown any direct relationship between population or housing density and violent crime rates; once residents' incomes are taken into account, the

Figure 3.24 Simple post and wire fencing to support a future hedge can be sufficient if there is good natural surveillance. Participatory housing in Malmo, Sweden. Architect: Ivo Waldhor.

Figure 3.25 Metal railings enhance and protect in this housing in Sydney, Australia.

effect of density decreases to non-significance" (Zelinka, 2002b). His research into unsuccessful housing estates in the USA of the 1960s and 1970s, such as Pruitt Igoe in St Louis, indicated that the problems were related to design and management and socio-economics rather than to density. "Crime is higher in low-density cities such as Los Angeles, Houston and Detroit than in other cities … attempts to design higher density on the model of the New Urbanist Movement (p. 158), have proved particularly successful." His overriding view is that crime is clearly more related to levels of income, education, urban design and management aspects of housing than it is to density.

Figure 3.26 The front steps and small yards and the balconies above foster a lively street life: Waterloo, Sydney, Australia. Architects: Peter Myers.

Higher densities can mean more eyes on the street, but the benefit of this is only gained if the overall design is of a high standard. The essential design features for successful high-density development are:

- Accessible locations with good transport links
- Location regarded as generally "sought after"
- Generous internal space
- An adequate infrastructure of amenities in the area
- High standards of management and maintenance. Generally when housing density increases, costs in the form of rents and service charges go up too
- Sufficient storage

Figure 3.27   Timber fencing can be attractive if well-maintained: early colonial housing in Sydney, Australia.

Figure 3.28 Gardens delineated by hedge planting can create a more soft affect than walls and fences: Holmefield, Heslington, York. Architects: York University Design Unit (John McNeil).

- Adequate facilities in the neighbourhood for children
- Spacious balconies where there are no private gardens
- Comparatively low occupancy levels and child densities
- Good security arrangements
- High standards of finish

To help make higher densities more acceptable an adequate level of communal facilities should be provided. An insight into providing this is per-

Figure 3.29 Post and chain fencing is sufficient protection to front gardens of these houses at Welwyn Garden City.

Figure 3.30 Street scene in Poundbury, Dorset. Note the small strip of planting to soften the junction between housing and pavement.

haps best given by looking at current patterns in the upper-priced private sector market and trends in other countries where people seem to prefer schemes with a range of services including recreation space (Fig. 3.32), gymnasiums and swimming pools, and a welcoming reception area with concierge service (Fig. 3.33). These facilities represent the way that people use their time, and they are becoming a necessary adjunct of high-density living. On a lesser level, glazing in a balcony and forming a conservatory can transform the idea of high-density living for many people (Figs. 3.34 and 3.35). In addition, space is needed for home working, computers, etc. Teenagers need space to entertain their friends and for their hobbies. This is much more possible in low-density housing where there is outside space

Figure 3.31   A strip of low planting separates housing from public space: Daglas Have, Frederiksberg, Copenhagen. Architects: Christian Tranberg.

Figure 3.32 Tennis court amongst housing at Greenland Passage, London.

in which to expand. Opportunity for flexibility needs to be built into the initial design to cater for changing social patterns and increases in living standards (Fig. 3.6). Otherwise the design will become outdated very quickly. In the social rented sector minimal affordable housing standards must increase and potentially expensive amenities must be funded and provided. "Cities will not work unless this is acknowledged" (Kaplinski, 2002, p. 14).

Some developers fear that increasing density will lower the sales potential of housing. A recent study (CABE/ODPM/Design for Homes, 2003) has proved this not to be the case. From investigating recently completed developments the study concluded that there was no reason to suspect that values

Figure 3.33 High quality reception area in housing for low-income people in East New York; built by H.E.L.P (Housing Enterprises for the Less Privileged). Architects: Cooper Robinson & Partners.

will be lower purely because of density. The important ingredient for success with all the schemes above PPG3's benchmark of 30 dwellings per hectare (12 dwellings per acre) that were researched was design quality, which clearly does have an impact on the overall value.

Figure 3.34 Glazed-in balconies are much appreciated by residents and afford a high level of surveillance: Copenhagen.

Child density

The most significant density issue is the number of children in a scheme. The likelihood of vandalism and antisocial behaviour is greater where dwelling mixes permit high child densities, and particularly where families are living in building forms that are unsuited to their needs. Studies in the past have indicated that not more than 25–30 per cent of the population of a housing development should be aged 6–16 (HDD, 1981, p. 5), but it is preferable for policies to be flexible in relation to building form and levels of management, both of which might mitigate the effects of child density. It must be remembered that children will not restrict their activities to playgrounds but con-

Figure 3.35 Spacious sheltered balconies are outdoor rooms: Heste, Gothenburg, Sweden.

gregate wherever opportunities allow including staircases, access decks, garages, and so on. It is therefore important to avoid an over-concentration of larger family housing in one group.

There are three occasions in the design and letting processes when child density should be considered. Firstly, at the briefing and design stage, the mix of dwelling sizes should plan for an appropriate child density. Secondly, at the planning permission stage the issue should be taken into account wherever possible. The real problem comes at the third stage: selling or letting of the property. Registered social landlords may be able to exercise some control,

111

but if houses are let on an individual "house by house" basis, without reference to the cumulative effect, problems can easily build up. There is even less likelihood that care will be taken in the private sale or private rented sector. The Essex Police Crime Prevention Design Adviser outlines the difficulties that can arise in Chapter 4 (p. 226).

Density and culture

It is most important to understand for whom the housing and its environment is being created. In this respect it is all too easy for architects to turn to models both in Britain and in other countries without understanding essential social and cultural differences between the people to be accommodated. The European model of urban living is vastly different to that of Britain. Historically, apartment living was most common in Europe, whereas in Britain the normal pattern has traditionally been the house in some form or other, with individual access at ground-floor level.

Japan offers special lessons. Its cities are far more densely populated than in Britain yet there is a much lower level of domestic crime (Table 1.1, p. 3). Japanese people have traditionally been accustomed to living close together in densely packed housing. In modern terms this means high-density, low-rise housing and "super-high rise" blocks exceeding 30 storeys. New housing blocks of four or more storeys with deck access are laid out in neat rows and set in an open landscaped environment. Orientation is the prime design criterion to gain maximum benefit from winter sunshine. Street parking for cars is frequently on two levels with mechanical platforms allowing one car to be parked beneath the other. There is no graffiti or rubbish strewn around. Bicycles need not be chained to a rail whilst the user is at the local shops. This is all possible due to a culture in which people at domestic level appear respectful of their neighbours and their neighbours' possessions. There are signs of change, particularly amongst young people, as they adopt western influences. However, the sustainability of Japanese urban living could be ensured by the high design quality and standard of finish achieved both within new dwellings and in the external environment (Fig. 3.36). The Japanese value new products and this is being met with a programme of over one million new houses each year in comparison to Britain's much lower figure of around 150,000.

Housing for elderly people

Elderly people and other groups with special needs are readily seen as exploitable. To avoid this problem some elderly people choose to live in sheltered housing. Category 1 sheltered housing complexes are designed either as

Figure 3.36 High-density housing is common in Japan where there is a much lower domestic crime rate than in Britain: Co-operative housing, U–Court, Kyoto.

bungalows or two- or three-storey flats grouped around one or more semi-public open spaces. Category 2 sheltered housing is usually in the form of a single building with heated internal corridors linking flats with communal facilities (Fig. 3.37). Sheltered housing should not be isolated. In crime prevention terms this means that it should be sufficiently close to other housing or the public to make natural surveillance possible from surrounding properties.

In the case of small groups of individual dwellings, it is preferable to enclose external spaces with walls, fencing and/or hedging to define territory but without creating a fortress feel. There should be a single well-defined

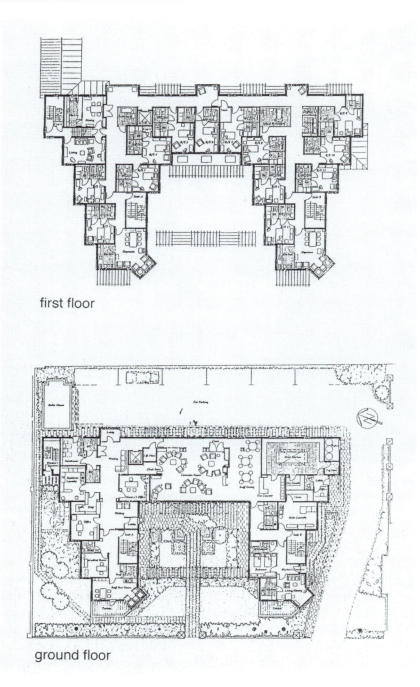

first floor

ground floor

Figure 3.37   Ground and first floor plans of Category 2 sheltered housing for elderly people, Alan Morkill House, St Mark's Road, London. PRP Architects.

entrance to the group with gates to provide a symbolic statement of privacy. The need for walls, fences and gates for individual dwellings depends upon the nature of the design. Where they abut public areas they would normally be needed. Elderly people welcome a small individual rear garden or patio. If, however, they have difficulty maintaining it, the space should be looked after communally by linking a small number together to form a shared garden. However, the area must appear private to that group of dwellings (Fig. 3.38) (Town, 2001).

Roads and footpaths

The quality of streets affects the way people feel about a place, yet too frequently roads dominate housing environment with little regard for overall quality. However, in recent years a new outlook has been emerging in Britain as reflected in the statement from the Office of the Deputy Prime Minister:

Figure 3.38 Shared rear gardens with individual patios: Campbell Court, Osbaldwick Lane, York. Architects: York University Design Unit (Terry Beechey).

"Most people live in streets of housing, and streets are an essential building block of urban living. Improving streets is not simply a design issue. Enhancing streets addresses wider social issues. It is about achieving safer environments through promoting a personal and communal sense of community – It is about social ownership of the public realm and helping to reduce the physical and cultural isolation fostered by streets with no thought to the needs of individuals and the community" (ODPM/CABE, 2002b, p. 8).

The important words in this statement are "social ownership of the public realm", for creating this can make a dramatic impact on reducing crime in residential areas.

It is now recognised that the character of a street can affect a driver's behaviour – and that of the would-be criminal offender. The perception of a street closely contained by buildings is different to one that passes through a wide-open space. Taking this into account, it is possible to control the speed of traffic through measures such as changing the perceived width of the road by narrowing it with walls, hedges and planting and foreshortening the views (Fig. 3.39). Changing the understanding of the street will affect the speed of traffic far more effectively than the use of

Figure 3.39   Roads, planting and buildings combine to create a harmonious street scene: Warrington New Town.

speed humps and chicanes (see p. for 20 mph zones). These should be regarded as back-up where the layout does not achieve low speeds. They do nothing to change the way streets are used; nor do they create a sense that the street belongs to the people living around. Tim Gill argues: "to significantly change the function of the street, more stringent measures such as changing the nature of the road to reduced speeds of 10 mph or less are needed. In any case, the road humps and steel gates that feature in standard traffic calming are hardly elements of high quality streetscape" (Gill, 2001, pp. 38–39).

Accessibility and permeability

Housing layout has changed considerably in the last few years from a largely cul-de-sac form to a pattern of through roads based on the principle of accessibility and permeability.

Culs-de-sac

These emerged from the Garden City Movement in Britain at the turn of the 20th century. In their designs for Hampstead Garden Suburb in London and Letchworth, located approximately 25 miles north of London (Figs. 3.40 and 3.41), architects Barry Parker and Raymond Unwin designed what, for the time, were unique street layouts. Instead of creating a conventional pattern of parallel streets connected together at either end, the streets were arranged in a hierarchy from wide through roads, via short and narrow connecting streets to small culs-de-sac. In order that culs-de-sac less than 150 m in length and 5 m wide could be constructed, a special Act of Parliament was necessary. Because of Parliament's worry about possible traffic problems, they stipulated a maximum density of eight houses to the acre.

The Garden City concept crossed the Atlantic to the USA, where the philosophy was related to the American way of life, including the higher reliance on and ownership of motor cars. It was reflected in the design of Radburn, New Jersey, built from 1928, which, with other schemes to follow before the Second World War, was to influence the theory of residential area planning and design in many countries until the 1960s. The major feature of a Radburn layout was the separation of vehicular traffic from the footpath system, with roads designed in a hierarchical fashion to eliminate unnecessary traffic in residential areas. Each house was designed to front onto a road or a cul-de-sac, where there was a garage or parking space. The main entrance was from the footpath on the other side.

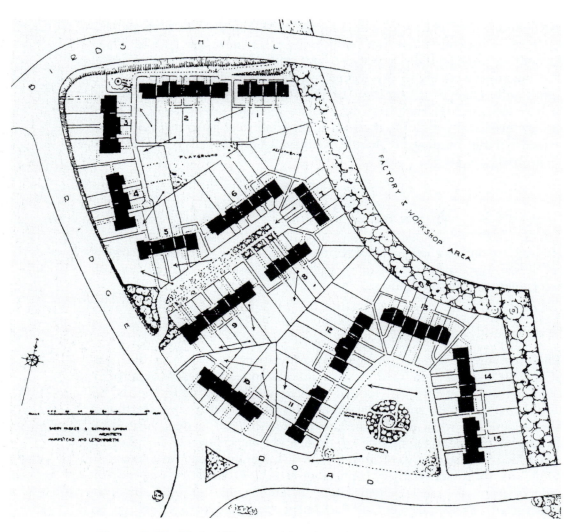

Figure 3.40 Birds Hill area of Letchworth, with its irregular layout of houses grouped around a cul-de-sac and a small green. From *The Art of Building a Home* (1901) by Barry Parker and Raymond Unwin.

The cul-de-sac was promoted as part of the Radburn system. In their 1939 manual, *Planning Neighbourhoods for Smaller Households*, the US Federal Housing Administrators observed that:

"Homes located on culs-de-sac . . . offer distinct advantages especially to families with small children. In addition to the reduction of the traffic hazard, the creation of such sites has many other advantages both to the buyer and the

Figure 3.41 Housing by Parker and Unwin in Letchworth.

developer. The cost of street improvements may be greatly reduced" (Colquhoun and Fauset, 1991a, p. 36).

When translated into large numbers of local authority housing estates in Britain in the 1960s, Radburn proved unpopular with residents due to the confusion over entrance, and children played on the road side rather than in the green areas. The arrangement opened both sides of a dwelling to the possibility of crime. The schemes also lacked one of the major Radburn principles, which was the development of a community organisation to "administer the public lands, enforce restrictions, and supply supplementary services such as recreation and day care facilities" (Colquhoun and Fauset,

1991, p. 36). In Britain, local authorities simply did not recognise this need at the time. In the USA, a number of Radburn Developments were built, which survive to this day in beautiful condition, having been maintained with great respect to their unique qualities.

The concept of the cul-de-sac was embodied in British design guides up to the 1990s. The Essex Design Guide (1973) was amongst the first to be produced. This encouraged the creation of small intimate groupings of dwellings around short mews courts (Figs. 3.42a and 3.42b) designed for both pedestrians and cars driven at very low speed. Design Bulletin 32, *Residential Roads and Footpaths* (DOE/DOT, 1977), also advocated small groups of housing designed around shared pedestrian and vehicular access ways and mews courts. This form of layout reflected the belief that the most effective way to reduce the possibility of crime was to limit access to possible offenders by designing the street layout so that only residents and people with "business" needed to be in the streets. At the time it was thought that limiting accessibility offered more in terms of security than

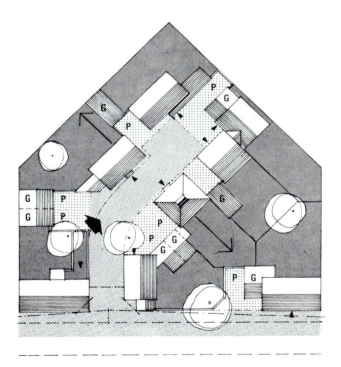

KEY

⬆ Viewpoint of Fig. 4.151d
P Parking
G Garage
▲ Front door
⟶ Main prospect
— 2 m. wall
⋯ Minimum highway area required in court
▓ Private zone
░ Public zone
▒ Adopted highway in public zone

Figure 3.42 (a) Mews court layout in the first edition of the Essex Design Guide. (Essex County Council Planning Department, 1973, pp. 96–97).

Figure 3.42 (b) Sketch of mews court (Essex County Council Planning Department, 1973, p. 97.)

territoriality and natural surveillance. Through the use of culs-de-sac and short horseshoe-shaped loops it was possible to minimise the intrusion of unwanted passers-by.

The cul-de-sac is perhaps best expressed in the form of a court where the characteristic features are as follows (Guinness Trust, 1996, p. 15):

■ A place contained by a small group of dwellings (a maximum of 25, normally fewer.
■ A single point of access/egress.
■ A constricted entrance gateway.

■ A pedestrian/vehicular surface, often partly used for parking.
■ High quality hard and soft landscape treatment.

The intimacy of a court is such that careful attention should be paid to the mix of dwellings. In particular, significant concentrations of large family houses should be avoided. Courts are generally better suited to small family houses or flats, with larger houses located on the main street (Figs. 3.43 and 3.44).

However, there are design problems with large cul-de-sac layouts that can be difficult to resolve. Walls and fences of back gardens to cul-de-sac houses tend to dominate the appearance of perimeter and collector roads. Highway engineers make this more of a problem by insisting on extensive sight lines along these roads, which create green swathes of unused land. In addition, without careful planning, pedestrians find the most direct routes along the collector roads.

Permeability

Permeability addresses these problems. The concept was the main theme of *Responsive Environments* (1985), written by a team of architects, urban designers and landscape architects at Oxford Brookes University. This drew attention to design principles forecast earlier by Jane Jacobs and Oscar Newman, the most important of which was to reduce the road hierarchy of routes by making a network of alternative ways through an environment. The theme was most expertly summed up by the Guinness Trust in its Housing Design Guide (1996):

> "*Traditional towns and neighbourhoods are permeable. This means that their streets, squares and courtyards are connected to each other to form a network, enabling quick, easy passage and easy route finding through the area (Fig. 3.45). Neighbourhoods and public places flow into each other forming a seamless and integrated settlement . . . Cul-de-sac layouts are not acceptable except for certain situations where they support responsiveness if they offer choice, which would otherwise be missing. But they must be added to a permeable layout, not substituted for it*" (Guinness Trust, 1996, p. 13).

David Taylor of Alan Baxter Associates, who wrote *Places, Streets and Movement* (1998b), for the UK Department of Environment, Transport and the Regions (DETR), comments that he deliberately avoided the issue of permeability and culs-de-sac due to the difference of opinion at the time between the police and the design theorists. Instead he recommended that "an assessment of potential risks should be made early in the development of the design, in consultation with the local Police Architectural Liaison Officer (or in London, the Crime Prevention

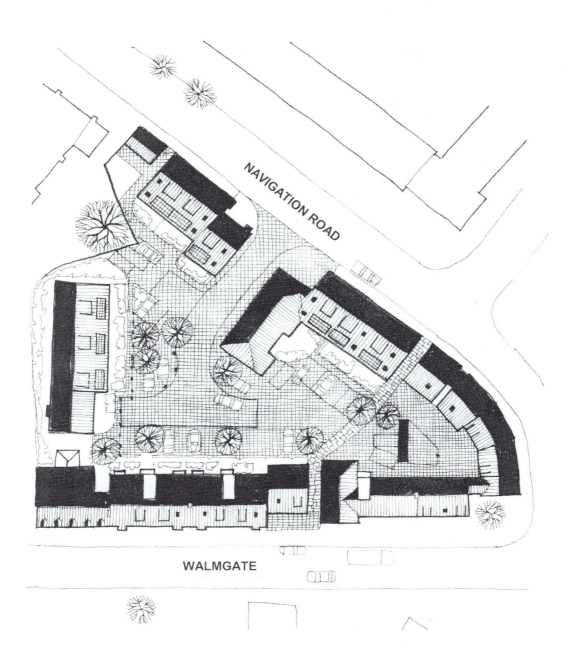

NAVIGATION ROAD

WALMGATE

Figure 3.43 Court development: site layout of Bretgate, York. Architects: York University Design Unit (John McNeil).

Figure 3.44 Harmony achieved between buildings and courtyard design: Bretgate, York.

Design Advisor)". There are significant local variations in the degree of risk. Crime prevention measures that are essential in one area may be less necessary elsewhere. The priority should be to understand the local context and to achieve a balance between security and other issues. For instance, some provision of culs-de-sac may be appropriate to the character of a particular area, but totally inappropriate elsewhere. Layout principles that work in private development may not be suitable for social housing. Streets should seem to belong to the adjacent housing and not to totally to a third party – i.e., the highway authority. People should take control of their street and it should no longer be regarded merely as a corridor for movement. In turn, this would offer greater security.

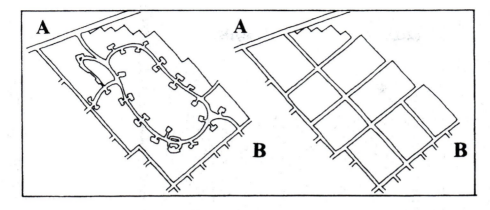

Figure 3.45 Small housing blocks in a permeable layout give more choice of routes than in the one large-block layout. In the example shown, the large block offers only 3 alternative routes, without backtracking between A and B. The version with small blocks has 9 alternatives, with a slightly shorter length of public route. (Bentley et al., 1985, p. 12.)

Robert Cowan was more outspoken in *The Connected City* (1997) when he related culs-de-sac to most of the bland formless suburbs built in the last half of the twentieth century. He commented that house-builders in Britain favour culs-de-sac:

> *"The minimal connection to the rest of the city means that builders' market staff can plug in their computer-generated, standard house types and standard layouts, without having to do any urban design. Some local authorities like them for the same reason: the simpler the planning application, the simpler it is for them to rubber-stamp planning approval"* (Cowan, 1997, p. 20).

Builders also market their housing as safe places in which to live. Residents can classify an intruder, but, argues Cowan, "The sense of safety, usually created by the way that culs-de-sac turn in on themselves, is limited to the residents. Innocent people passing by are less likely to feel safe as they walk past the cul-de-sac along pedestrian routes that are flanked by blank perimeter walls and fences, and that are not directly overlooked by windows" (Cowan, 1997 p. 20). His solution is the "connected city" – even an unconnected stretch of city (Fig. 3.46) can be connected with new routes and development.

By Design: A Better Place to Live, A Companion Guide to PPG3 (2001), produced for the UK Government by the Department of Transport, Local Government and the Regions (DTLR), is also more specific in recommending permeable layouts. "Routes should lead to where people want to go:

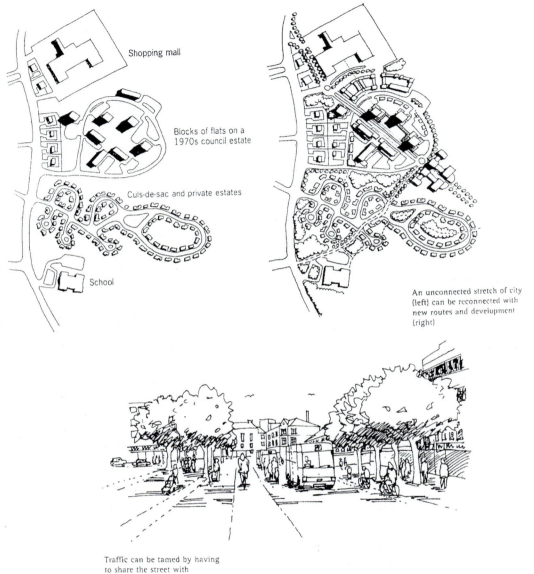

Shopping mall

Blocks of flats on a
1970s council estate

Culs-de-sac and private estates

School

An unconnected stretch of city
(left) can be reconnected with
new routes and development
(right)

Traffic can be tamed by having
to share the street with
pedestrians

Figure 3.46 An unconnected stretch of city (above left) can be reconnected with
new routes and development (above right). New roads can be integrated into the environment. (Cowan, 1997, p. 22 and 27).

providing for the optimum variety of journeys means creating well connected layouts. Introverted, dead-end layouts limit people's choice of how to travel, especially if they want to walk, cycle or use the bus."

The second edition of the Essex Design Guide, published in 1997, relates permeability to crime reduction:

> *"It should be possible for pedestrians and cyclists to move freely between all parts of the layout, both locally and on a wider scale ... A more permeable layout offers the pedestrian a choice of routes, which offers greater visual interest and therefore generates a higher level of pedestrian activity, and thus security. If there are more pedestrians around in the street there is a greater chance of casual social encounters and less chance of thieves being able to gain access unobserved to cars and houses. In order to allow free movement the ideal would be a deformed grid based on the small residential block"* (Essex County Planning Officers' Association, 1997, p. 11) (Fig. 3.47).

Permeable layouts have now become generally accepted in Essex and a number of schemes are illustrated in Chapter 4.

Despite this research and publication, there is still uncertainty about the merits of permeable over cul-de-sac layouts. There is no doubt that the average house purchaser in Britain still perceives living in a cul-de-sac as the more secure option. They see them as places where they can let their children play in safety, and the social advantage of a small group of houses is not insignificant. Is it that there is a difference between theory and practice? The guidance note produced by the Camden Police in London, *Secured by Design*, leaves open the possibility of using culs-de-sac with conditions as follows. It comments that research suggests culs-de-sac that experience burglary usually feature one or a combination of the following factors (Camden Police, 2003, p. 3). They are likely to be those that:

- back onto open land, railway lines, canal towpaths, etc.
- are very deep or complicated, i.e., culs-de-sac branching off each other
- are linked to one another by footpaths

In a paper for the *Journal of the Designing out Crime Association* (DOCA), D. Stubbs of the Thames Valley Police comments further by saying that "all these (research) works have centred on high density peripheral or inner city dwelling areas...the fact remains that too little pedestrian movement is generated (in suburban development) to create an acceptable level of what Jane Jacobs calls 'encounter rates', i.e., meetings or sightings of other law abiding people." He claims that there is a difference between "urban" and "suburban" environments. The movement patterns on the routes of a town or a city where people work and live are going to be greatly different from those on a housing estate where residential dwellings are the only main land use, apart from neighbourhood shops, schools or

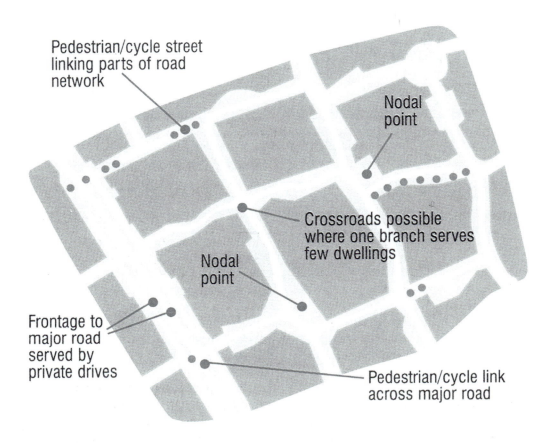

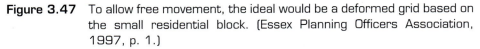

Figure 3.47 To allow free movement, the ideal would be a deformed grid based on the small residential block. (Essex Planning Officers Association, 1997, p. 1.)

community centres. His paper was particularly critical of footpaths/cycle links between culs-de-sac to create permeability – "they are used infrequently and become colonised by local youth as part of their social interaction"(Stubbs, 2002, pp. 11–19).

The answer surely lies in avoiding pre-determined views and considering sites on their individual merits within the context of their surroundings.

Tracking

Tracking is a new concept that relates the design of roads in residential areas to good urban design practice (Fig. 3.48). Instead of taking the highway

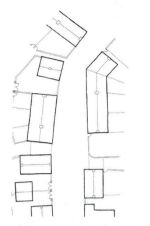

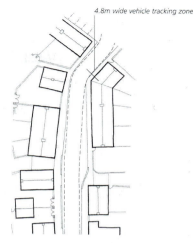

Buildings arranged to form street enclosure.

Footways laid out in front of buildings help to reinforce the space and enclosure.

Carriageway width checked by plotting vehicle tracking paths, using minimum widths quoted in DB32.

Figure 3.48 "Tracking" (DETR, 1998b, p. 55).

engineering requirements as the starting point for road design, the arrangement of buildings and spaces should be considered first. The road shape can be designed to vary in accordance with the spaces created. Then the size and shapes of the spaces should be checked against the highway engineering needs. In this way, housing can be laid out to suit an urban form with pavements and kerbs helping to define and emphasise spaces. Junctions between roads can help define a place and be considered as landmarks on a route through an area (DETR, 1998b, p. 55).

Car parking

Planning Policy Guidance Note No. 3 (PPG3) makes a change to the standard approach of planning departments in Britain to car parking, by recommending flexible policies that recognise that car ownership varies with income, age, household type and type of housing and its location. Developers should not be required to provide more car parking than they or potential occupiers might want, nor to provide off-street parking when there is no need, particularly in urban areas where public transport is available or where there is a demand for car-free housing. This is particularly relevant in housing for elderly people where the demand for car parking may be less than for family housing.

Parking is best located within the curtilage wherever this is possible. The projects illustrated in Figs. 3.49 and 3.50 successfully hide away the car within the fabric of the housing. Where curtilage parking is not possible, group parking should be in small areas screened by planting of a type and height that does not deter natural surveillance from the surrounding houses (Fig. 3.51).

Poundbury

Permeability was successfully adopted as the principle for the layout of Poundbury in Dorchester in the south-west of England, for which Leon Krier was the master planner and Alan Baxter Associates the lead consultants. The project has been the focus of much debate due to the architectural theories of HRH The Prince of Wales incorporated into its design. The total development will comprise some 3,000 houses and it will take a total

Figure 3.49   Cars parked within the curtilage: self-build housing at Nicholay Road, London. Architects: Architype.

Figure 3.50 Curtilage parking for disabled people: Rolls Crescent, Hulme Redevelopment, Manchester. Architects: ECD.

of 25 years to build, which will allow it to grow organically. A mixed-use "urban village" (p. 155) of housing, workshops, employment and shopping is envisaged. The first phase contains 250 dwellings, 50 per cent of which are owned by the Guinness Trust and cannot be identified visually from the sale housing. 15 or more architects were involved in the first phase, each designing a small area only, to avoid an estate image (Fig. 3.52).

The form of the development reflects urban village principles. Its permeable layout (Fig. 3.53) is intended to "engage" traffic, i.e., instead of excluding or calming traffic, it is "civilised" within urban spaces of human scale designed to avoid long vistas that allow drivers to accelerate. Junctions

Figure 3.51 Cars parked in a central square screened by railings, planting and trees but still well overlooked: Bishops Wharf, Skeldergate, York. Architects: Crease Edmonds Strickland (David Strickland).

have tight radii to reduce speeds, and limited sight lines make drivers slow down or stop. Car parking and garages with two spaces per dwelling, plus visitor parking, is provided by a combination of street parking on wider roads and garage/parking courtyards at the rears of the houses (Fig. 3.54). These courtyards include some housing to provide natural surveillance and reduce the possibility of burglary from what would normally be a highly vulnerable location. There is also mixed tenure in most of the housing blocks, which offers different kinds of natural surveillance. Where houses abut open space they are designed to overlook it, or a substantial wall gives privacy to rear gardens (Fig. 3.55).

Figure 3.52 Poundbury: a rekindling of the traditional town street.

The streets have been designed as coherent spaces from house wall to house wall using "tracking" as an essential tool in the placemaking process. Residents contribute communally to the quality of this space by designing and maintaining a small strip of land against the house wall, with plants, flowers and cobbles. David Taylor of Alan Baxter Associates believes that there needs to be a complete change of attitude in the design of streets. They should be looked at holistically to account for broader social issues, and comprehensively, so that all elements that make up the environment – movement, lighting, planting, children's play, safety and security – are considered together.

Holly Street regeneration

Holly Street, in the London Borough of Hackney, is also planned around the concept of permeability, and it is one of the best examples of decline and regeneration in public sector housing in Britain. The original redeve-

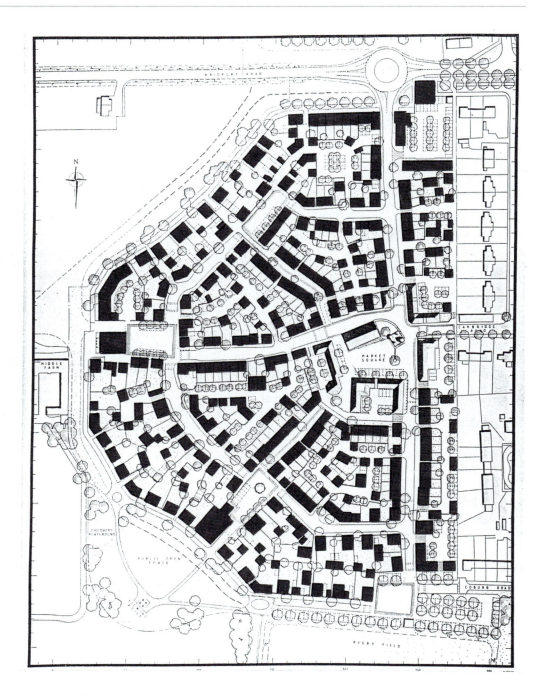

Figure 3.53 Poundbury: the layout of the first phase creates a network of spaces in which vehicles have full access. Master plan: Leon Krier. Lead Consultant: Alan Baxter and Associates.

Figure 3.54 Poundbury: rear courtyard, which contains housing to ensure natural surveillance.

lopment was completed in 1971 but it became reduced to a sink estate within five years. Holly Street comprised 1187 dwellings in four tower blocks and a series of five-storey blocks grouped around green courtyards. Particular problems were experienced in the five-storey blocks from noise and insect infestation, which proved expensive to remove. Internal corridors were long and dark and there was consistent graffiti. The estate suffered continuously from a concentration of some of the poorest people in Hackney and some dwellings were taken over by squatters. Hackney Council made various attempts in the 1980s to rectify the problems but suffered from lack of finance. Started in 1993, the new design, by Levitt Bernstein Associates, integrates a mixture of 960 family and single-person housing into its surroundings by largely reinstating the pre-1971 street pattern (Fig. 3.56). It is mixed tenure combining local authority, housing association and owner-occupied housing.

Figure 3.55 Poundbury: housing abutting open space.

In recognition of the need for social and economic regeneration to go hand-in-hand with physical change, a comprehensive programme of community development was put in place and local economic opportunities were encouraged. Children's and young people's interests were ensured through the creation of the Children and Young People's Interest Group and a detached youth worker was appointed. Widespread consultation ensured an effective contribution to policy making by local people and the results have been the subject of various reports. *Upwardly Mobile*, commissioned by Hackney Estate Management & Development in 1998, found residents completely in favour of the new estate. The most positive finding was

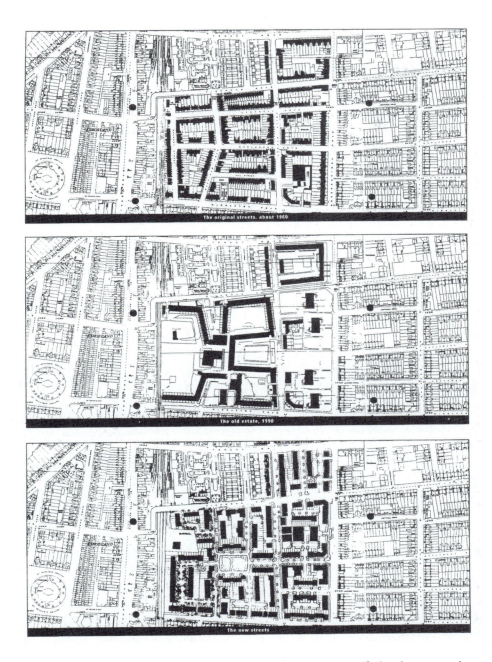

Figure 3.56 Holly Street, Dalston, London: three stages of development since 1960. Architects: Levitt Bernstein Associates.

that the downward spiral of decline and despair experienced previously had been reversed. There was a genuine improvement in community spirit (Fig. 3.57).

The increased feeling of personal and community safety is summed up by the following words of a resident:

"It was hell really. Concrete steps and long dark passages. The groups of people just standing were the most frightening. You never knew whether you might be the fifth one to pass them, the one they'd had a bet on for kicking... used to go up, get in, and go to the window to wave to my daughter to say I'd got in all right... Now it's wonderful, sometimes I can't believe I'm here. I just go in, close my front door. It's home. I never feel afraid in the neighbourhood now" (Wadham and Associates, 1998, pp. 9, 10).

The new neighbourhood is now policed by traditional beat "Bobbies" and community police, rather than by police in cars as before. 60% of residents re-housed from the old estate reported previously having had a feeling of danger, and a fear of the area. In the new Holly Street neighbourhood this

Figure 3.57 New human-scale urban housing at Holly Street.

had, by the summer of 1996, fallen to 16 per cent; by 1999 only 5 per cent of residents had any residual concerns over community safety (Colquhoun, 1999, pp. 79–81).

Street Design, Woonerfs, Home Zones

Woonerfs

Measures now used in Britain for reducing traffic speeds by design have been central to the Dutch "Woonerf" concept since 1968. Woonerfs have made a huge contribution to improving, not only the quality of the built environment in The Netherlands, but also in reducing street crime and the fear of crime in residential areas. "They have increased neighbourliness, reduced fear of 'stranger danger', lessoned isolation amongst older people and by increasing passive supervision from the streets – cut crime" (Ward, 2001, p. 4). The belief is that by handing the street to its residents, Woonerfs can provide a better quality of life. The Dutch are planning to bring traffic calming features with 18 mph speed limits to every suitable residential area in the country by 2006 (Figs. 3.58, 3.59 and 3.60).

Woonerfs in Germany

In Germany it is common practice to use the road and footpath space in a managed way to cater for pedestrian and vehicular movement and car parking (Fig. 3.61). The cars are overlooked even though planting screens them. Figure 3.62 shows a pedestrian-only area within a Woonerf, which can be used by emergency vehicles. Crime prevention through environmental design has become an accepted part of the planning and design of new housing in Germany. It started from a small beginning in 1990 when the state of Schleswig-Holstein (close to Denmark) founded the first crime prevention council in Germany. It has now established 65 at local level. There are some 1,700 crime prevention councils at local level throughout Germany, supported by co-ordinating bodies in all sixteen states. At national level, the German Forum for Crime Prevention arranges a national annual conference attended in 2001 by 1,300 people. The key to its success has been good political support and adopting a holistic approach; there is a focus on grass-roots level participation by municipalities and local communities.

Home Zones: the Woonerf theme in Britain

In Britain the "Woonerf" concept has only slowly been taken up. It was reflected in the design of shared pedestrian vehicular areas, of which Old

Figure 3.58 "Woonerf" at Entrepotdok, Amsterdam. The road is a shared surface with space for cars, people and parking of cars and bicycles.

Royal Free Square, Islington, is an excellent example (Fig. 3.67). It is also seen in 20 mph speed zones (Fig. 3.63), but most significantly, it has become central to "Home Zones", offering a highly imaginative way of creating streets that can, through taming the car, belong to the people who live in the housing they serve. Home Zones are designated by local highway authorities under powers in the Transport Act 2000. A Home Zone is a set of roads designed primarily for pedestrians and cyclists instead of motorists. Details vary from place to place but the concept involves abolishing "roadways" and "pavements" and replacing them with a level surface shared by all users. Cars are restricted to 10 mph and parking is

1. no continuous kerb
2. private access
3. bench around low lighting column
4. use of varied paving materials
5. private footway
6. bend in the roadway
7. empty parking lot: place to sit or play in
8. bench/play object
9. on request: plot with plants in front of facade
10. no continuous roadway marking on the pavement
11. tree
12. clearly marked parking lots
13. bottleneck
14. plant tub
15. space for playing from facade to facade
16. parking prevented by obstacles
17. fence for parking bicycles etc.

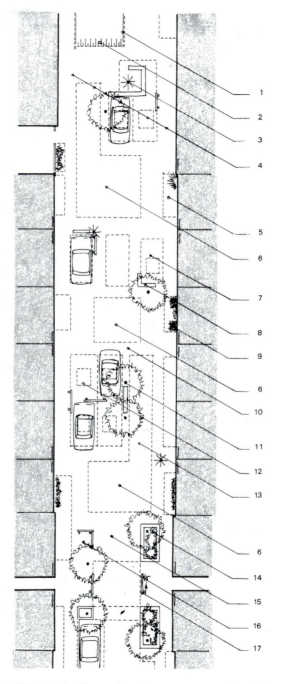

Figure 3.59 Detailed design of a Woonerf. Reproduced courtesy of ANWB (Colquhoun and Fauset, p.195).

Figure 3.60 Woonerf loop. Reproduced by courtesy of ANWB (Colquhoun and Fauset, p.194).

Figure 3.61 Woonerf in Cologne, Germany: a street designed to maximise the use of the space.

severely limited. Traffic calming, parking areas, trees and shrubs, seating areas, etc., are part of the proposals to slow traffic right down. Clear signs at entrances and exits reinforce the message to drivers that these are different kinds of streets. The aim is to change the way that streets are used and to improve the quality of life by making residential streets places for people, not just traffic (Ward, 2001, p. 4).

Success depends very much upon the involvement of the residents in the planning and design process. This can generate considerable community activity, which has a knock-on effect in terms of reducing fear of crime. The process includes community meetings, door-to-door surveys and design

Figure 3.62 Woonerf in Cologne: pedestrian-only area provides emergency access for fire engines.

workshops. Vehicle speeds are recorded with the help of the police – even school children are involved in this. Residents are encouraged to take part in simple education courses that provides them with the skills to do things for themselves, such as making bids for funding.

Since 1999 the Department for Transport, Local Government and the Regions (DTLR) has provided £30 million to pilot Home Zone development throughout Britain. This compares with 6,500 projects created since 1968 in The Netherlands and many in Denmark, Germany and Austria. In the USA the concept is reflected in some cities in "Smart Growth" mixed-use streets.

Figure 3.63   Entrance to 20mph speed limit zone: North Hull Housing Action Area:
Note the uncoordinated street furniture.

The authoritative publication on British practice is *Home Zone: Design Guidelines*, by the Institute of Highway Incorporated Engineers (2002). Its key design principles [pp. 90–91] are as follows:

- There must always be enough residents to form a viable community through a Home Zone.
- Vehicles should not have to travel more than 400 m along Home Zone streets.
- Home Zones should not have traffic flow of more than about 100 vehicles in the afternoon peak hour, which is the time when there could be conflict between vehicles and people, including children playing.
- A high proportion of residential buildings should have active fronts to the streets (i.e., windows of habitable rooms, doors and entrances) to provide good

opportunities for natural surveillance and to foster a sense of local "owner-ship" of the street.

- Home Zones must be clearly marked at their entrances and exits to ensure that all street users recognise the different nature of the area.
- Home Zones should be designed to encourage vitality in residential streets, with a high level of social interaction between residents.
- Home Zones must provide children with a safe and attractive area outside their homes, which will provide a place to meet and play with their friends.
- Any communal features, including play equipment, must be located carefully so as not to cause nuisance to local residents.
- The route for vehicles through a Home Zone should be as narrow as is practicable with a minimum width of 3 m in order to contain a speed of not more than 10 mph.
- Home Zones must be accessible to disabled people and legible to blind and visually impaired people.
- A continuous raised kerb should not normally be provided.
- On-street parking should normally be provided and arranged so that it does not dominate views of the street or impinge upon other activities that will take place in the Home Zone. In new development the amount should be deter-mined by the number and type of dwellings and the application of the appro-priate parking standards.
- Opportunities for indiscriminate parking should be removed through the design and location of street furniture, planting or other features, so that it is only possible to park within the designated on-street spaces.
- The creation of gateways is recommended at entrances to Home Zones, along with a change in surfacing material or texture. This informs drivers that they are entering an area of special character within which they must behave accordingly. Alternatively, a narrowing of the carriageway with a road hump at entrances can have the same effect upon drivers.

Stainer Street, Northmoor, Manchester

Designed and implemented by Manchester City Council, Manchester Methodist Housing Association, Urban Solutions (Manchester Engineering Design Consultancy) and Ian Findlay Architects, the Home Zone at Northmoor formed part of a multi-million-pound regeneration of 1400 small Victorian terraced houses in Longsight, Manchester. The pilot area comprised four streets, in which houses had no front gardens, and only small rear yards. There was speeding traffic, rear alleys full of rubbish that attracted burglars, few recreational facilities for children, empty houses that added to the sense of neglect, and high levels of crime. The demand for car parking was low – some 35–40 per cent cars/dwellings.

Design features (Fig. 3.64) include:

■ Converted parallel parking on both sides of the road to echelon parking
■ Installing 20 mph gateways to the area
■ Installing attractive finishes to the street – a continuous asphalt overlay with a pattern printed on it to mark the entrances to the street and create small areas that appear to relate to the adjacent house
■ New street lighting
■ Planting trees and installing street furniture

The Manchester City Council and the Manchester Methodist Housing Association have acquired houses in order to create a "green" street through

Figure 3.64 Stainer Street Home Zone: Northmoor, Manchester.

the development overlooked by new three-storey properties to provide good surveillance.

The residents participated fully in the development of the proposals. Participation began at the Residents' Association Christmas party in 1999 where a Home Zone video was shown. Residents were kept informed by newsletters and leaflets. Proposals were displayed at an "open house display" and a fun day. The display was set up in a vacant property and staffed for two weeks, day and evening. Models, plans and photographs were used to explain how the Home Zone proposals would work. Visitors were asked to fill in a questionnaire.

During the fun day one of the streets was closed for a day and a band-stand was set up with live music. There were circus performers, street games, face painting and barbecues. A four-screen cinema, dubbed the "two-up two-down", was set up in an empty house. A full-scale mock-up of ideas for the Home Zone was set up, to see how they would work in reality. Part of the street was grassed over with trees and shrubs added, and a fire engine was on hand to test the design for emergency service access.

The project was funded from the Local Transport Plan, Single Regeneration Budget, Housing Association and Housing Corporation sources. The project won a top best practice award in 2001 from the British Urban Regeneration Association.

The Methleys, Chapel Allerton, Leeds

This is a neighbourhood Home Zone scheme for 307 Victorian terraced houses, including back-to-back properties all fronting a grid of roads, and two separate complexes of flats. There was a mixture of privately owned, privately rented and dwellings in multiple occupation. The residents' survey indicated a 2.1 persons/household average and a car ownership of 0.86 cars/household.

The scheme was designed and implemented by Leeds City Council Department of Highways and Transportation. Key measures included (Fig. 3.65):

■ Extensively treating Methley Drive by bringing the road up to footpath level and providing semi-circular planting areas to give the road a more informal feel and slow traffic down. Local people have imprinted large areas of brick-work with their own designs and names.

■ On the surrounding side roads, gateways have been created with road narrow-ing and changes to the colour of the surface of the highway.

■ Traffic calmed to 20 mph. Speed cushions are provided on the main "rat-run" through the area.

■ Home Zone signing designed with the local community to demonstrate the unique character of the area and advertise the 20 mph speed limits.

Figure 3.65 The Methleys Home Zone: Chapel Allerton, Leeds.

Residents participated in the development of the proposals through questionnaires asking whether people favoured a Home Zone in principle. A separate questionnaire was used for children's views. There was a 45 per cent response rate mostly in favour, but there were some reservations about the proposal to use play street legislation to designate specific play space in the street.

The project cost £150,000 and was completed in November 2001.

Old Royal Free Square, Islington, London

Although this scheme was not designed as a Home Zone, it demonstrates the design principles extremely well. The original hospital on the site closed in

1986 and was bought by the Circle 33 Housing Trust and the New Islington and Hackney Housing Associations for housing purposes. Two architects, Levitt Bernstein Associates and Pollard Thomas and Edwards, designed the scheme, which was completed in 1992 (Fig. 3.66). It combines a mixture of new development and the conversion of the former hospital buildings. The housing provides accommodation for families, couples, single people and people with physical disabilities. The new development at the Liverpool Road end of the site reflects the scale of the hospital buildings with matching gateways of housing on either side of the entrance to help emphasise the transition from public space to semi-public space. The focus of the design is a new square (Fig. 3.67) that reflects those of the nineteenth century in the surrounding area. Within the square, a garden is enclosed by railings and gates designed by the residents and their children in collaboration with the

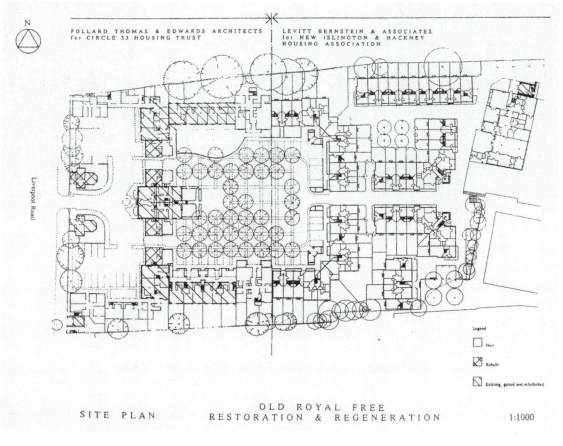

Figure 3.66 Old Royal Free Square: site layout. Architects: Levitt Bernstein Associates and Pollard Thomas and Edwards.

Figure 3.67 Old Royal Free Square: urban space of great quality.

sculptor, Jane Ackroyd. Beyond the square at the Upper Road end of the site the housing is in two- and three-storey form grouped around narrow streets (Fig. 3.68).

The urban quality of the scheme is outstanding. The blockwork treatment of the shared pedestrian/vehicular ground treatment is at the heart of the design and is well overlooked from the surrounding housing. It has created an environment that clearly belongs to the people. Strangers are noticed by the residents and particularly by the children playing in the streets. The design was only possible at the time because the two housing associations were willing to accept maintenance responsibility for the shared surface (Institute of Highway Incorporated Engineers, 2002, pp. 60–61).

151

Figure 3.68 Old Royal Free Square: narrow spaces contrast with the large central square.

Footpaths and cycleways

Generally streets that are designed for low traffic speeds less than 20 mph are safe for walking and cycling and segregated pedestrian and cycleways are only really necessary when they can provide a more direct and safe route from one place to another than is provided by the road. They should be accessible and direct, and should lead to shops, bus stops, schools and other community facilities. They can be elegant, tree-lined routes in high-density areas (Fig. 3.69) or simple tarmac routes. There should be a clear view along the route but to provide interest they should be set within a series of contrasting spaces,

Figure 3.69 Elegantly designed footpath route between new housing and a school in the Manin-Jaures area of Paris. Architect: Alain Sarfarti.

rather than along one long continuous corridor. It is important to avoid long lengths of footpath in narrow open space where people could feel unsafe. Footpaths separated from the road system should be at least 3 m wide to allow for use by emergency vehicles (Fig. 3.70) and wider if there is cycling. At appropriate intervals, barriers should be provided to prevent access by private vehicles, particularly motorbikes.

Planting adjacent footpaths and cycleways should be designed with low-growing plants next to the curb and higher species and trees at the rear. Where main footpaths run next to buildings there should be some form of barrier to prevent people looking into windows, but this planting should not obscure natural surveillance. Elderly and infirm people always appreciate seating along main footpaths but they can be a source of nuisance. Their siting must always consider the possible effect on surrounding dwellings of loitering by young people and vandalism. In this instance the use of single seats or stools set several metres apart could deter young people gathering whilst providing the opportunity of a seat for an elderly person. In some locations the use of leaning bars might be a useful alternative to seats.

Figure 3.70 Footpath designed to take service and emergency vehicles: sheltered housing for elderly people, Valley Lodge, Grange Estate at Ben Rhydding, Ilkley. Architects: York University Design Unit (John McNeil).

Where there is space the seat could be set back to create space between walkers and loiterers (Camden Police, 2003).

Urban Villages, New Urbanism and Smart Growth

Urban Villages in Britain and New Urbanism/Smart Growth in the USA arose in the late 1980s and early 1990s out of a similar interest in both countries for higher density housing as a reaction to suburban sprawl and a landscape dominated by the car. It is also seen as a way of reducing crime and fear of crime in the environment. In the USA, much of the population live in single-use residential neighbourhoods and go shopping in stand-alone commercial shopping centres. Most are happy with this segregated pattern, believing it to be more secure; but questions are being asked as to whether these single-use land patterns are as safe as people imagine. Regrettably, from a statistical point of view, the research does not yet give a clear-cut answer.

Urban Villages

The Urban Villages concept received much support from HRH Prince Charles in the early 1990s out of concern for the future environment of Britain (Aldous, 1992). It involves mixed-use development, with each village covering 30 hectares (100 acres) and accommodating 5,000 residents. Housing is built to an average density of 50 to 60 dwellings per hectare (20 to 25 dwellings per acre). There is a focus on public transport and reducing car travel by building workspace as part of the development. Developers and landowners are expected to guarantee a commitment to the urban village principles and residents are engaged in the management of the village through the establishment of a "Community Trust".

Poundbury in Dorchester (p. 130) was the first demonstration project but most emphasis has been directed towards building on brown-field sites. Silvertown in the London Docklands and Crown Street in Glasgow are also well-known examples.

Crown Street, Glasgow

The overall concept is to create the "liveable city" in which "urban life can have a vitality but also dignity and calm (Colquhoun, 1999, p. 307). The elements of this are the traditional Glasgow street grid and the city block, where the front is clearly public and the back fully private (Figs. 3.71 and 3.72). Another important element is the tenement, which the plan (by CZWG) considers to be Scotland's, especially Glasgow's, traditional building

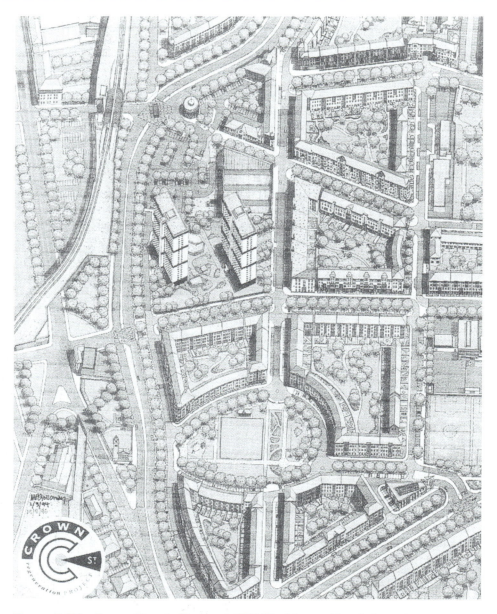

Figure 3.71 Crown Street, Glasgow. CZWG's Master Plan is based on a permeable grid of traditional streets.

Figure 3.72 New tenement housing in the Gorbals, Glasgow: car parking is in the centre of the streets between the blocks. Architects: Cooper Cromer Associates.

form. Its design meets modern living requirements with the ground and first floors of a four-storey block comprising three-bedroom maisonettes with their own front and back door and a private rear garden. Above these are two upper floors of one-, two- and three-bedroom flats accessed by a separate communal staircase. Throughout the development, car parking is in the centre of the street which is designed with trees to form a boulevard (Colquhoun, 1999, pp. 308–309).

West Silvertown Urban Village, London

West Silvertown Urban Village at the Royal Docks in London comprises 1000 dwellings on 11 hectares (27 acres). Two-thirds of the new development is private housing built by Wimpey Homes with the remainder being social housing for rent provided by the Peabody Trust and East London Housing Association (ELHA). A genuine attempt towards sustainability was made in the design through mixing tenures on the site. The layout is permeable with a grid pattern of tree-lined urban streets, crescents and courts (Figs. 3.73 to 3.75). The planning strategy included landmarks in key locations, one of which is the "Crescent" located around a central piazza overlooking the River Thames. This contains 53 flats, including 20 dwellings for elderly people on five storeys above shops on the ground floor.

New Urbanism and Smart Growth

The New Urbanism and Smart Growth movements are concerned with creating "walkable" neighbourhoods of higher density housing on small plots of land. This change of thinking reflects demographic and cultural change in the USA. There are now more elderly people in American society and fewer households with children, which has created a move amongst some people in the higher income group towards an urban life-style. Perhaps more importantly, existing car-dependent suburbs in many regions have physically declined and are less attractive to house-buyers. House values are stagnating and, in addition, suburban traffic is increasingly unbearable.

New Urbanism is a set of urban design principles for building these new walkable, mixed-use neighbourhoods. The Congress for the New Urbanism (CNU) is an organisation of architects, planners, government officials and developers. The Charter of the New Urbanism, written in 1996, lays out in a code a set of principles ranging from regional policies like balancing jobs with housing in each town, to neighbourhood-scale principles of mixed use and mixed income development, to local architectural principles like having buildings face the street. The main criteria are listed below:

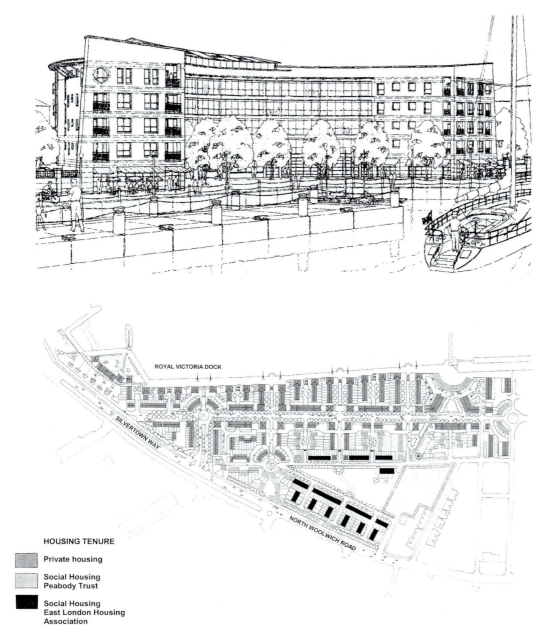

HOUSING TENURE

Private housing

Social Housing
Peabody Trust

Social Housing
East London Housing
Association

Figure 3.73 West Silvertown Urban Village: permeable layout of streets (below). Perspective of the crescent (above). Architects: Tibbalds Monroe Ltd.

Figure 3.74 West Silvertown Urban Village: tree lined streets create a strong urban form.

Land use
- A balanced mix of uses within neighbourhoods
- Higher density housing and commercial uses towards neighbourhood centres; a corner store (subsidised if necessary) in all neighbourhoods containing 500 residences
- A civic space (square, plaza, green area) at each neighbourhood centre
- Each neighbourhood should have one prominent, honorific site at the neighbourhood centre

Street design
- Avoid culs-de-sac where natural conditions do not demand them

Figure 3.75 West Silvertown Urban Village: crescents provide streetscape variety.

- Street blocks should be less than 200–300 metres in length and less than 700 metres in perimeter
- All streets within the neighbourhood should be fronted with housing rather than serving as collector roads with no purpose except handling traffic
- Street geometries should be designed so that speed is limited to 50 kph (30 mph) on main streets and 35 kph (20 mph) on local streets
- One-way streets should be avoided in all but the most needed places in the central area
- Hide the garage and put porches back in front

Streetscapes

- Think green ... every street should have indigenous shade trees planted no more than 10 metres apart
- All streets in residential areas, other than alleys, should have pavements on one side, 1.5–2 metres wide
- All streetlights and other street furniture should be placed within the tree strip except main street benches which should back up to building fronts
- Softer and more pedestrian-friendly street lighting design
(*ICA Journal*, 2002, pp. 1 and 7)

These design principles are considered important in reducing crime and the fear of crime. Al Zelinka writes:

> *"Mixed-use, walkable communities – including a mix of housing types within a neighbourhood – allow people of diverse backgrounds to co-exist or informally conform to the accepted behaviour of their neighbours ... community policing is made much easier with designs that include pedestrian friendly streets, a diversity of people of different ages, incomes and cultures who get to know each other. Driving around spread out suburban areas is very inefficient for police patrols, and many such areas never see such police presence. If we do not provide opportunities through our planning and design policies for diversity to co-exist, then homogenous patterns emerge which are conducive to criminal activity"* (Zelinka, 2002a).

Smart Growth shares the same values as New Urbanism but adds principles to encourage community and stakeholder collaboration in the planning process and to direct development towards existing communities already served by infrastructure.

Crawford Square, Pittsburgh

While this scheme was built in the mid-1990s, before New Urbanism became a major influence in the USA, it demonstrates the design and community sustainability principles extremely well. It also demonstrates how dilapidated, crime-infested, urban neighbourhoods in American cities are having life brought back into them. Located at the edge of the downtown area of Pittsburgh on an 18 acre (6.5 hectares) site, the development revised the original street grid (Fig. 3.76). The high density of 28 dwellings per acre (76/ha) was achieved with a mixture of two- and three-storey apartments, town houses and single-family houses. The design of each street was carefully considered in relationship to urban design guidelines, produced by the Architects, UDA of Pittsburgh (Fig. 3.77). These specified materials and colours, as well as the design of bay windows, dormers, porches, fences,

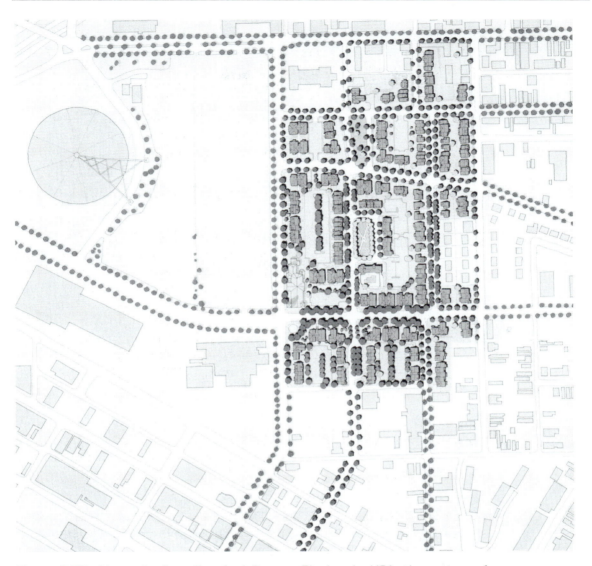

Figure 3.76 New urbanism, Crawford Square, Pittsburgh, USA: the pattern of streets extends the existing city grid. Architects: UDA Architects.

etc. All ground-floor dwellings have front and rear gardens (Fig. 3.78) (Colquhoun, 1995, pp. 53–54).

The scheme, which was planned for an economically mixed population with a wide range of incomes, comprises 350 rental units and 150 houses for sale. Some subsidy was available from the Department of Urban Housing and Development (HUD) to enable less well-off households to afford to rent or

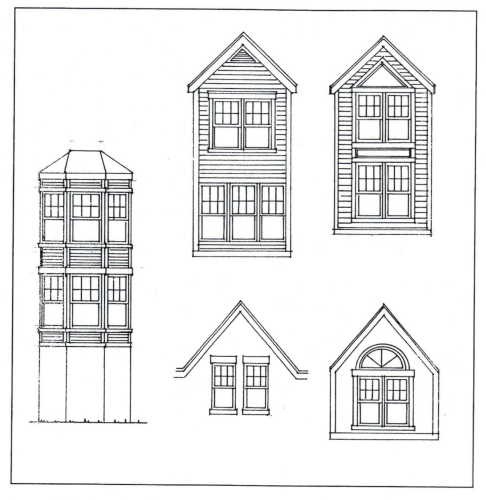

Figure 3.77 Crawford Square: Architectural Design Guidelines. Special features such as dormers, bay windows, decorative trim or decorative windows are encouraged for street façades.

buy. The funding was administered through a locally established development association and there is a Community Association to organise community development and common maintenance for which a small compulsory charge is made.

The architecture of the new housing has produced a scheme in character and in scale with typical Pittsburgh neighbourhoods. The buildings all have the same general form as typical Pittsburgh houses and each street has

Figure 3.78 Crawford Square: the new housing has created a new link to the Pittsburgh downtown. Photo: Tom Bernard.

its own character: the variety and individuality of each building establishes the scheme as a neighbourhood rather than a development.

Middleton Hills, Madison, Wisconsin

Middleton Hills is a new housing development in the "new urbanism vocabulary". Designed by Andres Duany and Elizabeth Plater-Zyberk (DPZ), it is a "neighbourhood for the future, built with a sense of the past – and a clear understanding of what makes people feel at home" (Zelinka, 2002a, p. 1). It consists of 400 single-family homes, townhouses, apartments and live/work units (Fig. 3.79). An integral part of the neighbourhood is the presence of small shops and businesses to sustain daily needs and provide local employment (Fig. 3.80). The design has rediscovered a sense of community, lost in the USA through the development of low-density housing, and separately

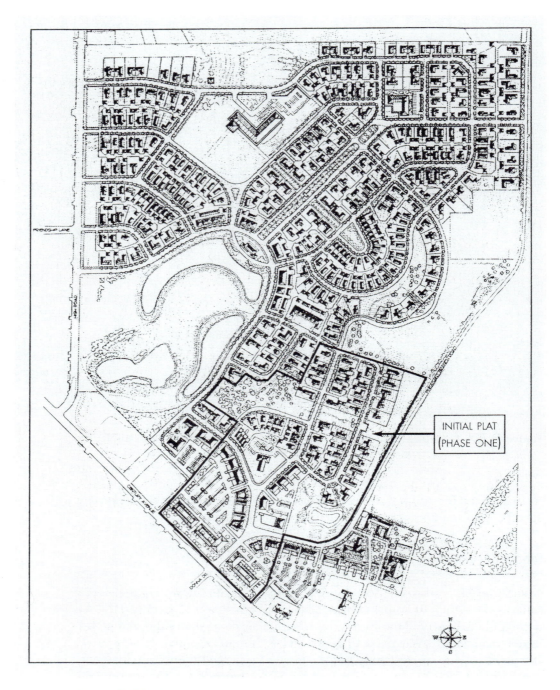

INITIAL PLAT
(PHASE ONE)

Figure 3.79 Middleton Hills, Madison, Wisconsin, USA: new housing designed in the local "new urbanism vocabulary". Architects: Andres Duany and Elizabeth Plater-Zyberg of DPZ Architects.

Figure 3.80 Middleton Hills: perspective of the neighbourhood store reflects the design influence of Frank Lloyd Wright.

zoned shopping malls and business parks. As with all housing designed to new urbanist principles, its emphasis is on people and on quality of life in a self-sufficient neighbourhood.

The design of the buildings is based on the regional tradition of Prairie Arts and Crafts. The styles are influenced by the architecture of Frank Lloyd Wright and his Midwest contemporaries. Establishing the architectural character of the neighbourhood is seen as essential to creating a cohesive "village" atmosphere. Design codes were developed to assure the architectural and visual integrity of the community. Image is considered vital for ensuring minimal crime (information by courtesy of Brian A. Spencer, A1A, Architect).

Open space

Green space is vital to human contentment. It is important both from an individual viewpoint and from a community perspective. Christopher Alexander wrote in *A Pattern Language* that "In order to nourish themselves, people need green open spaces to go to; when they are close they use them. But if the greens are more than three minutes away, the distance overwhelms the need" (Alexander, 1977, Accessible Green Pattern.) He defines the term "green" as being a place large enough so that, at least in the middle of it, you feel you are in touch with nature, and away from hustle and bustle. He suggests a green is shaped so that it forms "one or more positive room-like

167

spaces". It should be surrounded with trees, or walls, or buildings, but not roads or cars (Alexander, 1977, p. 309).

In the UK, open space is the subject of the Government's Planning Policy Guidance Note 17, *Planning for Open Space, Sport and Recreation* (PPG17). This advocates that high quality, well managed and maintained open spaces and good quality sports and recreational facilities can play a major part in improving people's sense of well-being in the place they live. "As a focal point for community activities, they can bring together members of deprived communities and provide opportunities for social interaction" (PPG17, p. 4). They also have a vital role to play in promoting healthy living and preventing illness, and in the social development of children of all ages through play, sporting activity and interaction with others.

The new edition of the Guidance Note, published in 2002, dropped the long-established mandatory standard of 6 acres (2.5 hectares) of open space per thousand population. Now local authorities can set their own standards through undertaking audits of existing open space, sports and recreation facilities, with an emphasis on quality rather than quantity of open space. Audits of quality will be particularly important as they will allow local authorities to identify potential for increased use of open space through better design, management and maintenance. However, there is a requirement that planning applications for development from 0.2 hectares have to be drawn to the attention of Sport England (and equivalent bodies elsewhere in the UK). The Guidance Note provides a typology to illustrate the broad range of public open spaces. This includes provision for children and teenagers – play areas, skateboard parks, outdoor basketball hoops, and other more informal areas (e.g., "hanging out" areas, teenage shelters).

Open space is one of the most difficult aspects of the built environment to design to avoid the possibility of crime and perception of crime. If open space is to be valued by residents, then it must feel safe and secure. Areas where people are in fear of themselves and their property will never be used. This will have a knock-on effect on the way they feel about their individual homes. The following factors can also contribute to the psychological fear of crime in open spaces:

- Lack of formal and informal surveillance
- The potential for antisocial behaviour
- Social factors – open spaces used as points of congregation for groups of young people including drug users
- Evidence of vandalism
- Lack of legibility and lack of signage
- Aural isolation
- Poorly lit areas
- Passage through areas where someone may be hiding

- Lack of information about the layout of the open space and to whom problems can be reported
- The wrong kind of plant material
- Inadequate or non-existent seating
- Poor management and maintenance

The issue of perceived risk is particularly prevalent in women's use of open space. Women generally express much greater levels of concern for personal safety than men do, even though the risk is actually less, and these concerns influence their reluctance to walk through open space areas after dark.

Larger spaces can facilitate all sorts of activity – recreational green space, play areas, sports facilities, nature reserves, walking and cycling routes, and educational projects (Fig. 3.81). The introduction of communal events and activities, e.g., jogging, cycle paths, informal areas for ball games, etc., will help to make a natural open space popular. They could also incorporate specific leisure facilities for teenagers and features such as seats and benches, children's play areas, etc.

Smaller open spaces within housing developments, whether maintained publicly or by a management agency, should form part of a spatial system in which each area has its own function. Small areas that have no purpose can be a source of nuisance to residents and a cause of fear. Designs must be robust and carefully considered in respect of how spaces are likely to be used. The important aspect is that open spaces serve a function and can be used in a natural and uninhibited way. They must, by design, feel safe. The determining factor for most people will be size and natural character but the essential determinant is the presence of other users. Woodland areas are frequently perceived as unsafe with potential aggressors lurking behind the trees. A sense of isolation from assistance can also be a problem. CCTV is not a significant help except at access points and vulnerable areas, e.g., children's playgrounds.

British practice is also described in a number of local planning and design guides. The Essex Design Guide recommends that the most effective public open spaces are "large, multi-purpose informally supervised parks" but it sees a role for additional smaller, more localised open spaces in order to create a varied townscape. These should be in the form of a well-landscaped and properly maintained open space, similar to a Georgian square (Fig. 3.82). In privately owned housing, they should be maintained by a management company set up by the developer to which all residents subscribe (Essex County Council and Essex Planning Officers' Association, 1997, p. 15).

The City of Nottingham Guide, *Community Safety in Residential Areas* (1998) (see p.) also provides useful advice on the design of open space. Figure 3.83 indicates its recommendations for relating open space to housing designed in a cul-de-sac layout (Nottingham City Council, 1998, p. 13). An

Figure 3.81   Entrance to neighbourhood park: Hulme, Manchester.

effective edge treatment of a housing fronting a major walkway and adjoining open space is shown in Fig. 3.84.

The City of Toronto in Canada has been at the forefront of designing out crime for a number of years and has produced some excellent guidance publications (p. 230). Its recommendations on open spaces are as follows (City of Toronto, 2000, p. 38):

- Front housing onto the open spaces so there is natural surveillance
- Legibility enhances safety. Feelings of apprehension and insecurity increase when users do not have a clear understanding of the physical layout of the area they are in.

Figure 3.82 "Georgian Square", Great Notley, Essex.

- Good lighting enhances perceptions of safety and allows for greater night-time surveillance.
- Diversity of design can attract a higher intensity of proper use. Variety in form, colour and texture of landscape elements as well as (in larger spaces) a range of activities contributes to an interesting environment.
- For smaller parks, signage in the form of maps and a descriptive text promotes a feeling of safety because people feel greater control over their environment when they know where they are and how to get to where they want to go.
- Organised use of spaces can increase surveillance, limit domination by any one user group and reduce the possibility of inappropriate behaviour.
- Resident participation in the design, management and maintenance of the spaces. This fosters a sense of ownership and pride and builds a constituency of users with an interest in keeping the spaces safe.

171

Public Open Spaces:

Good Design

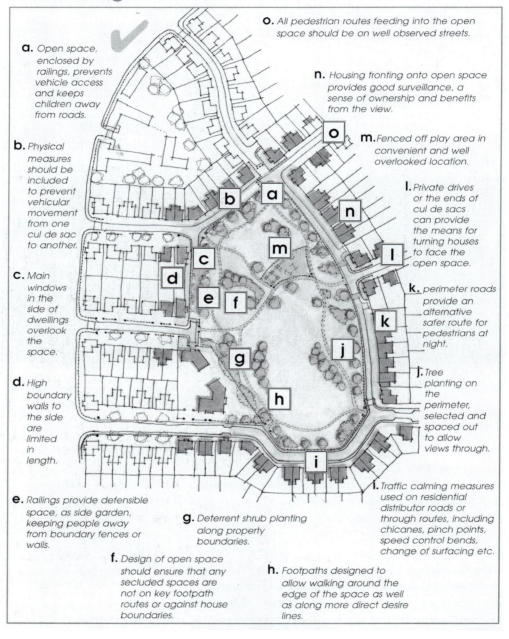

o. All pedestrian routes feeding into the open space should be on well observed streets.

a. Open space, enclosed by railings, prevents vehicle access and keeps children away from roads.

n. Housing fronting onto open space provides good surveillance, a sense of ownership and benefits from the view.

m. Fenced off play area in convenient and well overlooked location.

b. Physical measures should be included to prevent vehicular movement from one cul de sac to another.

l. Private drives or the ends of cul de sacs can provide the means for turning houses to face the open space.

c. Main windows in the side of dwellings overlook the space.

k. perimeter roads provide an alternative safer route for pedestrians at night.

d. High boundary walls to the side are limited in length.

j. Tree planting on the perimeter, selected and spaced out to allow views through.

e. Railings provide defensible space, as side garden, keeping people away from boundary fences or walls.

g. Deterrent shrub planting along property boundaries.

f. Design of open space should ensure that any secluded spaces are not on key footpath routes or against house boundaries.

h. Footpaths designed to allow walking around the edge of the space as well as along more direct desire lines.

i. Traffic calming measures used on residential distributor roads or through routes, including chicanes, pinch points, speed control bends, change of surfacing etc.

Figure 3.83 Design guidance for public open spaces (Nottingham City Council, 1998, p.13).

Figure 3.84 Housing overlooking the seafront promenade: Ferrara Quay/Marina Walk, Swansea Maritime Village. Architects: Halliday Meecham Partnership.

Children's play

Play for a child is an essential part of their learning, which should be taken seriously in neighbourhood and housing design, even though communal areas such as playgrounds, seating and drying areas have the potential to generate crime, the fear of crime and antisocial behaviour. The planning and design task is to provide environments that are stimulating and safe for children of all ages but which prevent play being a source of nuisance to others. In particular older children, who are often the least well catered for on

173

housing estates, congregate on playgrounds, deter young children from using them, and are abusive to adults living around.

Forms of play provision vary from small incidental play features to equipped playgrounds, skateboard parks, youth shelters, etc. Design should take account of the separate needs of different age groups; for example, doorstep play for toddlers (Fig. 3.85); boisterous game playing and exploratory activity among older children (Figs. 3.86 to 3.89); and general socialising between young teenagers who often need places to hang around where they can feel free of adult interference. This age group – 11 to 15 – is particularly difficult to cater for: it features high amongst the statistics for vandalism. It is worth considering providing informal meeting spaces or a shelter for this age group (Fig. 3.90), sited so that there is adequate surveillance without residents in nearby housing being adversely disturbed. They should be located in such a way that people using adjacent footpaths and cycle ways will not be subject to harassment or otherwise put in fear. Areas for ball games are important but they should be located away from housing as they tend to attract older children with consequential additional noise (Fig. 3.88). Careful consideration needs to be given to whether play-

Figure 3.85 Doorstep play: Home for Change, Hulme, Manchester.

Figure 3.86 Children play table tennis and other games in this housing court in Cologne, but there is a rule that at 9.00pm, everyone goes home.

grounds should be locked at night to prevent damage, graffiti and general misuse.

Strategies should be developed through community development and youth workers who are familiar with local issues. It is important to use existing facilities to the full. Schools, particularly secondary schools, can make their facilities available during evenings and school holidays (see p. 179). After school clubs (p. 181), play schemes and other provisions can provide imaginative ways in which to absorb the energies of young people. There may be a cost for this but its impact on reducing crime, vandalism and antisocial behaviour could be significantly less in the long term.

Figure 3.87 Slade Green, Bexley, London: accommodating boisterous play at a distance but within sight of housing.

Landscaping

In most large-scale housing developments there are two main levels of planting within the design. Structure planting can screen the development from the surrounding area where this is required and it can define the pattern of main roads and footpaths (Fig. 3.91). It can also form shelter-belts where sites are exposed to strong winds. Within a development, buildings and landscaping should form part of the same integrated design with landscaping having a clear function within the scheme. It should assist in creating enclosure and spaces of individual character and contribute to the spatial quality of the development as a whole. Planting can be used to create

Figure 3.88 Ball games Area at Slade Green.

or reinforce containment, to form gateways and to mark events in the hierarchy of spaces. In open layouts, the planting itself can form the space. Planting should not impede natural surveillance and must not allow the possibility of hiding places. It can be used advantageously to prevent access into private and semi-private areas, but defensive planting is about selecting the right type of plant material for each situation; for example, open-branched and columnar trees are best where surveillance is important. Climbing plants are useful to cover walls subject to graffiti, and thorny plants can help keep people away in vulnerable areas.

It is most important that landscape proposals are designed with management and maintenance in mind (Fig. 3.92). Small areas of grass are totally unsuitable as the maintenance is expensive. A good proportion of evergreen

Figure 3.89 Children play in the central space between two parallel streets: Neighbourhood renewal in the Noordereiland district of Rotterdam.

plants are beneficial to secure an all-round effect, and planting should be dense and located in concentrated areas where it can have much greater impact and be more vandal-resistant than sparsely planted species. Shrubbery that is not kept down to a level that ensures adequate surveillance will encourage crime. These issues should not be left until the completion stage of a project but should be considered as part of the overall landscape plan during the design of the scheme. Wherever possible, residents should be involved in the design and choice of the plants as this will encourage a sense of ownership of the public spaces and go some way to ensuring future care and supervision.

Figure 3.90 Youth Shelter at Slade Green.

Schools

Schools, their open spaces and their playing fields are important focal points in a community, yet so often the buildings are set back within their site behind high fencing installed to reduce the possibility of crime and vandalism. The school appears remote and physically not part of the community. Long gone are the ideas of linking the buildings with housing, shops and other community buildings to create a square or a village green. "Dual-use" playing fields were provided with additional open space to make it possible for the community to have access after school, and there was an on-site resident caretaker to provide a degree of supervision and surveillance.

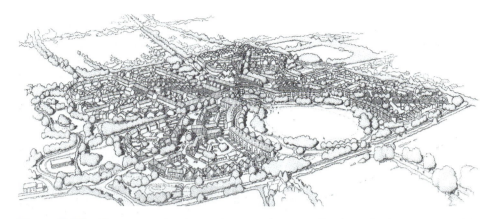

Figure 3.91 Structure planting enhances the overall urban design concept. New Osbaldwick Village, York. Masterplan: PRP Architects.

Figure 3.92 Well-maintained planting at Oakwood, Warrington. Architects: Warrington and Runcorn Development Cooperation. Chief Architect, Hugh Canning.

The extent of arson of school buildings in recent years in many parts of Britain is a sufficient reason for fencing, but there surely must be alternatives. The Essex Design Guide recommends that houses should overlook school playing fields to provide informal supervision; playing fields should be an obvious part of the greenspace system and they should be a focus for the pedestrian and cycle network. (Essex County Planning Officers' Association 1997, pp. 15–16). The new Millennium School at Greenwich, London, is carefully designed to sit in its landscaped setting and security does not appear an obvious issue (Figs. 3.93 and 3.94). Research at Parrs Wood High School in Didsbury, Manchester, by Salford University and Sheffield Hallam University proved that, by design, many of the likely problems of security could be reduced. The architects for the new school worked closely with the headteacher who wanted the school to be designed to resist criminal damage, protect children from unwanted intruders and deter bullying. Pupil security was achieved by having a single point of entry and a central reception, around which pupils and teachers were forced to flow as they passed to the different curriculum centres. Externally the school was built without fences. Instead, 40 CCTV cameras were installed around the perimeter to prevent burglary, to be monitored by a security guard. The arrangement works well and could continue to do so provided the 24-hour security surveillance can be maintained (Davey et al., 2001).

Another solution available is to encourage schools to become actively involved in the local community so that communal parts of the buildings can be used after school hours, thereby reducing the risk of crime and vandalism. In return, schools can raise valuable income from the community using its facilities. The Education Act of 2002 makes it more possible for schools to provide services for the local community. An "extended" school is one that provides a range of services and activities beyond the school day to help meet the needs of pupils, their families and the wider community.

Some schools are already taking advantage of this by providing extended services including childcare, adult education and community sports programmes. A few are starting to provide health and social care. Guidance on the possibilities is available from the Department of Education and Skills, which explains about how schools can provide these services, working together with local partners. Schools will likely need to make some changes in the way they operate covering practicalities such as working in partnership with other groups and agencies and having more flexible opening hours. This should make them more lively social centres and less vulnerable to crime (see www.crimereduction.gov.uk/active communities27.htm and www.teachernet.gov.uk/extendedschools for more information on these possibilities).

The design of the school buildings themselves has an important part to play in reducing crime. Barry Poyner's advice on design in his book, *Design*

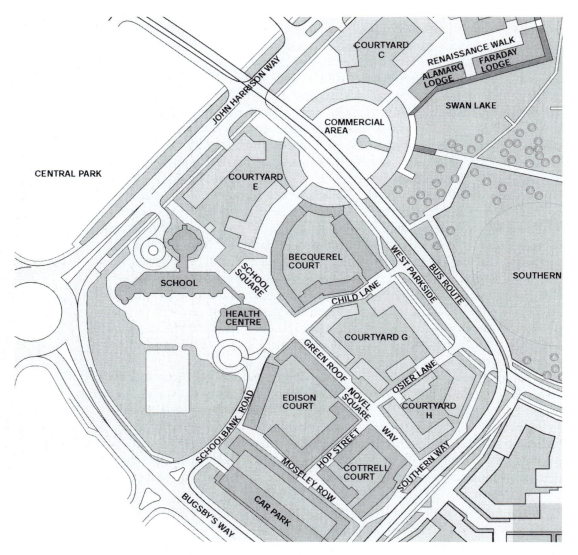

Figure 3.93 The new school in the Millennium Village, Greenwich is designed with housing and a health centre to create a "school square". Plan by courtesy of English Partnerships.

Against Crime: Beyond Defensible Space (1983), is still relevant. His six tips to aid the prevention of burglary and vandalism in schools are:

- Schools should have neat and well-maintained buildings and grounds
- They should be located near a busy area
- They should be visible from the street or surrounding houses

Figure 3.94 Entrance to the new Millennium School, Greenwich.

- Their design should be compact and avoid recesses where offenders cannot be seen
- It should not be possible to climb the roof
- Their design should be easy for the caretaker to survey

Local shops and facilities

A small number of shops and other commercial facilities in any neighbourhood can add considerably to its sustainability, making for a lively mixed-use environment at a focal point. If shops and other facilities cannot initially be

Figure 3.95. Parrs Wood High School, Didsbury, Manchester is not fenced but protected by CCTV cameras.

provided, it is worth considering reserving sites for the future, leaving them undeveloped in the first instance.

A local centre of shops and other facilities can have the affect of reducing the fear of crime but, on the other hand, if the area is taken over by gangs of young people at night, its impact can be just the opposite. Local shops are therefore best integrated into housing, with simple arrangements for servicing that avoid rear-unloading areas. Car parks with large areas that create a feeling of a no man's-land between the shops and the surrounding buildings should be avoided. CCTV surveillance looking over the public areas and car parking is generally recommended.

Robust door and window frames, doors, windows, locks and glass can reduce the risk of burglary and vandalism. Quick repairs are important, as wilful damage will otherwise continue.

Shutters

More than anything else in the built environment, shutters create a fortress-like atmosphere and their installation can be self-defeating giving an area a "dead appearance" (DOE, 1994a, p. 6). They provide a surface for graffiti, which not only gives out signals about an area's vulnerability to crime, but can also deter the public from using such locations, thereby losing the benefit of passive surveillance. In turn, places that lack activity, or appear deserted, can be attractive to criminals who perceive that they are less likely to be detected. An open grille design is preferable as it can let light from the premises onto the street during normal trading hours and can help to maintain the attractiveness of the area. Shutters of this type also enable passers-by to see inside, which can help deter criminals.

Designing out vandalism and graffiti

In areas particularly vulnerable to vandalism and graffiti, careful design and specification is needed to minimise the risk of damage to buildings and their external surfaces. The following items should be given special consideration:

Materials

- Vertical tile hanging, weatherboarding and large flat areas of sheet materials should not be used in vulnerable locations.
- If timber is used in high-risk areas then it should be close-grained with an impregnable preservative finish.
- Areas of small setts or other blocks should be embedded to prevent their removal.

Applied surfaces

- Strongly textured surfaces generally suffer less graffiti than smooth ones.
- Walls with strongly patterned surfaces or bold contrasting colours are less liable to receive graffiti. The pattern should not be too large otherwise graffiti could appear within one area of colour.
- Damage to applied surfaces is particularly pronounced when the surface colour is very different from the colour of the material below.

- Material used below the surface finish should be as durable as possible.

Components and services

- External light fittings should not be accessible.
- Wall-mounted light fittings should be recessed or concealed where possible.
- Rainwater pipes located near intensely used areas should be concealed or recessed.
- All pipes and cables should be concealed where possible.

Street lighting

Benefits of good lighting

Well-designed street lighting can reduce the fear that many people have of going out after dark. While there may be a cost involved in raising the standard of lighting above the level normally accepted by street lighting engineers, the savings on reduced crime could be considerable. Recent examples of good British practice are to be seen in Stoke-on-Trent and Dudley where crime against households in the areas concerned was cut by approximately 25 per cent and 41 per cent respectively. People felt safer and night-time pedestrian street use increased dramatically, providing more eyes and ears to make the streets safer overall. (Webster, 2003; Painter and Farrington, 1999).

In her article *Ray of Hope*, published in *Regeneration and Renewal*, Kate Painter of the Institute of Criminology, Cambridge University, writes:

> *"The benefits of good lighting are reaped widely by all parts of local government service such as housing, and education . . . it is worth considering moving money from housing, education, social services and police budgets to public lighting in a "joined-up" inter-agency environment"* (Painter, 2003, p. 23).

She advises that street lighting is an inexpensive means of reducing street crime and it has no civil liberties implications. Ken Pease of the University of Huddersfield sums up the benefits by saying: "Precisely targeted increases in street lighting generally have crime reduction effects. Street lighting improvements can reduce day-time crime as well as night-time crime, inviting speculation that lighting increases community pride, sense of ownership and surveillance" (Parker, 2001, p. 18).

Lighting requirements

Street lighting should be for the convenience of pedestrians, not just motorcars. The design should enhance the quality of the space at night (and in the

Figure 3.96 Cromer Street, King's Cross, London. Street lighting is designed specifically for the pedestrian space it serves.

day) rather than merely light it (Fig. 3.96). Traditionally, engineers have related standards and costs of street lighting to the movement of traffic and preventing accidents. There is now emerging an opinion that priority should also be given to reducing crime and the fear of crime through higher and more site-specific lighting. Improvements in street lighting will not in themselves reduce crime but will tackle the opportunity to commit crime through increasing natural surveillance.

Canadian experience

There are a number of simple questions in the *Toronto Safe City Guidelines* (2000) that can form a useful checklist for the design of street lighting in residential areas (City of Toronto, 2000, p. 38):

Minimum standards

Does the lighting allow visibility along and around routes? Lighting should adequately illuminate paths, inset spaces, access and egress routes and signage. Shadows from buildings and landscape elements should be considered when laying out the lights in order to minimise dark corners and insets.

Consistency of lighting

Is the lighting consistent, in order to reduce contrast between shadows and illuminated areas? It is vital to avoid dark spots, which can offer as much opportunity to the criminal as general darkness, and in addition can cause much personal anxiety. Every effort should be made to avoid distorting people's features and making them as readable and recognisable as possible.

Proper placement of lighting

Does street lighting illuminate pedestrian walkways, rather than the road or people's windows? The placing of light standards should take into account planting, including the eventual height and breadth of mature trees and bushes, and other potential light blocks.

Protection of lighting

Are the light fixtures protected from casual vandalism?

Maintenance

Are lighting fixtures maintained in a clean condition and promptly replaced if burnt out or broken? The maintenance of lighting should be worked out during the design stage and responsibility for maintenance accepted.

Planning for night-time use

Architectural drawings should depict night-time use, including the position, quantity and type of lighting. The design should not be left just to the street lighting engineer.

Design process

The general process for designing a good lighting scheme is as follows (Genre, 2002, pp. 3–4):

- Determine first the seeing task.
- Illuminate first what is necessary to see (usually objects, not light sources).
- Quality lighting is largely an issue of good placement. This is not just for the purposes of glare reduction and navigation. Certain lighting angles are discomforting to the brain, such as lighting from below, as in ground lighting for

security reasons. This is generally unsafe, as we are accustomed to perceive light from above.

- In most cases, a combination of direct and diffuse light is best. This combination increases depth perception.
- Large brightness ratios should be avoided.
- Quality is better than quantity. The quality of light and the reflective factors of the surfaces are important. White light is clearly preferable.

Lighting in public spaces must be adequate for people to have a good look at another person when he or she is still a reasonable distance way away. This is perhaps not more than 12 to 15 meters. Up to a point, more lighting is beneficial but too much light produces glare. In this respect it is important to consider the brightness with which a path is illuminated. Generally speaking, lighting needs to be bright enough to provide direction, but not so bright that pedestrians have difficulty seeing into the darker areas. Light spillage can be detrimental to certain areas, so lighting levels should be gauged to suit local context.

Lighting mounted on buildings can enhance the visual appearance of an area at night and reduce street clutter, but it must be away from bedroom windows. Lights in prominent positions can be used to define an area and create spaces. For instance, two lights located on each side of the road can help create a gateway effect. Carefully positioned lighting can also help create a feeling of ownership of spaces to the surrounding houses. The choice of light fitting is important but local authority street lighting engineers have traditionally been reserved in order to keep maintenance costs to a minimum. This is understandable, but the minimum specification may do little to enhance the quality of an area.

Street lighting should be designed with the landscaping to ensure that trees do not block the light and in this respect it is necessary to consider the full height to which trees may grow.

There can be security problems with non-adopted roads, including shared drives, with no street lighting. Rear access roads to car parking and garages that have no lighting can also present problems. Most residents do not themselves have the financial means of providing street lighting and local authorities will not accept responsibility. There are limited grants available but, as Kate Painter says on page 186, joined-up thinking is needed to relate savings from crime reduction to the cost of providing and running the lighting.

CCTV

There are currently around 2.5 million cameras in use in Britain and the numbers are increasing rapidly. It is becoming so much part of the everyday scene that "It is almost becoming another public utility, like drainage, gas, water, telephone and electricity services. Designers need to be involved in this development. However it is not a substitute for people" (Parker, 2001b, pp. 17–18).

This increased use of surveillance raises important issues. Home Office guidance emphasizes that it is by no means a universal solution and that it will only be effective as part of an integrated package of crime prevention measures, and that sensitive and professional management is essential for success (Fig. 3.97). Furthermore, in most cases, the installation of CCTV does not require planning permission so there is little public debate over its use and location. In some countries CCTV is perceived as intrusive and a restriction to personal freedom and civil liberty. European Union and recent British Human Rights legislation (Human Rights Act 2000) and Data Protection can place considerable constraints, and users need to put in place adequate codes of practice and procedures. In The Netherlands and Denmark its use in public places is rare; predominately it is confined to private areas. It is also much less employed in the USA than in Britain.

CCTV can be costly to install and to operate so it is important to maximise the potential for success as follows:

■ It is essential to make an honest appraisal of the problems to be addressed. Is the area in question suffering from a consistently high level of crime and do the crimes follow a pattern? Is the crime data of good quality and up-to-date? Sometimes public fear of crime is so high that it becomes necessary for this reason. However, if it is hoped that CCTV operators watch every move and will call the police immediately, the reality can be a disappointment.

■ It is important to assess whether CCTV is a useful tool at all: is the type of crime susceptible to open surveillance? Thirdly, local residents must give their approval.

■ Equally important is liaison with the police – will they treat calls from the control room as high priority? For residential areas this may not be the case. It is essential also that the full implications of installing CCTV are understood. This includes a commitment to its management and the total costs involved.

■ Grants may be available for the installation of CCTV cameras but not for overall management and running the systems. It is essential therefore to be sure that the running costs are in place and sustainable.

A recent evaluation of CCTV undertaken by the Scarman Centre as part of the UK Government's current Crime Reduction Programme found that the projects with the best results tend to be in areas which have already been identified as having crime/disorder problems. The less successful ones were those that tried to identify an area that fits the statistical requirements of the project. It is vital to include from the outset someone in the project with technical knowledge. Most important is dialogue with the community to

Figure 3.97 CCTV camera and sign at Belgrave Street, within the King's Cross Estate Action Area, London.

ensure that CCTV is the best solution to the problem (Scarman Centre, 2003).

Gating alleys

The Alleygater's Guide

The London Metropolitan Police Guide *The Alleygater's Guide to Gated Alleys* advises that only 15 per cent of all domestic burglaries were caused by means of access through the front door or windows. Burglars prefer to break into a house through a door or window at the back or the side where they will not be seen. In terraced housing access to the back is frequently via alleys, alleyways, paths, snickets, ginnels, passages or whatever local name is used for the narrow walkways between the houses, which provides access from front to back without going through the house. As they are only publicly visible when crossing the road to the next alleyway, a criminal can use an alleyway without being seen, even in broad daylight and, if they know the alleyways in an area well, they will use them as escape routes. Some burglars break into a house in the day, hide stolen property in the alleyway and collect it at night under the cover of darkness.

Lockable gates that cannot be climbed over (Figs. 3.98 and 3.99) helps keeps down the number of burglaries. In some parts of London, it has been proved that a gate can bring down rear access burglaries by up to 90 per cent. There are other benefits from putting gates in. They stop fly tipping of rubbish and litter, and fouling of alleyways by dogs. Children can play safely in the alleyways. "It helps the people in the street get their alleyway back" (Beckford and Cogan, 2000, p. 4). The design of the gates is important. They must be non-climbable with no centrally located horizontal bars or anything that would give a burglar a foothold. They must be strong and solid with a clear line of sight down the communal alleyway. Metal is better than timber, and fitted with a "slam to lock" automatic deadlocking mortice lock. Lighting should be located above gates to illuminate anyone attempting to climb over in the dark.

Dutch experience in Haarlem

Gating alleys can be extremely effective providing residents give it their full support. The City of Haarlem in The Netherlands proved this beyond doubt in the mid-1990s when it decided to encourage burglar proofing of back paths. A group of residents prepared to develop a plan to secure their back paths collectively was selected to develop a pilot scheme with 50 per cent of

Specification

- The gate should open inwards.

- All the sections should use a minimum 3mm thick steel.

- Surrounding the gate is an outer box frame (like a door frame) measuring 40mm x 40mm. This is topped by 150mm blunted rods. The rods can be welded to the top of the gate instead of the frame having a top. If a top section is included,

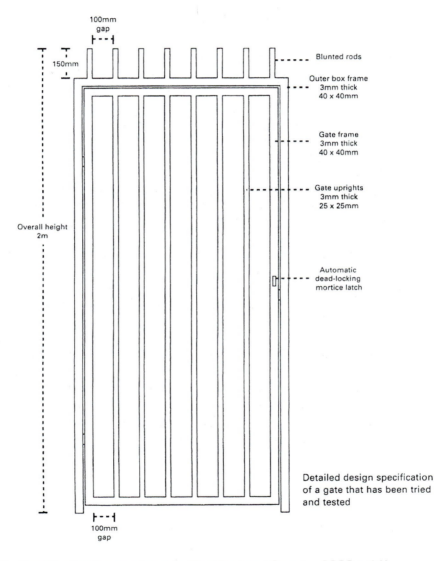

Figure 3.98 Specification for an alley gate (Beckford and Coogan, 2000 p.11).

Figure 3.99 Gating to a courtyard: King's Cross Estate Action Area, London.

the costs from the city. The scheme included securing the paths with gates and installing lighting. The first schemes were tested in 572 houses after a year and the results were remarkably positive. 85 per cent of the residents say they were very satisfied with the measures taken. 48 per cent felt unsafe before the measures that were taken. 87 per cent felt much safer after the measures were taken. In the year before the measures were taken 35 burglaries were committed; the next year there were 15, a decrease of 57 per cent. Therefore the risk of burglaries decreased significantly, and the perception of safety rose considerably. The pilot project was seen to be so successful that a much larger subsidised programme was launched in following years with remarkable effect (Wallop, 1999, pp. 3–4).

Figure 4.1 Kop Van Zuid, Rotterdam: typical of the quality approach to high density housing design in The Netherlands.

CHAPTER 4

Design guidance

Introduction

This chapter looks at design guidance produced by government, police and local government sources. "Secured by Design" is a Police initiative that was launched in 1989. The Dutch Police Labelling developed out of this. Local authorities have traditionally produced planning design guides that contain information on designing crime out of the built environment. Essex County Council was one of the first to do so. Nottingham City Council and others have produced guides specifically related to crime prevention. The City of Toronto in Canada has a long-standing international reputation for its effective policies in the area of crime prevention through environmental design. The European Parliament Prestandard "Prevention of Crime by Urban Planning and Design" reflects its concern that people within the European Union should enjoy living in a crime-free environment. This chapter draws out the key principles from these publications to provide a compendium of design criteria.

UK Government guidance

Department of the Environment, Circular 5/94, "Planning Out Crime"

Since 1994 this has been the main source of government guidance for designing crime out of the built environment. It states that the causes of crime and vandalism are complex, but advises that the environment has a role to play. It recognises that desolate, sterile and featureless surroundings can create feelings of fear, alienation and anonymity.

The Circular established that crime prevention was capable of being a material consideration for local planning authorities when determining applications for planning permission. It stressed the importance of addressing crime prevention at the design stage – once a development has been built, the main opportunity to incorporate crime prevention measures has been lost. It emphasises that crime prevention depends on a wide range of measures. Initiatives in housing estates, for example, must be based on a package of measures which address a range of issues – not just crime itself – and involve several agencies of which the planning system is one, but when co-ordinated with other measures one contribution of planning can be significant.

The Circular also states that "there should be a balanced approach to design which attempts to reconcile the visual quality of a development with the need for crime prevention". It also states that "Used sensitively, the planning system can be an instrument in providing attractive and well managed environments that help discourage anti-social behaviour" (p. 1).

It established the consultation on planning applications between Police Architectural Liaison Officers (Crime Prevention Design Advisers) and local planning authorities. It also refers to the Secured by Design scheme.

The Circular sets out some of the principles of designing to reduce crime, including:

- Mixed use development: avoid incompatible land uses that could create conflict.
- Discussions between planning authorities, developers and designers should take place early in the design process.
- Layouts should be designed to reduce the risk of criminal activity towards people and property.

Crime and Disorder Act 1998

Until 1998 there was no legislative support for crime prevention in the UK, but Section 17 of the Crime and Disorder Act 1998 rectified this. It recognised that crime can only be tackled through dealing with the root causes and it gave a clear message that communities should not have to tolerate living in fear of crime. It placed statutory responsibility upon each local authority and its police counterpart to include crime considerations in their undertakings, "to exercise its functions with due regard . . . to the need to do all it reasonably can to prevent crime and disorder in its area".

The obligation to consider crime and security issues in formulating development control functions is therefore placed more strongly upon planning authorities. This does not mean that security considerations will always take precedence as local authorities are expected to use their judgement in weighting security factors against other considerations (DETR, 1998b, p. 47).

Community Safety Partnerships were established at the same time. These link the police with local authorities and recently health authorities. Safety Funds are held by local authorities, and money can be available for physical improvements to reduce crime.

Planning Policy Guidance Notes (PPGs)

Designing out Crime appears briefly in a number of the UK Government's Planning Policy Guidance Notes as follows:

PPG1: *General Policy and Principles*. Sets out the principles of sustainable development. Annex A, relating to "Handling of Design Issues", advises that in considering the design of proposed new development, local planning authorities, developers and designers should take into account advice contained in DOE Circular 5/94.

PPG3: *Housing*. Emphasises the importance of local context on the scale and shape of new development. It recommends that local authorities should adopt policies to promote designs and layouts that are safe and take account of public health, crime prevention and community safety.

PPG7: *The Countryside: Environmental Quality and Economic and Social Development*. Provides guidance on land use planning in rural areas, including policies for housing and new development.

PPG12: *Development Plans and Regional Planning Guidance*. Sets out the need to acknowledge local context and encourage alternative transport in development plans. One of the relevant social considerations to be addressed in development plans is to look at measures for crime prevention (including through better design).

PPG13: *Transport*. Emphasises the need for integrated transport policies to help achieve sustainable development. On housing its principal advice is that "housing development should be located, wherever possible, so as to provide a choice of means of travel to other facilities". It includes a section on "design, safety and mix of uses" which states that local authorities should consider how best to reduce crime/fear of crime through the design and layout of developments. It develops this further by saying "places that work well are designed to be used safely and securely by all in the community, frequently for a wide range of purposes and throughout the day and evening. Local authorities in partnership with the police should promote designs and layouts that are safe (both in terms of road safety and personal security) and take account of crime prevention and community safety considerations".

PPG15: *Planning and the Historic Environment*. Sets out the Government's policies on the conservation of the historic environment.

PPG17: *Planning for Open Space, Sport and Leisure*.

Good Practice Guidance in Planning Out Crime

The aims and content of Circular 5/94 are currently subject to revision by Architect/Planners Llewellyn-Davies and Community Safety specialists Holden McAllister Partnership. The Guide (planned for late 2003) will set out principles of good practice in creating safe, sustainable communities. The principles are not intended to be rigidly prescriptive, as each location should be considered as an individual place, nor are the principles intended to be exclusive.

At the London Conference, *Improving Safety by Design* (April 2003) Jon Rouse, Chief Executive of the Commission for Architecture and the Built Environment (CABE), presented a paper on the new guide. He explained what CABE means by good design:

- Functionality and fitness for purpose. Safety is vital – if the environment is not safe it will not function and it will have no delight.
- Sustainability
- Sensitivity to place
- Good value and efficiency
- Aesthetic attractiveness
- Innovation
- Flexibility
- Benefit to the end user

His key attributes of safe, sustainable places are:

- Establish a positive link between crime prevention and the wider urban and rural renaissance.
- Design based on criminological research but site specific.
- Nothing is prescriptive.
- Local context fully taken into account.

The Guide will contain eight key design principles (Rouse, 2003):

- **Access and movement:** Places should have well-defined routes, spaces and entrances that provide for convenient movement and security. A development should be easy to get to and to move around in, allowing good surveillance. Routes should be permeable where appropriate and segregation of cars, pedestrians and cyclists should be avoided; alleyways and underpasses should not normally be necessary – wide pedestrian crossings as on the Continent are preferable. Spaces should be understandable; good signage is important but a sense of direction should be achieved through design.
- **Activity:** Places should be created where an appropriate level of human activity creates a reduced risk of crime and a sense of safety at all times. The balance between spreading social and commercial facilities throughout a development or concentrating it in one location should be determined on a local basis with the police. It is essential to consider young people – skateboarding can have a big impact on the environment.
- **Adaptability:** Places and buildings should be able to adapt to changing requirements and security concerns. Quality of public space is more important than quantity. If open space creates problems for people living around it, it may be preferable to privatise it or remove it altogether. In this respect cul-de-sac layouts tend to create more open spaces of little use.
- **Management and maintenance:** It is essential at the briefing stage of a design to clearly identify how the scheme will be managed and maintained to discourage crime in the present and in the future. This includes the need for concierges, and neighbourhood wardens where appropriate. The community should be involved in management and maintenance and every effort should be made to avoid concentrations of people with life circumstance problems that may increase the likelihood to offend.
- **Ownership:** Places should promote a sense of ownership, respect, territorial responsibility and community. The key to ownership and design is that it fosters "social capital" through neighbours being able to recognise and get to know each other. Public, private and communal space should be well defined but if too high, barriers can create fear and a lack of safety. Gated communities should only be used when all else has failed.
- **Physical protection:** Places should have, where necessary, well-designed security features – locks and grills, including those products that are tested to recognised security standards. Careful selection of fittings and fixtures should reduce their impact on the overall environment.
- **Structure:** Places should be structured so that different uses do not conflict. This requires appropriate interaction between uses and users and with surrounding areas and communities and appropriate uses in appropriate places.
- **Surveillance:** All publicly accessible spaces should be safely overlooked. This may be achieved by one or a combination of the following:

– "Natural Surveillance" by people going about their normal lives
– "Organised Surveillance" by the police or wardens
– "Technological Surveillance" by CCTV
– Appropriate lighting

Bank Top, Blackburn

Jon Rouse illustrated his principles by referring to proposals to improve a typical inner urban area in decline at Bank Top in Blackburn. This is an area that possesses two predominant types of housing – parallel streets of nineteenth-century terraced narrow frontage artisans' housing, and council housing designed in the 1970s on Radburn principles of vehicle and pedestrian segregation. Unlike similar housing areas in the South of England, the nineteenth century housing is not subject to gentrification but is subject to some clearance by the local authority. The council housing is in need of re-shaping along the lines of a traditional street pattern. An audit was undertaken in 2000 to assess levels of crime and its perception, with the results indicated in Table 1.2 (p. 9).

Design solutions by Levitt Bernstein Associates and Llewellyn Davies to both problems are illustrated in Figures 4.2 and 4.3. Essentially they restructure the area to provide greater permeability along main routes whilst offering greater protection along back alleys.

Jon Rouse's paper concluded that:

- Planning out crime should be mainstream policy.
- Local residents should be rewarded for taking a role in neighbourhood management.
- Right to buy of council housing should be restricted in certain circumstances.
- There should be flexibility in the use of funds to deal with housing layout, as well as the internal condition of the house.

UK Police guidance

Secured by Design

Secured by Design (SBD) is a UK Police initiative that was launched in 1989 to support the principles of designing out crime. It was drawn up in consultation with the Department of Transport, Local Government and the Regions (formerly DETR), as well as trade and industry organisations. It is supported and managed by the Association of Chief Police Officers (ACPO) and the Association of Chief Police Officers for Scotland (ACPOS) and it has the backing of the Home Office. Its aim is "to support one of the government's key planning objectives – the creation of secure, quality places where people wish to live and work".

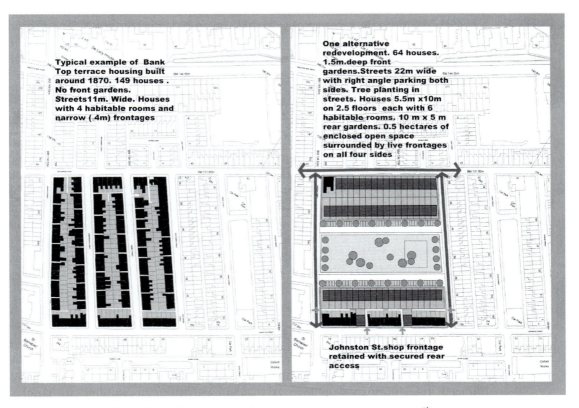

Within the figure:

Typical example of Bank Top terrace housing built around 1870. 149 houses . No front gardens. Streets 11m. Wide. Houses with 4 habitable rooms and narrow (.4m) frontages

One alternative redevelopment. 64 houses. 1.5m.deep front gardens. Streets 22m wide with right angle parking both sides. Tree planting in streets. Houses 5.5m x 10m on 2.5 floors each with 6 habitable rooms. 10 m x 5 m rear gardens. 0.5 hectares of enclosed open space surrounded by live frontages on all four sides

Johnston St. shop frontage retained with secured rear access

Figure 4.2 Bank Top, Blackburn: Redevelopment proposals for the 19th century terraced housing. Architects: Levitt Bernstein Associates and Llewellyn Davies.

The key features of SBD are:

- It is the corporate title for a group of national police projects involving the design of new housing, estate refurbishment, sheltered housing, multi-storey dwellings and commercial premises and car parks.
- It is primarily an initiative to encourage the building industry to adopt recommended crime prevention guidelines in both house and estate design and thus gain approval and to use an official police-approved logo in the marketing of new houses.

It functions on two levels:

- The Developers Award is a certificate given to building developments which, following consultation with local Police Architectural Liaison Officers (Crime Prevention Design Advisors), are built to conform to the ACPO guidelines

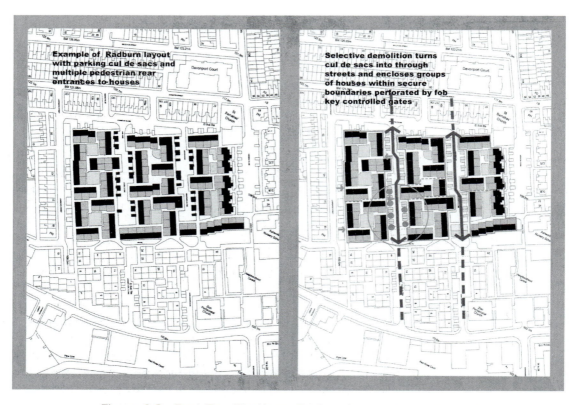

Figure 4.3 Bank Top, Blackburn: Radburn housing layout changed to a more traditional street pattern. Architects: Levitt Bernstein Associates and Llewellyn Davies.

and so reduce the opportunity for crime. SBD Design Guides state minimum standards for Secured by Design Awards.

■ Licensed Products – Secured by Design licensed company status is awarded to those companies producing security products, including doors and windows, which pass standards and tests nominated by the police service as "Police Preferred Specification".

SBD is promoted by Architectural Liaison Officers (Crime Prevention Design Advisers). The Design Guide places strong emphasis on controlling access: making sure that anybody who is in an area has a legitimate reason to be there. Spaces, especially private spaces, are well defined, helping to provide a clear sense of ownership amongst residents. Natural surveillance is encouraged in these well-defined public spaces and routes. The principles of Secured by Design are now incorporated in the Housing Corporation's Scheme Development Standards as a test of compliance of receipt of the

Corporation's Social Housing Grant (The Housing Corporation, 1998, Section 1.4.2).

SBD design guidance

New housing

Key principles are as follows:

- **Roads and footpaths** that are clear, direct, busy and well used are desirable. They should not undermine the defensible space of neighbourhoods. Where it is desirable to limit access to, say, a particular group of residents and their visitors, design features should be used such as rumble strips, change of road surface (by colour or texture), pillars or narrowing of the carriageway. This helps to define the defensible space psychologically, giving the impression that the area beyond is private. Footpaths should be wide enough for use by emergency vehicles.
- **Landscaping:** planting should not impede the opportunity for natural surveillance and must avoid the creation of potential hiding places. As a general rule shrubs should have a mature growth height no higher than 1 m and trees should have no foliage below 2 m, thereby allowing a 1 m clear field of vision. Walls and hedges should not obscure doors and windows and the position of trees should avoid them becoming climbing aids into property or obscuring lights and CCTV. Spiny or thorny types of plants are recommended as they help prevent loitering.
- **Street lighting:** This should comply with BS 5489.
- **Communal areas:** Communal areas, such as playgrounds, seating or dry areas, have the potential to generate crime, fear of crime and antisocial behaviour. They should be designed to allow supervision from nearby dwellings with a safe route for users to come and go. Boundaries between public and private space should be clearly defined and open spaces should have features that prevent unauthorised vehicular access. Toddler areas should be designed so that they can be secured. Consideration should be given to the provision of informal association areas for members of the community, particularly young people. These must be subject to surveillance but sited so that local residents will not suffer from too much noise. In addition they should be sited in such a way that people using adjacent footpaths and cycleways will not be subject to harassment or otherwise put in fear.
- **Dwelling identification:** clear naming and numbering of properties is essential to assist both residents and the attendance of Emergency Services.
- Consideration should be given to the provision of vandal-resistant location maps at convenient points.

- **Dwelling boundaries:** It is important that appropriate demarcation between public and private areas is clearly indicated. Dwelling frontages, which are open to view, may have low walls, fences or hedges. Vulnerable areas, such as side or rear gardens, need more defensive barriers with walls or fencing to a minimum height of 1.8 m. There may be circumstances where open fencing is required to allow for greater surveillance. Where the risk is increased with gardens adjoining open land, footpaths or other areas, additional deterrent features such as a trellis top or thorny shrubs must be considered.
- Boundary walls, bins and fuel stores, low flat roofs or balconies, should be designed so as not to provide climbing aids to gaining access into the property.
- Footpaths that give access to the rear of properties must have gates placed as near to the front building line as possible, to the same height as the adjacent boundary fencing. These gates must have a key-operated robust lock and not be easy to climb or remove from hinges.
- **Car parking:** Curtilage parking arrangements are preferred, but where communal parking is necessary, it must be in small groups, open to view and well lit. Garages should be located towards the front of the dwellings, but not at the risk of reducing opportunities for natural surveillance. Entrances to garages should be designed to be within boundaries of the secured area.

The Police Architectural Liaison Officers (Crime Prevention Design Advisers) are always keen to ensure that there are windows in end gables to ensure good natural surveillance (Fig. 4.4). It is also important to liaise with the Fire Officer to ensure that there are no conflicting requirements between security and means of escape.

Refurbishment: In the case of refurbishment, SBD advises of the importance of involving existing residents who will have first-hand experience of the crime risks and the practicality of any proposed security improvements. Also, their co-operation is crucial in ensuring that security features are properly used.

Sheltered housing: The recommendations for sheltered housing emphasise the importance of good lighting to deter intruders and reduce the fear of crime, which is particularly vital to elderly people. It also advises on standards for lighting and gates.

Multi-storey dwellings: For multi-storey dwellings, SBD standards are connected with the communal areas and the space around the blocks (Fig. 4.5). These are indicated below:

- **Public areas:** Public access to blocks should be limited. An access control system should be provided. This may be a managed concierge system, a Proximity Access Control (PAC) system and door entry phone system, or a combination of both. There should be no unnecessary paths, which could be used to gain unobtrusive access and escape. Good signage should be

Figure 4.4 Wiltshire Road housing, London SW9. Windows wrap around the corner to offer good natural surveillance. Architects: London Borough of Lambeth, Technical Services Department.

provided to deter unauthorised access and assist Emergency Services, tradespersons, etc.

- **Natural surveillance:** There should be natural surveillance of all public spaces including galleries, communal areas, drying areas, landscaping, and garages and parking areas. Recesses, blind corners and hiding places must be avoided.
- **Formal surveillance:** A monitored Close Circuit Television (CCTV) system covering the site area with particular focus at key access points may be required. Consideration should be given to providing residents with visual access control.

Figure 4.5 Northwood Tower, Walthamstow, London: refurbishment of high-rise housing is usually to SBD requirements. Architects: Hunt Thompson Associates.

- **Lighting:** The following areas must be lit: main site access, garages, garage forecourts, car parking areas, all footpaths and associated areas to the main building, refuse store, drying areas, secluded areas and similar locations around the site. Also at the main entrance door, secondary access doors and fire exit doors. All lighting must be automatically controlled by photo-electric cell or time switch. Fittings and service wiring should be vandal proof.
- **Block boundaries:** Private gardens or patios to ground-floor dwellings or communal facilities should be secured. The estate layout should provide each block with a clearly defined defensible space, and fencing where appropriate.
- **Car parking:** Curtilage car parking is preferred with communal parking in small groups, close to the blocks and open to the view of the residents from regularly habitable rooms. Garages should be located to maximise opportunities for natural surveillance.

Secured by Design has been shown to reduce burglary by over 50 per cent. Therefore, hypothetically, the adoption of the scheme over the entire housing stock could be said to save over £12 billion. In terms of sustainability, therefore, the use of the Secured by Design scheme would appear both logical and cost-effective (Knights et al., 2003, p. 7).

West Yorkshire survey of SBD schemes

A survey carried out in 2000 in the West Yorkshire area of England by Rachel Armitage of the Applied Criminology Group at the University of Huddersfield proved that "Secured by Design" estates experienced between 54 and 67 per cent less crime than equivalent non-SBD estates.

The evaluation was commissioned and funded by the West Yorkshire Police and the Kirklees Community Safety Partnership. Of the 150 estates included in the research, 75 were Secured by Design. The study found that burglary offences were lower on the SBD estates and were significantly lower than the national average as reported in the British Crime Survey. In addition, it revealed that the burglary reduction did not switch the crime rate into other types of crime on the estates. Residents' surveys revealed an overall perception that crime and disorder had been reduced. It proved that Secured by Design was "not just about crime statistics, but about making communities feel safer and more desirable places to live".

The study sought information from Registered Social Landlords (Housing Associations), builders, architects and quantity surveyors on the cost of designing to SBD requirements. The outcome was a general consensus that certain developers will choose their products based upon price, not quality. In this instance, the additional cost of building to SBD standards may be as high as £1,250 (for a 3-bedroom property). Alternatively, certain developers have typically high standards of non-SBD dwellings, in which case the difference could be as little as £90 (for a 3-bedroom property). In the case of Registered Social Landlords, as all dwellings have to comply with Scheme Development Standards, the extra cost was in the region of £440. In the case of refurbishment this was £600 (Armitage, 1999).

The Royds regeneration, Bradford

The planning of the Royds regeneration in Bradford, West Yorkshire, by Architect/Planners WSM (Webb Seeger Moorhouse) adhered closely to Secured by Design, and the local Architectural Liaison Officer, Stephen Town, was involved throughout the whole process. The Royds covers three local authority housing estates on the south-west corner of Bradford that were subject to major regeneration. The estates were built in the 1950s and contained a total of 3,350 dwellings accommodating 12,000 people. The housing and environment were in a poor state of repair, whilst the people suffered a low economic base with high unemployment. It had become a dumping ground for some of Bradford's problematic council tenants. Levels of crime were high and drug taking was rife. In 1995 burglaries were seven times the national average.

In 1995 the Royds Community Association secured a £31 million SRB grant to stimulate a seven-year programme of physical, economic and social regeneration activities that cost a total of over £100 million. One of the most striking features of the Royds project is that it is very much a community-based initiative. It acts itself as the accountable body for SRB funds, in contrast to many projects where the local authority assumes this role. Elected community representatives form a majority on the 24-strong board, with the local council and local business also represented.

Right from the beginning the Royds developed a holistic approach to regeneration covering economy, crime, health and housing. It was concerned to build up a sustainable form of regeneration, thinking ahead to when SRB funding came to an end. The physical element involved a major programme of housing refurbishment, selective demolition of unpopular walk-up flats and replacement with homes for sale and development for social rent by housing associations (Fig. 4.6). Physical redesign was carried out with a view to reducing crime and the signs are that this has been very successful (Table 4.1).

The economic programme included support for job advice, local businesses, an employers' club, building an enterprise park and initiating three community-owned businesses. Members of an employers' club guarantee to consider local residents when taking on new workers, and contractors with the Royds were expected to take steps to ensure that local people were trained and engaged for work in the building industry. The enterprise park and

Figure 4.6 The Royds, Bradford: new private housing mixed into existing social rented housing.

Table. 4.1. The Royds, Bradford: burglary statistics

Year	Forced entries	Failed attempts
		within total
1.4.97 to 31.3.98	307	54
1.4.98 to 31.3.99	215	30
1.4.99 to 31.3.00	133	19
1.4.00 to 31.3.01	89	10
1.4.01 to 31.3.02	95	17

There is no record of a successful forcible entry into any refurbished dwelling.
Source: West Yorkshire Police (Webb, 2003).

community businesses aim to become viable projects, which will be able to run long after SRB, generating a stream of income to help support other community activities.

The social programme included building a healthy living centre, with local GP, dentistry and health facilities (Fig. 4.7). The building brings in a useful guaranteed rental stream for the association. Two community centres have also been built, which are also generating small but useful income streams. Other initiatives include educational work, training, provision of play areas, advice services, environmental work, such as tree planting, railings and gates (Fig. 4.8) and a local food initiative.

Dutch Police Labelling

Principles

The Dutch "Police Labelled Secured Housing®, Politiekeurmerk Veilig Wonen®" represents some of the most advanced CPTED strategies to date. It has incorporated the principles of Christopher Alexander's pattern language and applied them to safe urban design. In addition it links social

Figure 4.7 A new healthy living centre at the Royds is a focal point within the community. Architects: WSM, Webb Seeger Moorhouse.

Figure 4.8 The Royds' community gates.

aspects of how neighbourhoods work with the physical environment. It differs from the British Secured by Design in that the list of requirements is not only confined to buildings, but is also extended to urban development planning and the direct living environment. After experimenting in the district of Middle Holland, the Ministry of the Interior in 1996 ordered that the Label became accepted on a national scale. By the end of 1998 it was completely accepted and included in the "New Estates Handbook" and the "Existing Building Handbook".

The Dutch system combines three elements into a set of requirements:

- The more scientific notions of the prevention of crime.
- The potential know-how of the police.

■ The know-how of building, urban development and housing.

The scheme involves the issue of three partial certificates. These certificates – "Secured Dwelling", "Secured Building" and "Secured Neighbourhood" – can be issued separately and together when they constitute the complete Police Label Secured Housing® New Estates or Police Label Secured Housing® Existing Building. The aim of the Label is to reduce the risk of crime as much as possible by way of design and management of the living environment. This can be achieved by reducing certain types of antisocial behaviour and offences (such as theft of or from cars, theft of bicycles and vandalism), and by reducing the fear of crime. To this end, the Police Label Secured Housing® has linked a clear list of requirements to the Label that will guarantee (the occupant) that the requirements have been met.

The process involves the commissioning party (housing corporation, project developer, speculative builder, etc.) and designers seeking support in the preparatory stage from specially trained plan advisers within the police – Architectural Liaison Officers – or external specialists. They are given advice on how the Label requirements can best be incorporated in the design.

The scheme also includes setting standards for building elements – door sets, windows and frames, hinges and locks – which are submitted to a manual test (also called the "burglar test"). Most manufacturers' products now comply.

The full Label will only be issued on completion of the development and after an independent inspection has taken place. Advice from the police is free but there is a charge to cover the cost of the inspections. The police or other organisations involved do not accept liability in providing the service.

The requirements for police labelling are in five categories:

■ Urban planning and design
■ Public area
■ Layout
■ Building
■ Dwelling

The first three are concerned with residential environment. Good public lighting, adequate car parking in the right locations, and security features within the dwelling design are considered basic requirements. Most other requirements are not mandatory to allow design flexibility.

Standards

The standards are much more specific in terms of design and management than Secured by Design. The key statements on the built environment are as follows:

Urban planning

- **Variety** of housing type, size, price, ownership and level (low-rise or high-rise) and therefore variety of target groups in the area.
- **Building height and scale:** not more than five floors high. Higher buildings functioning as features within the urban development are allowed, if used on a small scale. Low-rise terraced housing should not contain more than 20 dwellings in one block; a maximum of 10 is preferred.
- **Number of dwellings and main entrances to traffic**: A residential area with up to 500 houses should have no more than one or two main entrances for motorised traffic. A residential area with more than 500 houses should have no more than two to four main entrances.
- **Routes for cyclists and pedestrians** must be socially safe. Good surveillance is necessary.
- **Open space:** There must be sufficient space in the residential area for recreation and public green belts, parks and gardens.
- **Rear paths** must be overlooked. Facilities in the neighbourhood must be appealing and can serve as a meeting place within the residential area. Outside shopping hours the place will not present an uninhabited deserted atmosphere, which will stimulate crime and/or fear of crime. Facilities "that draw a great number of people" should be situated on the outskirts of the residential area. These should create as little nuisance as possible in the neighbourhood.
- **Community centres** are to be located to avoid any nuisance to people living in the neighbourhood. However, community centres are preferably located in the centre of the residential area. From the surrounding houses people should have a good view of the (entire) community centre.

Public areas

- **Facilities for young people:** Play facilities and meeting places for young people of all ages should be available – located in such a manner to enable natural supervision. Play facilities for young children should be seen from the living rooms of the surrounding dwellings. There should be benches in play areas for parents to supervise their children. There should be facilities for teenagers, such as squares and fields suitable for sports like football. Facilities for teenagers should be located within the sphere of influence, but not necessarily within view of the dwellings. Play facilities should be resistant to vandalism and well manageable. They should be located to guarantee access to residential buildings by fire engines, refuse collection, etc.
- **Walls/surfaces/partitions and graffiti:** Blank walls and surfaces need to be considered to reduce the impact of graffiti – the use of graffiti-resistant coating or a coating material that is easy to clean is recommended.

- **Management and supervision of public areas:** Agreements on (the role of safety) in managing and supervising the environment must be laid down in writing by all relevant parties. The plan contains agreements on the way in which a lasting "clean comprehensive and secured living environment" can be guaranteed. The plan provides for procedures regarding co-operation and communication with occupants and other parties involved. Informal supervision is stimulated and, if necessary, supported by hiring, for example, a salaried caretaker for this purpose.

Layout

- **Layout and location of single-family dwellings:** There should be a clear distinction between the public front side of the dwellings and the rear, which is screened off and difficult to access by burglars and other unauthorised persons. This is achieved by:
  - Good surveillance of the fronts and entrances of the dwellings from public spaces
  - The fronts of the dwellings are flat or the projections and recesses do not interfere with surveillance and security
  - Dwellings have a front and/or side garden, with clear separation between public and private space
  - The accessibility of the rear of dwellings should be restricted. Options for this purpose are:
    - back gardens that do not border public areas
    - the building block is fully enclosed (connected dwellings, possibly with garages)
    - there are no (continuous) rear paths.
- **Layout and location of residential buildings:** All housing should be capable of being well supervised and secure. Entrances should be highly visible – avoid trees, shrubs, sheds and other obstacles blocking the view of the housing. Access routes should be short and well overlooked. Outside parking places are located to ensure good accessibility from the entrance.
- **Rear paths** (basic requirement). Any rear path should be secure, overlooked and not be inviting to unauthorised persons. Rear paths should be at least 1.5 m wide, straight with no sharp bends, twists or forks. Rear paths should be provided with (public) lighting. There should be a point of light at the head of the path and further lighting at least every 15 to 20 m. They should preferably be dead end. Each side of the path should serve a maximum of 10 back gardens or residential properties (there are other detailed options).
- **Fencing of the grounds** (basic requirement). Fencing of the grounds provides a barrier against burglars, but does not restrict the view of the residential property or the building block. 1.8 m fences/walls are generally required. The fencing between the grounds can be a pergola, garden fence, wall or hedge-

row. Visibility of the rear side for instance remains possible by using partially non-solid fencing (at a height of 1.2 to 1.8 m).

- **Blocks of storerooms/garages** (basic requirement). A block of sheds or private garages should be positioned in such a way that an area that is socially secured and has natural surveillance is created.

The standards for dwellings recommend that all dwellings should have a balcony to offer natural surveillance of the public and semi-public spaces below. This could be in the form of a "French balcony", i.e., French doors with a balustrade.

Success of Dutch Police Labelling

To date, occupants have shown great enthusiasm. Research carried out by NIPO (the market and opinion research institute) has shown that as high a percentage as 90 per cent of the people surveyed agrees with the proposition that the Police Label increases the feeling of safety, and 70 per cent want to have a Label on their next house. All measures are highly approved of, particularly improved public lighting, improved door and window furniture, proper external lighting attached to their house, a clear view of the street and parking places, all of which are considered important aspects.

Since labelling began in 1997, the national burglary rate has dropped from 120,000 to 86,000 offences in 2000. The cost of these offences was estimated to be in the region of 2 billion Euro per annum. The results of Police Label Housing since 1997 (to the end of 2001) were as follows:

- 220,000 residential certificates awarded
- 32,000 new build projects awarded certification
- 95 per cent reduction in the risk of burglary in secured dwellings
- 70 per cent of people asked knew of the scheme and in municipalities this rose to 88 per cent.

Police Labelling is clearly successful in The Netherlands. It is helped by the higher percentage of people than in Britain living in rented accommodation, which makes it far easier to implement. If Secured by Design in Britain were to be extended to embrace the environment more fully it would need more skill on the part of planners, architects, developers and crime specialists and a will to work together. There would be a cost involved but this would be quickly recouped in savings from crime reduction (Hesselman, 2001).

De Paerel, Hoorn, The Netherlands

A new development at Hoorn illustrates that the Dutch Police Labelling does not affect quality of design – it proves that the measures are not noticeable.

Hoorn is situated some 30 kilometres north of Amsterdam and is a port on the Ijsselmeer Lake. The site on which the development was built is close to the town centre and overlooks the Ijsslmeer on one side and a marina on the other. The development comprises a mixture of 67 terraced houses, 67 apartments and 13 penthouse flats. The apartments are in 4-storey blocks overlooking the lake, whilst the houses are in 3-storey form built above basement parking and storage. (Figs. 4.9 and 4.10). The houses are arranged in terraces enclosing small greens at the rear, with pedestrian street access on the front side. The design reflects the scale and street character of the surroundings and the building image is bright and colourful (Figs. 4.11 and 4.12).

The basement parking was originally to be open but was enclosed for reasons of security. Access is now via electronically controlled doors. The police liaison officer recommends a maximum of 15 garages in such a situation. He also considers that the basement parking is acceptable as all the houses above are privately owned, but it might not be suitable in other situations. Balconies provide good surveillance of the street below. They are large enough to accommodate four people sitting and eating together and are designed to be sheltered from the winds. Doors and windows are carefully designed to provide good surveillance. Corner windows, in particular, offer wide views. Entrance doors have carefully sized and positioned glazed panels. This and other details and specifications relate to Police Labelling standards, although in some instances the specification determined with the police liaison officer was higher to suit the purpose.

Figure 4.9 De Paerel, Hoorn, The Netherlands: model of the scheme. Architect: Inbo Architecten B.N.A.

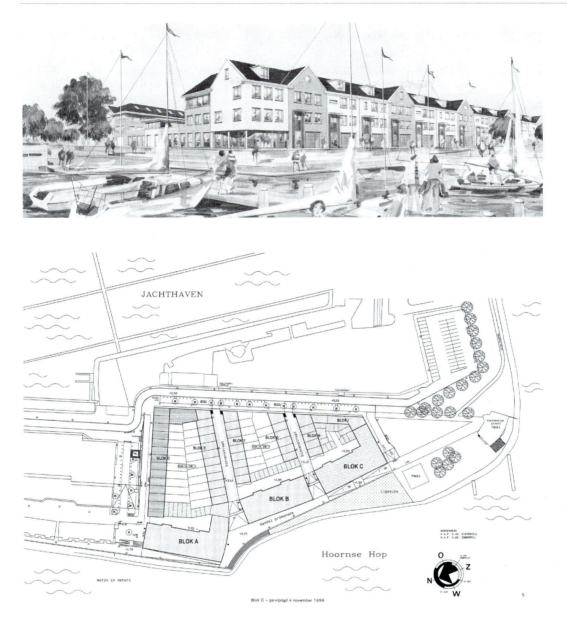

Figure 4.10 De Paerel: perspective and site layout.

219

Figure 4.11 De Paerel: windows carefully arranged to provide natural surveillance at street level.

UK local authority guidance

Research was recently commissioned by the Office of the Deputy Prime Minister (ODPM) to establish the extent to which crime prevention is included in the development plan policies and/or supplementary planning guidance, and is a significant factor in local planning authority decisions on planning applications. The research, which was conducted by the University of Manchester amongst all local planning authorities in England, concluded that just over three-fifths of currently adopted devel-

Figure 4.12 De Paerel: upper street level. Residents have adopted territory in front of their homes.

opment plans contain specific policies relating to planning out crime. Relatively few planning authorities have specifically produced guidance on crime prevention. Where it exists, it is in the form of supplementary planning guidance or leaflets. Planning out crime has been relevant for only a small proportion of all development control work. Where there was guidance it has been mainly concentrated on housing estate layouts, car park designs, boundary fencing and landscaping. Some of the better guidance, including practice from overseas countries, is now reviewed (Williams and Wood, 2001).

Essex Design Guide, 2nd edition

Lessons from experience in Essex are most important, as the County Council was one of the first local planning authorities to produce a Design Guide for residential areas and therefore has long experience of working with developers and architects through its guide. When the first edition of the Guide came out in 1973, *The Architects' Journal* compared it in significance with Le Corbusier's *Vers une Architecture*, saying "It will definitely influence the environment in the future". It most certainly has, although perhaps not in the way Le Corbusier would have imagined (Fig. 4.13). (*The Architects' Journal*, 1973). Essex is now bearing the brunt of the economic growth of the South-east of England, and all along the M11 corridor new housing is springing up. A second edition of the Design Guide was published in 1997 (Essex County Planning Officers' Association, 1997), which has very different recommendations leading to a most distinctive range of architectural solutions (Figs. 4.14 to 4.16).

Figure 4.13   Typical Essex mews court: Brentwood Place, Brentwood. Architects: David Ruffle Associates.

Figure 4.14 Essex Design Guide: high sense of individual dwelling identity to avoid an estate image.

Main recommendations

These are framed to produce sustainable development and are as follows:

- A site appraisal is now required for all development sites larger than 1 hectare (2.5 acres) (p. 6).
- Developments larger than 500 dwellings must incorporate mixed-use development of an employment and/or retail nature (p. 9).
- Sustainable issues must be addressed for development sites larger than 1 hectare (p. 9) This means addressing a number of issues as follows:
  - Proximity to a town centre or similar facilities and public transport access.
  - The need for a mix of residential and employment uses.
  - Close proximity to a bus route (400 m max), primary school (600 m) and a secondary school (1500 m).

Figure 4.15 Essex Design Guide: a country/town street.

– The development must safeguard the existing ecology, improve the natural habitat and minimise heat loss from buildings.

- The layout structure on development sites larger than 1 hectare must be both permeable and legible (p. 10). Any residential development containing a road over 100 m in length must be designed to reduce speeds to 20 mph (30 kph) by means of physical constraints.
- Where residents are prepared to enter into agreement not to own cars, it is possible to lay out a residential development as a Car Free Zone (p. 77).

Police views of the Guide

The Essex police force generally welcomes the design guide although there is some reservation about permeable layouts. They claim a degree of rigidity in

Figure 4.16 Essex Design Guide. Beaulieu Park: greenspace at the entrance to the development.

the interpretation of the guide by the planning authorities whilst designs should be considered on a site-specific basis. At times it is not always sensibly possible to provide off-street car parking, and parking at the rear of groups of dwellings can offer easy access for burglars into rear gardens, and from there into the backs of the houses.

Assessment of plans by the police

The police advise of the importance of assessing how society is changing and what issues could confront communities in the future. This means considering two common denominators of crime potential: crime patterns and long-term planning.

To assess possible future crime patterns for a proposed housing development on a green-field site, the police look at surrounding areas to see the existing patterns. On a brown-field site they research the past record in the area, particularly youth crime. They review long-term planning proposals for the whole area and consider the environmental impact of this on the site that is currently subject to development. They examine the distribution of affordable sale and rental housing within a development, giving careful consideration to the interaction of people. Entry points are important, as is the distribution of different kinds of housing for the elderly, families, young people, etc. The practice in Essex is for affordable housing to be developed in clusters with separate vehicular access to the sale housing. Developers prefer this as it reduces its impact on the marketability of the sale housing. This is an issue that goes beyond the scope of police advice but in terms of creating communities it raises obvious questions.

For the police, looking at long-term planning issues also means considering how a development within an area might change over the years. They consider "what if" factors on a wide basis. Initially the focus of the community might be a school, but this declines as children grow older. "Community spirit" cannot be forced upon people. Residents' Associations are valuable but need to be embodied into the proposals from the planning stage if their use is not to be limited to a small number of interested people. The engagement of women in this process is essential, as they are the key investors in home and community.

Feedback from the police

It is very important to review older estates to determine success and failure. Initially, families with small children occupy developments. How these children engage with the environment as they grow older offers many clues to future design. Teenagers will congregate in certain types of space, particularly beneath archways, on play areas, etc. Later they will own their own cars resulting in up to four cars per dwelling, which can be a huge problem in areas of predominately family houses.

Density

The police consider that in private sector housing density can be an issue if design does not fully reflect the long-term use of the development. Flats mixed into housing can help secure higher densities without increasing child density. However, the police in Essex experience problems when flats are let to teenagers. Also individual people purchase housing for rent and there is little control of how they are used. Large wheely-bins, which are difficult to incorporate into the design of higher density housing, are left out on the street. It all depends upon the quality of management of the housing and its environment, which in the private sector is usually very minimal. Problems occur with the lack of maintenance of communal planting. Bushes and shrubs are allowed to grow too intensely and too high, blocking off views into the street from houses behind. There is also concern about high fencing around schools that have consequently become separated from the community they serve. Instead, schools should appear to be part of the physical fabric of the community and owned by it. Hedge planting in double rows to a height of not more than 1.2 m would be far less imposing than a 3 m fence.

Developers' and architects' views

The police in Essex are also concerned that developers still need convincing of the benefits of Secured by Design. They fear that any mention of crime in sales documents will reduce the marketability of the housing even though it can lead to lower insurance premiums. Some architects similarly tend to shy away, relegating their thoughts on the subject to a low priority.

Great Notley

One of the largest developments in Essex to be designed in accordance with the principles of the second edition of the Essex Design Guide is Great Notley near Chelmsford. Developed primarily by Countryside Properties plc., it is suburban in form. The layout is based on a central spine road leading to a green (Fig. 4.17) with pedestrian and cycle routes within a landscaped corridor. This main spine road serves a variety of loops, access roads and culs-de-sac (Fig. 4.18), and it is the main public transport route through the scheme. The housing is highly varied in appearance helping to avoid an estate feel.

Nottingham City Council Design Guide: "Community Safety in Residential Areas"

The Nottingham Guide for designing out crime in residential development was produced in 1998 by the City Council's Conservation and Design Service (part of the Development Department). The guidance goes beyond the police "Secured by Design" in advising on the integration of new developments into the wider community: "it considers the environment of the whole neighbourhood and not just that of new development within it". In its objectives it also links reducing crime with creating a more sustainable environment by ensuring ease of maintenance, long life and adaptability.

Its recommendations on layout design include a number of important principles, which are less clearly defined in other guides. In particular, it

age centre

village green

Figure 4.17 Great Notley: variety of layout form (Reproduced by courtesy of Countryside Properties plc).

Figure 4.18 Great Notley: entrance to a housing court.

differs from other more recent guides on the use of culs-de-sac. The recommendations are:

- **A mixture of street types** should be provided including through routes and short culs-de-sac. This provides a choice of residential setting and helps establish settled communities by providing an environment to suit any age groups and lifestyles together. In a development with a mixture of street types, the culs-de-sac feed activity and movement along the through routes maximising surveillance on those roads. Culs-de-sac have less movement but develop a sense of ownership, because residents recognise each other and have reason to notice others. A perimeter block of through roads can be any shape provided dwellings face outwards towards streets or open spaces and the rear gardens interlock with one another.

- **Dwelling numbers in culs-de-sac** should ideally be limited to 16 to ensure residents have the likelihood of knowing each other and identifying strangers.
- **The number of culs-de-sac** within any perimeter block should ideally be limited to four. This ensures that the blocks are kept to a reasonable size.
- **Traffic calming** is important as it increases safety by reducing vehicle speeds. They can also reduce crime through creating a sense of identity and ownership of the street amongst residents by defining "territorial" boundaries. For example, chicanes along a route help divide it into clearly demarcated sections, especially if planting and street trees are used to signify "gateways".
- **Parking courts** are only acceptable in new developments if they have a single restricted access controlled (with gates or automatic barrier) by the residents and are not backed onto by rear gardens. They must be well observed from surrounding dwellings.
- **Access to private space**: communal grounds around blocks of flats should have lockable gates to allow access to residents only. Sometimes it will be preferable to define the space immediately adjacent to ground-floor flat windows as a small private garden or terrace exclusive to them.

There is also good advice on the design of open space and how to relate housing to it. This is illustrated in Fig. 3.83.

Canada: Toronto Safer City Guidelines

Toronto (and Canada as a whole) is a very safe place in which to live. Yet many people still feel afraid to use public spaces and public amenities. They fear for their personal safety on streets and transit systems, in parks and multi-storey car parks. The majority of the frightened people are women, whose fear of crime in public spaces frequently relates to the following issues:

- Poor lighting
- Isolation
- Lack of sightlines ("not visible to others")
- No access to help
- Hiding and entrapment spots (including "trees and shrubs")
- Inadequate security

Consequently Toronto City Council promotes "a City where all people can safely use public spaces, day and night, without fear of violence, and where people including women and children and persons with special needs, are safe from violence" (p. 11). Its Design Guide, *Toronto Safer City Guidelines*, is far more inclusive than most UK guidance and embraces the concepts of 2nd generation CPTED. It offers excellent advice that is relative to the British situation. Most measures are low cost and do not interfere with innovative design.

The Guide lists questions to keep in mind during the planning and design of development. These are:

- **Learning from experience**: What kinds of concerns have come up in similar developments in the past? What kinds of situations were developed?
- **User groups**: Who will use the place frequently? Who will use this space? What might their concerns be? How might they be consulted?
- **Day and night**: How might the spaces be used during the day and in the evening? Is the issue of evening use addressed?

With these questions in mind it gives three main factors to consider in the design process:

- **Awareness of the environment**: the ability to see and to understand the significance of what is around and what is ahead, through adequate lighting, clear sightlines and the elimination of entrapment spots.
- **Visibility by others**: the ability to be seen, reduction of isolation, improvements to the mixture and intensity of land use, and intelligent use of activity generators.
- **Finding help**: the ability to escape, communicate, or find help when in danger, through improved signage and legible design.

Its detailed design objectives are as follows:

- **Intensification of land use:** by filling in "empty space", especially at grade, with human scale housing, commercial and community services that are complementary to the needs of the existing residents (p. 56) (Fig. 4.19).
- **Housing for elderly people** and those with mobility impairments should be located near to essential services such as shops and public transport. Larger houses for families with young children should relate to the location of playgrounds. "This is not only for ease of access, but also avoids 'running the gauntlet' past teenage hangouts."
- **A meeting space** or a community centre for people to organise and involve themselves in defining the problems and creating the solutions.
- **Sightlines:** avoid tall, solid privacy fences, overgrown shrubbery and other thick barriers adjacent to pedestrian paths which could shield an attacker; low hedges or planters, small trees, wrought-iron or chain link fences, lawn or flower beds, benches and lamp posts all denote boundaries while allowing users to see and be seen.
- **Movement:** avoid underpasses or at least design them so it is possible to see what is at the end of it.
- **Isolation – ear and eye:** natural surveillance is important. The Guide advises on the use of CCTV in some especially dangerous or isolated spots: "There

Figure 4.19 Street housing in Toronto, Canada: Frankel Lambert town houses. Architect: Annau Associates (Photo: Lenscape, Toronto).

may be need for formal surveillance in the form of audio monitors, video cameras and staff. But it is important not to over-depend on formal surveillance hardware: a video camera, aside from its cost, will only help if there is a 24-hour attendant who knows what to do in a dangerous situation and who can be supervised to ensure that priority takes preference over reading the paper. In some cases, one person is expected to monitor up to 40 screens – too many to watch all day. Hardware can also easily be vandalised and it takes long periods to repair" (p. 31).

■ **Vandalism:** The Guide advocates an imaginative approach to solving vandalism problems which in turn enhance a sense of ownership: "The City of Toronto has funded murals painted by neighbourhood young people on walls subject to constant graffiti. An informal 'shortcut' through the grass can become a more formal path. Residents should become involved in landscaping around their housing. This is preferable to using prison-like 'vandal-proof' materials and treatments" (p. 36).

- **Legibility:** Significance is given to the "ability of people to place themselves in their surroundings". The degree to which users of an area can find their way around – the "legibility" of a space – influences the feeling of security. Legibility is the creator or inhibitor of security. Good design lessens the need to depend on signs in order to find one's way around, but signage is important at entrances and near activity nodes so people know where they are going, where there are telephone and public conveniences and where the nearest "safe" place (e.g., busy street) is located. House numbers should be clearly visible from the public road. The Guide lays important emphasis on the design of residential streets, referring to the Dutch "Woonerfs" as a model. It recommends traffic calming measures and the avoidance of "dead-end" streets.
- **Lighting:** The Guide emphasises the need for well-designed street lighting (see pp. 187–189.)

Towards a European standard

The European Urban Charter asserts the basic right for citizens of European towns and cities to a "secure and safe existence, free as far as possible, from crime, delinquency and aggression". This basic right to a safe community has been enshrined into national and local crime reduction programmes in many countries in Europe. This right is now incorporated into a European Prestandard, prENV 14383 *"Prevention of crime by urban planning and building design"*, that is being prepared by CEN/TC325 (CEN – Comité Européen de Normalisation – European Committee for Standardisation – the official body controlling the production of new standards). The preparation of the standard started in 1996 and it may be 10 years before it has been finally approved, as it requires the consensus of and agreement from all European countries and all European stakeholder organisations – police, architects, planners, security and insurance.

Why standardisation is necessary

The Dutch planner, Paul van Soomeren, explains that the standard will not be legally binding in any way. It will be voluntary across countries, institutes and the people concerned. Standardisation is seen as necessary because they are "a key component of the United European market and they facilitate communication and co-operation between different participants or stakeholders working in one process or implementing a project; e.g., in this instance, crime prevention. It also helps collaboration making processes more transparent" (van Soomeren, 2001).

Purpose of the Standard

The task of the CEN is:

> *"The preparation of European standards on building design and urban planning and housing design to provide performance requirements for the prevention of crime in residential areas, both new and existing housing, including local shops, in order to ensure safety and comfort and to minimise fear of violence. Standards on building products and security devises are excluded."*

The Prestandard aims to provide those engaged in urban planning, housing design and environmental crime prevention – as well as all stakeholders like local authorities and residents – with advice, guidance and check lists on effective multi-agency action to minimise the risk of crime and the fear of crime. It will encourage a greater understanding of the motivation of the offender in order to counterbalance this by specific physical security measures through planning and design. It intends to promote collaboration between the police and professional designers and ensure that police officers are specially trained to advise on the relationship between crime and the built environment.

There are two parts of the Prestandard related to housing design – Part 2, "Urban Planning" and Part 3, "Dwellings".

Part 2: Urban planning and crime reduction

Part 2 reflects that urban planning has an impact on the different types of crime and fear of crime by influencing the conduct, attitudes, choices and feelings of offenders, victims, residents, police, etc. It recognises that crime can be subdivided into specific types (such as burglary, vandalism), also that crime and fear of crime are different phenomena. Fear of crime is an important issue but it has to be separated from the much broader set of feelings people have about the whole of their living space and about the degree to which they feel deprived of a good social and physical living environment.

It recognises that a securer and safer city or neighbourhood is the result of a safety policy aiming at the physical and social environment, but policy-makers and practitioners should never focus on planning and design only. Every newly built neighbourhood, public space or building needs good maintenance. Actions need to be integrated and be of a multidisciplinary nature involving as necessary a wide range of people – local authorities, law enforcement specialists, environmental specialists, maintenance and management personnel, social workers, teachers and citizens, all of whom are stakeholders in the process.

It recommends procedures for planning a neighbourhood:

- Classify an area and its characteristics.

- Identify possible crime problems – burglary, car crime, theft, etc.
- Target crime and fear of crime potential – identify the area, the crime problems and the "stakeholders" who have a vested interest in the issues.
- Prepare urban planning and design guidelines.
- Develop urban design strategies.
- Consider management strategies.

It recommends linking "stakeholders" with the "responsible body", i.e., the regional or local planning authority, to prepare a mission statement that guides working groups for individual projects on the processes and steps required, documentation, etc., to determine the safety and security objectives. The eventual decisions are made by the responsible body and monitored by an independent auditor.

The Prestandard's planning and design objectives and process, including requirements for schools, are described in more detail in the Appendix.

Part 3: Dwellings

Part 3, "Dwellings", provides guidance on the design of residential neighbourhoods, dwelling design and the building envelope, designing out crime in residential blocks with shared entrances, and the management and maintenance of building in multi-occupancy. Its principal planning and design recommendations relate to:

- Assessment of potential risk factors in individual neighbourhoods
- Image
- Territoriality
- Design and layout of public space, semi-public space and private space
- Garages
- Fencing
- External lighting
- Management

It advises on risk assessment of required protection level and advises on risk analysis for individual dwellings and dwellings in a residential block with shared entrance(s). It advocates the establishment of a team of professionals for a project – town planners, designers, developers and professionals with crime prevention expertise. This joint approach should consider the various factors that can influence the opportunity to commit crime. It recommends that fear of crime, whether real or perceived, should be fully taken into account in the design of the environment. The detailed objectives are listed in the Appendix.

Figure 5.1 A refurbished central space in a Copenhagen city block of housing provides a community focal point.

Chapter 5

Creating safe and sustainable communities

Community and sustainability

The previous chapters have dealt with physical, social and economic aspects of designing crime out of the environment. However, it is now recognised that the most important measure is to create sustainable communities by looking at all issues together in a holistic way through the engagement of the local people. The task is too important to leave to developers, who often want a quick way out and no long-term commitment. This chapter explores the main principles of this.

Community has many definitions, but a useful one is:

"the web of personal relationships, groups, networks, traditions and patterns of behaviour that exist amongst those who share physical neighbourhoods, socio-economic conditions of common understandings and interests" (Community Development, 2001).

The web of personal relationships can include extended families, networks of neighbours, community groups, religious organisations, local businesses, local public services, youth clubs, parent and teacher associations, playgroups, elderly people's groups, and many more. How these come together in the interest of the community as a whole is vital to its sustainability. Coming together can be through a variety of sources such as tenants' and residents' committees, local community forums, neighbourhood management committees, the establishment of Development Trusts and others.

Sustainable development is concerned with creating neighbourhoods with facilities needed to enjoy a civilised life, in which people, young and old, can live in harmony and in safety, enjoying the social and other benefits of being part of a lively society. It was defined in 1987 by the United Nations World Commission under Gro Harlem Brundtland on Environment and Development as: "Development that meets the needs of the present without compromising the ability of the future generations to meet their own needs".

The Brundtland Report devised concepts that are referred to as "capital" – resources that need taking full advantage of. These are "social" – people are a resource; "economic" – making the best use of resources; "technological" – ensuring a knowledge base; "environmental" – making the best use of natural resources; and "ecological", which includes habitats, species and ecosystems.

Neighbourhood sustainability means embracing all these concepts in a holistic manner. Creating "balanced", mixed-use, walkable communities is fundamental and density is an important issue. This needs to be seen in the context of three different views of community – village, urban street and suburban. The village and suburban communities are attractive ideals to which people aspire, but urban areas are different. Rudlin and Falk suggest that "if we are to make cities more popular (than the village or suburban ideal) we need to develop new models of urban communities... the village or suburban community transplanted into the city simply will not work" (Rudlin and Falk, 1999, p. 110). Much of the success will rest on the quality of design and, through this, the effective reduction of crime.

Balanced communities

The notion of using planning to create balanced communities in terms of age profile, tenure, etc., has proved difficult in the past, particularly where it involved social planning. In the 1950s, Aneurin Bevan spoke of recreating "the living tapestry of a mixed community" where "the doctor, the grocer, the butcher, and the farm labourer all lived on the same street". The creation of balanced communities is once more high on the current agenda –

regenerating inner urban areas with the hope that it will significantly tackle social exclusion and all its accompanying problems including reducing crime (Minton, 2002b, pp. 10–11).

In her publication *Building Balanced Communities*, Anna Minton believes a balanced community in terms of age and tenure is the key to sustainability. She also believes that education and health and housing are important issues.

Her main principles are:

- **Social housing:** Do not build concentrations of single tenure social housing.
- **Private ownership**: Bring private ownership into public housing areas. This has proved successful in Europe and the US (and in Britain). In Holland it is now enshrined in a national policy entitled "Urban Restructuring". In the US, the HOPE VI programme (Housing Opportunities for People Everywhere) aims to attract higher-income people to low-income neighbourhoods.
- **Affordable housing:** Build a proportion of affordable housing in all new developments. This can take on the most sophisticated architectural forms. In the London Borough of Sutton, the Peabody Trust has developed the Beddington Zero Energy Development – known as Bed Zed – and created a sustainable community through a common low energy design approach using a combined heat and power unit to serve the whole scheme (Bill Dunster Architects). Of the 82 dwellings, 34 are outright ownership, 23 for shared ownership, 15 for social housing and the remaining 10 are available for reduced "cost rent", specifically for nurses and teachers (Fig. 5.2).
- **Quality development:** Invest at reasonable levels to ensure quality development. A particular problem for housing associations is that the total cost indicator system used by the Housing Corporation to assess grants to housing associations can force upon associations design decisions that they would prefer not to be made. Land cost can be a substantial element of the total cost, which at times has led to associations developing in poor neighbourhoods, to which people do not wish to move. Housing Development cost should therefore be more flexible and site specific.
- **Schools:** There must be a national recognition of the issue relating housing and schools in the creation of mixed, balanced communities. In the USA "magnet schools" are placed in blighted areas with the aim of enhancing the neighbourhood and improving educational opportunities for young people. These schools have been key to the retention of middle-class families in US cities since the 1970s and are widely seen as contributing to de-segregation. In Britain, parents are reluctant to send their children to schools that are under-performing, particularly at secondary level. This is one of the main causes for middle-income people choosing to live in the suburbs.
- **Health and poor housing** need considering together. Research shows a strong correlation between poor housing conditions characteristic of socially excluded areas and poor health, adding to the growing cost of health provision.

Figure 5.2 BEDZED: a small mixed tenure community share the benefits of the Beddington Zero Energy Development, London. Bill Dunster Architects.

She recommends introducing "magnet policies" that attract economically active people with spending power back into the area. This is best achieved through a carrot and stick approach, which offers incentives to live in low-income areas, often in the inner city, and limiting the supply of green-field sites. She also suggests a return to the land values and ownership theories of the Garden City movement, which were based on ploughing back into the community the benefits of land sales. The first garden cities flourished on this principle but few people dare tackle what is such a politically sensitive issue (Minton, 2002a).

From a crime perspective, there are great advantages to be gained from mixed use, mixed tenure, walkable communities. There is a variety of housing types and tenure within a neighbourhood, which allows the opportunity for people of diverse backgrounds to co-exist or informally conform to the accepted behaviours of that neighbourhood. When the make-up of households and employment patterns are different, there will probably be someone at home nearby most of the time to provide some measure of natural surveillance. The alternative is found in the USA where people live in single-use residential neighbourhoods, and go shopping in stand-alone commercial shopping centres. Most people are settled in this segregated pattern, believing it to be safer; and most local governments in the USA promote this land-use pattern through policy and regulations. Unfortunately, research does not provide a clear answer on whether mixed-use, walkable communities are safer. However, according to Mark Kroeker, the Chief of Police in Portland, Oregon, USA, community policing is made much easier with designs that include pedestrian-friendly streets, a diversity of house types and densities, and a diversity of people of different ages, incomes and culture who get to know each other. "Driving around spread-out suburban areas is very inefficient for police patrols, and many such areas never see any police presence. If we do not provide opportunities through our planning and design policies to co-exist, then homogenous patterns emerge which are conducive to criminal activity" (Minton 2002b, p. 10–11).

Balanced communities are now being created through adding an element of low-cost housing into new private developments. The Greater London Council is insisting in certain situations on as much as 50 per cent affordable housing due to soaring house prices that exclude key workers – even teachers and doctors – from getting into the market. Despite the evidence pointing to a lack of community interaction, there is a growing body of opinion among experts that suggests that social housing tenants fare considerably better in mixed areas than in their previous homes. They seem to have greater aspirations and they are not condemned for having a certain postcode.

A means of creating this balance in existing council estates is through demolishing local authority housing that is difficult to let. This can provide the opportunity to bring private development into areas that previously contained only social rented housing. It can produce significant social change, but private developers frequently insist on a critical mass of private housing to make their development financially possible. A few developers are pepperpotting private and social rented housing with interesting results. In the Royds Regeneration in Bradford (p. 210) this approach has proved particularly successful. The new Marquess Road development in the London Borough of Islington (p. 29) included private housing and shared equity housing with social rented housing in the same block. At Hulme in Manchester, council housing has been demolished and some land redeveloped for private housing. In Scotland, one of the best examples is Crown

Street in Glasgow (p. 155), which is a mixed tenure development of tenements and town houses with communal back gardens.

Hulme, Manchester

The regeneration of Hulme in Manchester is seen in many quarters as the planning model for the future reflecting the design and sustainability principles previously described. It started in 1991 as the result of a successful City Challenge bid of £35 million for pump priming a programme of housing renewal and social and economic regeneration with major renewal and infrastructure works. The scheme involved the demolition of 2,500 deck-access dwellings including the notorious Hulme Flats. Eventually, there will be 1,250 rented dwellings and 2,000 built for sale by Bellway Urban Renewal.

The planning approach was to produce an Urban Design Guide to characterise the vision of the area and the principles of the massing and positioning of the buildings. The planning criteria were as follows:

- Development of streets which promote sociability, community and natural surveillance, all designed to limit traffic speed to 20 mph.
- Permeability, i.e., a neighbourhood with strong links to surrounding areas, which is easy to move around in (Fig. 5.3).
- A sufficient density to support a wide range of shops and services.
- Development, which is sustainable economically, socially and environmentally, achieved by encouraging urban ecology and allowing the area to adapt for future change.
- A street hierarchy using 3-storey housing along the principal routes and 2-storey in residential streets (Fig. 5.4).
- A careful treatment of corners and vistas and landmarks – traditional points of reference in the city (Fig. 5.4).
- Dwellings to a national energy rating of 9.

So far these principles have been fully incorporated into the designs. The housing is varied and colourful. The private housing fronts on to the grid street pattern with car parking at the rear in gated courts. The success of this will depend entirely upon the willingness of residents to make the arrangement work through a long-term acceptance of closing the gates after entering.

Most noted of the individual projects is Homes for Change, which was envisaged as a community within a community. Its planning began in 1991 when a group of residents approached the project managers for the development at Guinness Trust to consider a mixed-use scheme with small businesses. The outcome is a startling building which incorporates managed workspace, shops, studios and a performance area that doubles up as a meeting room and café (Figs. 5.5 and 5.6). Its deck-access form is a reminder of

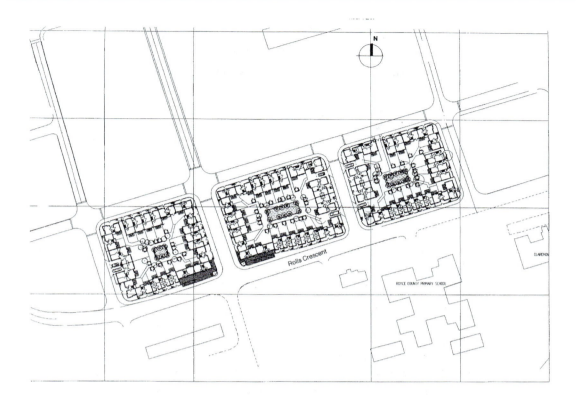

Figure 5.3 Rolls Crescent, Hulme, Manchester. Housing related to a permeable street pattern. ECD Architects.

past housing but in this case the decks are imaginatively used by residents (Fig. 3.85). The arrangement works because the residents all share a commitment to its success.

In their book *Planning for Crime Prevention: A Transatlantic Perspective*, Richard H. Schneider and Ted Kitchen review Hulme. They suggest there is evidence of crime reduction in Hulme but emphasise the importance of the scheme being carefully monitored over a period of time "so that we know what ordinary people think about the problems (if any)". They also stress that Hulme is not like many other parts of Manchester, and also unlike many other British cities (Schneider and Kitchen, 2002, p. 256).

Selling social houses to rebalance communities

A second approach to rebalancing existing communities in the UK has been explored by the Joseph Rowntree Foundation. In a five-year experiment on its own New Earswick estate at York of selling on the open market every

Figure 5.4 Rolls Crescent, Hulme. 3-storey housing on corners provide focal points.

second home that becomes vacant – and by marketing the properties to better-off people – the Foundation found that the estate's decline was halted. The initiative was prompted by mounting complaints of local children's antisocial behaviour. The Foundation's aim for the estate as a whole is now to achieve a ration of two-thirds rented homes to one-third owned. It ensures that all properties are in good condition before being put on the market,

Figure 5.5 Homes for Change: Hulme: access decks can work when there is a community that supports the design concept.

although houses are reported to be easier to sell than flats. Sales contracts include buy-back clauses and a ban on sub-letting. The outcome to date has been a marked improvement in the perception of the village and property values are increasing.

It is not, however, as the Joseph Rowntree Foundation admits, a solution for a desperately unpopular estate. It may not therefore be a model for

Figure 5.6 The community shop at Homes for Change.

British public sector estates with large numbers of difficult-to-let housing, unless it is accepted that a sufficient number of existing properties are cleared in a given area to provide developers with a critical mass of new houses to build and sell. Where this has been planned at Gipsyville, a council estate of some 2000 dwellings in Hull, private developers, after a very difficult start, have successfully sold new private housing. In addition the local primary schools are reporting greater achievements due to the greater mix of social background in their classes.

Density and sustainability

Sustainable neighbourhoods

The further issue to consider in respect of sustainability is density. The Urban Task Force, established by the UK government in 1998 and chaired by architect Lord Rogers of Riverside, advocated densities of at least 50 dwellings per hectare (20 dwellings per acre). This would sustain mixed-use development with public amenities such as a group of shops, a primary school and transport facilities within walking distance of home. In this way, Lord Rogers claimed there was a link between density and community that contributed considerably to urban sustainability (Urban Task Force, 1999, p. 61). Brian Edwards considers that only by achieving densities above 80 units per hectare (32 dwellings per acre) can public transport be sustained and streets designed to provide safe walking and cycling facilities. Above this density, he claims, development readily supports local shops, schools, local employment, etc. In reality, solutions must be site specific. It is much easier to create higher density developments in London and in the centre of other large cities. It is more difficult elsewhere where people seek a suburban life-style (Edwards with Hyett, 2001, p. 103).

Living over shops

There is a widespread belief amongst the police, planners and property owners that housing over shops has some potential to make town and city centres safer places by encouraging people back to live there. Bringing empty, unused space into residential use actively enhances security by helping to protect against break-ins to commercial premises below. Evaluation, in 1995, of a government's living over the shop scheme proved that it was good value for money, even though it was expensive to implement due to the complexity of negotiating deals with the property owners, but the rewards could be great. A study produced for the London Planning Advisory Service in 1998 estimated that some 73,000 additional residential units could be created in London alone from existing and vacant and under-used shops and upper floors (Urban Task Force, 1999, p. 253).

However, research undertaken by Sheffield Hallam University and the Empty Homes Agency, published by the Joseph Rowntree Foundation in 1997, found that this potential was not being realised as much as it could. Their research indicated that in most schemes there was little contact between residents and the occupiers of the commercial properties below. Only 2 per cent of the residents would know what to do if the burglar alarm went off in the shop. Most liked their homes and found them safer than, or as safe as, their previous homes. The results suggested that housing over shops is a satisfactory solution for the social group for whom it was designed but they did not necessarily suggest it was suitable as a general housing solution (Joseph Rowntree Foundation, 1997).

Sustainable housing

In his book *Rough Guide to Sustainability*, Brian Edwards considers that sustainable housing addresses three important issues in parallel (Edwards with Hyett, 2001, p. 102):

- Energy-efficiency, waste minimisation, resources, etc.
- Community and social welfare
- Economic prosperity, especially employment and education

The Scandinavian publication *Good Nordic Housing* supports this view. This was produced in 1995 by the five Scandinavian housing ministries to outline what they jointly considered to be the features of a good home and a good residential environment. Their 10-point summary offers a simple overview of the major features to consider in creating sustainable communities (Bjorklund (ed.), 1995, p. 45). Good Nordic housing:

- Is to be found in surroundings where resource management is combined with proximity to nature and outdoor recreation.
- Encourages long-term sustainability through the resource management of building materials and built-up areas, of water, of energy for heating and transport as well as through facilitating the recycling and sorting of household refuse and making compost.
- Is to be found in a neighbourhood close to shops, public transport, cultural activities and schools as well as recreational opportunities and outdoor activities for all age groups.
- Forms part of a context which offers opportunities for social contact and influence on one's own environment.
- Is to be found in a building or group of homes with a character of its own and which is suited to and enriches its surroundings, in combination with luxurious and varied vegetation.
- Has space for seclusion and company, for cooking, for meals, for work at home and room for one's circle of friends and for hygiene and storage, as well as for all the members of a household to have their own bedroom.
- Can be reached and used by persons of impaired mobility and orientational capacity as well as people who require care and attention in the home.
- Is light and sunny, warm and sheltered with beautiful rooms and layout, with views in different directions.

- Provides opportunities for good health and well-being with freedom from exposure, noise and allergy-provoking materials.
- Is to be found in surroundings with conditions for feeling at home and with security against break-ins and attacks.

There is much to learn from the experience of Scandinavian countries where there appears to be a greater appreciation than in Britain of the value of design in both new housing and regeneration. The Danish journal, *Arkitektur dk*, is one of the few architectural journals in the world that still regularly illustrates housing design. The following projects in Copenhagen in Denmark and Malmo in Sweden illustrate very different approaches to creating sustainable communities.

Urban renewal, Copenhagen

Figures 5.1 and 5.7 illustrate urban renewal and housing improvement in the centre of Copenhagen. The project was concerned with the preservation of large areas of nineteenth-century housing and updating the interiors to meet modern standards. The housing formed urban blocks with central courts previously full of redundant buildings relating to earlier uses. These have been removed, freeing space for common use by all the residents or, in some cases, creating semi-private space for the enjoyment of residents of a single building or stairwell. These spaces now provide opportunity for children's play, neighbourhood parties, sunbathing, etc., together with storage for refuse, bicycles and clothes drying. Access to this space is restricted to residents only and they are extremely safe and secure. Their success as space arises totally from the willingness of the residents to share and care for the spaces together. They are completely safe and free from crime.

Egebjerggard, Copenhagen

Egebjerggard, near Copenhagen, is another outstanding example of a sustainable community. It is part of the Ballerup Municipality and of Greater Copenhagen. Built between 1986 and 1996, it was a full-scale social experiment in urban development, attempting to incorporate holistic thinking and relationships between ecology and social conditions into the development of a new sustainable urban community, which, in turn, produced an extremely safe and secure living environment.

The planning concept that served as the basis for architectural design was to recreate "the lost town", with more social life and more potential for interaction. There were to be streets, lanes and squares, which were to be

Figure 5.7 Urban Renewal: Copenhagen: communal space created in rear courtyards of city blocks by removing redundant buildings.

populated. There was to be a wide range of choices – a mixture of socially
rented housing, housing co-operatives and private housing, plus housing for
young people and housing suitable for elderly and handicapped people. Each
housing group has its own identity and architectural character. Most houses
have been designed with a street frontage, which the residents say they prefer,
even if it means having north-facing back gardens. The main traffic route is a
long loop with frontage development along most of its length, designed to

limit the speed of traffic to 15 km/hr. The careful integration of the roads and buildings, street lighting, planting and public art in a coherent piece of urban design is most admirable (Figs. 5.8 and 5.9).

Social concept: Egebjerggard contains a mixture of people and housing tenure that reflects modern Danish society. There was a policy to locate "problem families" amongst other families, but on the basis of not more than one to every six to eight households, all of whom had to agree to the principle. This was considered preferable to locating problem families together. In the neighbourhood centre, there are a variety of shops, including a supermarket, baker and pizzeria. Nearby are the schools, out-of-school buildings for children and young people, sports facilities, etc. Less visible services, such as home help and other services for the elderly and handicapped, are provided. Many of the housing groups have common rooms that can be used for meetings, parties, and various other kinds of activity. The project also includes space for establishing local businesses

Resident participation in the planning of Egebjerggard was artificially created at the beginning but, as people began to move in, residents who were members of participation groups encouraged others to join in, and this way a community network was formed. This has led to open and friendly attitudes between residents. Newcomers are instructed that the responsibility for, and the work involved, in making the development a success, is everyone's concern.

Physical design: There is a huge variety of housing. The earlier concept of fronting buildings on to the street was regrettably replaced in later phases with more formal layouts of crescents and rear car parking. The individual row housing on the streets revives the small town houses of the past with their private side and garden at the back (Fig. 5.10). Several later schemes are inward-looking into a courtyard rather than outwards towards the street. These offer more social contact and the potential for more activity on a small scale amongst families, especially for small children, but at the same time they have less contact with the street. Because of this introverted orientation towards neighbourhoods, there are unclear spaces and a doubling of paths – the front of housing is at the back and the back yards are at the front. The last phases of housing have blank end gables and little defensible space at the front, so it is easy to look into the houses through the large windows. Consequently there are more blinds.

Crime: There are a few problems of graffiti, vandalism, break-ins and assaults but crime rates are less than half of the Municipality's average. The most vulnerable locations were the rear parking areas in the last houses built, which were not adequately overlooked. By far, most people wish to remain in the development, which now has a long waiting list. It is everything that a civilised sustainable community should be.

Figure 5.8 Egebjerggard, Copenhagen: site layout. A full-scale social experiment in urban development. The numbers on the plan refer to different housing phases and buildings. Of particular note are the following:

1. School complex
5. Shops
6. Lake overlooked by young people's housing in the block at the head of the lake.
20. Sheltered housing for elderly people
23,29. Later housing not relating to roads.

Figure 5.9 Egebjerggard, Copenhagen: the shopping centre fronts onto the main loop road that runs through the development.

Bo01 Housing, Malmo, Sweden

Malmo is the commercial centre of southern Sweden and a city with a long-standing commitment to integrated and strategic approaches to city-wide sustainable development. In 1987 it fostered an adventurous experiment in user participation in housing at Monbijougaton Street, as a means of creating sustainable development. 70 potential tenants came together with an architect, Ivo Waldhor, to build within a single apartment block a development in which every household had a dwelling that was designed specifically to their individual requirements. This produced a most imaginative development illustrated in Fig. 3.24 (*Architectural Review*, March 1992, pp. 25–29).

Figure 5.10 Egebjerggard: street housing.

The City of Malmo continued this willingness to experiment with Bo01, which is a new sustainable city district built on reclaimed land by the Vastra Hammen (Western Docks). The development was the subject of an international exhibition of experimental sustainable housing in 2001. Renewable energy is produced locally and supplied to the site. Green spaces are seen as essential to enhance the level of biodiversity within the site and the area uses the most up-to-date eco-technology for the treatment of water and waste.

The site overlooks the sea with a wonderful view of the new bridge linking Sweden and Denmark. The layout is highly permeable. Car access is by means of an informal loop road through the scheme, serving small grouped parking spaces. There is a varied mix of housing forms ranging from five-, six- and seven-storey apartments overlooking the seafront (Fig. 5.11) to two-storey houses within the development. The site was divided into small sites, each of which was designed by different architects (Fig. 3.7). Mixed use is in the form of shops on the ground floor of the apartments overlooking the seafront. There are also workshops located nearby.

The planning and design took on board CPTED principles to a point, and the design has strengths and weaknesses from the security point of view. Some housing is grouped around small, gated communal gardens (Fig. 5.12). Spacious balconies give considerable potential for overlooking of public spaces. Large windows are a common architectural feature but sometimes

Figure 5.11　Bo01: Experimental mixed-use housing in Malmo, Sweden.

they are located too close to opposite windows in adjoining housing so there could be a loss of privacy inside the dwellings. Some alleyways are not over-looked, but could be gated if there were any problems (Fig. 5.13) (Arkitektur dk, 2002, pp. 9–21).

Regeneration and sustainability

Neighbourhood renewal in the UK

The newly elected New Labour government in 1997 immediately turned its attention to the state of Britain's housing. Its Social Exclusion Unit reported back in 1998 that there were 3,000 neighbourhoods in England experiencing serious problems with run-down housing. It set out a policy to address the problems with the aim of ensuring that in 10 to 20 years time no one would be seriously deprived by where they live (Social Exclusion Unit, 1998).

It saw Neighbourhood Renewal having two key objectives:

- Significantly improved outcomes in deprived neighbourhoods in five key areas: health, jobs, crime, education and housing.
- A narrowing of the gap between deprived areas and the rest of the country.

Figure 5.12 BoO1, Malmo: large windows in this court provide good natural surveillance but reduce privacy.

The Social Exclusion Unit recognises that local people know best what the priorities of their neighbourhood are. Community participation is therefore a key theme. The neighbourhood renewal fund is used in any way that tackles deprivation in the most deprived neighbourhoods. It is available for both capital and revenue expenditure; the emphasis is on helping to bend mainstream programmes to better tackle deprivation.

Figure 5.13 BoO1, Malmo: alleyways such as this would be less successful in Britain but could be gated.

New Deal for Communities: Within New Deal for Communities, the UK government has committed large sums of money for the intensive regeneration of neighbourhoods. The programme supports plans that bring together local people, community and voluntary organisations, public agencies, local authorities and business to tackle problems such as high levels of crime and run-down environment. Crime and antisocial behaviour rank high in the list of priorities for action because of the effects they can have on driving business from a community, trapping people in their homes and encouraging the economically active to leave the area altogether.

These programmes provide opportunity for creating sustainable communities. They need to be linked with CPTED to create communities that are safe, are perceived to be safe and are considered by others to be safe. This means looking at the physical environment in a holistic manner with social, economic and other issues, to produce a wide range of measures that encourage people to remain or move back into urban areas. Housing should be considered within a regional or sub-regional framework of strategies of urban renewal and the location of new development. Much effort must be put into improving the environment and to ensure a good social infrastructure, particularly good schools. "Gap funding" is needed where there are no sources of finance, particularly where the market is failing.

Slade Green regeneration, Bexley, London: Community Safety Action Zones (CASZs)

The concept of Community Safety Action Zones (CSAZs) in Bexley, on the south-eastern edge of London, came from the development of their Community Safety Partnership, which brings together the Borough Council, Police, Health Authority and Probation Service and local communities. In 2001 the Home Office provided funding for a three-year Communities Against Drugs (CAD) scheme, which enabled the partnership to develop proposals for an area-based approach to crime and disorder, targeting short-term reactive action and introducing longer-term preventive proposals in areas identified as "Community Safety Action Zones". These could look at local level into measures to combat crime and antisocial behaviour including:

- Designing out crime
- Installation of CCTV
- Removal of graffiti
- Health promotion
- Outreach youth work in the form of dedicated work with young people and the families of young people involved in disorder
- Early intervention work with parents
- Introduction of education programmes in schools

A multi-agency approach was considered necessary to deliver sustainable projects that could make a real difference. Projects would be targeted to the needs of each particular zonal area. There was resident involvement at all stages from identifying the problems to agreeing priorities and helping to develop and deliver solutions. The Safety Partnership hoped that this approach would help rebuild those communities who felt isolated and that it would reduce the disproportionate fear of crime; in this way making Bexley as a whole a safer place in which to live and work.

The Partnership looked at crime statistics and found that certain areas were experiencing higher than average levels of crime and disorder. Efforts were therefore targeted on these on the Dale View Estate and, at Arthur

Road, Slade Green, which was designated as the first CSAZ. All the indicators of poverty blighted the area, and ill health, burglary and drugs were epidemic.

One response to these problems was to obtain antisocial behaviour orders against some of the young people identified as the main trouble-makers. This meant that gangs were not able to associate freely. However, the action zone was about more than crime – it also dealt with quality of life and regeneration issues. The housing was renovated and the environment improved. Youth shelters, where young people can congregate without causing nuisance to others, were built at a cost of £6,000 each. Lighting was improved and the Orbit Housing Association, which has responsibility for much of Bexley's former stock of council housing, erected street cameras to monitor low-rise blocks of flats, their car parks and their playgrounds. Residents in the areas of highest burglary rates were given free locks. The estate has been "greened" with flowers and shrubs and a community garden in the centre with a barbecue, seating and a sculpture of three pigs (Fig. 5.14). An intensive and continuous clean-up saw some 450 abandoned vehicles removed in just three weeks. Fly-tippers became council targets and the graffiti patrols toured each day. Outreach staff worked, and still work, with

Figure 5.14 Community meeting area at Arthur Street, Slade Green, Bexley, London.

the vulnerable, the old, those with drug problems, the mentally ill and young people identified as likely to commit crime.

Involving the community did not prove difficult but as Natasha Bishop, Bexley's Community Initiatives Policy Manager advises, "It is not hard to engage communities, but it takes time and energy and you can't do it too quickly.... If you move too quickly, you are probably not consulting. The key to engaging people is finding out what they want and what their priorities are."

Before the Community Safety Action Zone was put in place, only 22 per cent of residents said they felt safe at night; that figure has now risen to 93 per cent. Gilian Davies of the Slade Green Forum says that: "This has become a nice area to live again. People have begun to stand up for themselves." The police are pleased with the outcome. The Bexley Police Commander, Robin Merrit, comments that there has been considerable benefit from the partnership approach with authorities working together: "There has been an increase in resources, but more than that, there has been a shared view.... This part of the borough was on the verge of being lost. Slade Green was at the 11th hour. We know that if things had got any worse we would never have got it back" (Muir, 2003).

Participation

Principles

The concepts of "participation" and "inclusion" are now at the heart of creating sustainable communities in many countries around the world. They are important means by which people can assess issues of crime and fear of crime in their neighbourhood, and understanding the process of participation is therefore important. The benefits of participation in Britain are summed up in a recent report from the Office of the Deputy Prime Minister:

> "The opportunities for meeting and working closely with other people, for developing new skills and for building confidence that can lead to greater community cohesion. Increasingly these are being recognised and efforts are being made to build community involvement into all stages of policy and action" (ODPM, 2002a, p. 15).

Participation means different things to different people. This can best be seen by looking at the "ladder of participation", developed over 30 years ago by Sherry Arnstein. In her terms, the more intense forms of participation at the top of the ladder require techniques that engage people in plan making and design. The ultimate is that the community is involved in construction (self-build) and is responsible for local management. This includes the community benefiting from any economic gains from investment and development. The mid-range is merely token participation whilst the lower end is defined by Arnstein as non-participation – objective methods of information gathering which can inform the planning and design process but do not enable people to really engage in the processes (Moughton, 1992, p. 14).

Table 5.1. Sherry Arnstein's ladder of participation

1. Citizen control	Degrees of Citizen Power
2. Delegated power	
3. Partnership	
4. Placation	Degrees of Tokenism
5. Consultation	
6. Informing	
7. Therapy	Non-participation
8. Manipulation	

Arnstein, 1969, pp. 216–224.

Participation promotes a sense of community by bringing people together to enable them to set their own goals and strategies. It identifies the community's assets as well as its problems and reinforces community values whilst building human and social capacity. Participation does not imply that there is not a role for institutional leaders and organisations. Rather, it helps develop creative partnerships between the community, local government, regeneration agencies, etc. It helps to make the most from resources available to the community. For the community, it offers an increased sense of having influenced the decision-making process and its consequences. They feel more attached to an environment they have helped to create, and if given the opportunity, they will manage and maintain it better. The user group benefits from learning more about itself and this helps it build its ability to take responsibility and action itself, which is at the core of sustaining local communities. Many grant-making organisations prefer, or even require, community involvement to have occurred before handing out financial assistance.

For the professional, it provides more relevant and up-to-date information than was possible before. Creating a methodological framework can enable the use of rational decision-making methods without affecting the creative process (Sanoff, 2000, pp. 8–13).

To persuade people to take part, they must feel that change can and will occur. Participation must therefore be active and directed, and the people involved must experience a sense of achievement. They must be encouraged to use the process as a means of learning through becoming aware of problems: "Learning occurs best when the process is clear, communicable and encourages dialogue, debate and collaboration" (Sanoff, 2000, p. 37). It is most effective when the process integrates bottom-up resident-led initiatives with traditional top-down approaches to create a partnership between residents, community organisations and management. People need to be allowed to participate at their own levels of interest and expertise. There will always be various levels of involvement, depending upon individual differences, the role of community and willingness to commit time and energy. Different groups may choose to be involved at different stages of the process, especially in larger projects. People may also participate more in some stages of the process than others. Therefore, the number and type of participants can change during the course of the planning process.

Stages of participation

Stage 1: Define objectives: Planning a participation programme should first include the identification of objectives (Sanoff, 2000, p. 16):

- Why is the process needed?
- What form of resolution is required?
- How will the group work toward a solution?
- How will decisions be made?
- What is the schedule?
- Who will receive and act on the final product?

Stage 2: Research, environmental and social assessment. The foundation for later planning and design is a thorough environmental assessment of the area. This involves residents in assessing their everyday physical environment, and its strengths and weaknesses. They review the past and explore the present trends affecting the community. Social assets could include residents' experience, existing community organisations, local businesses and schools. Those controlled by outsiders to the community, such as local authorities, regeneration agencies, etc., can become assets to engage in the process.

Researchers must become well informed about the community, both historically and sociologically, through records, interviews, observations and some form of participation in the life of the community. The community decides how this all should be done; the professionals act as facilitators in this process.

Techniques: There are numerous techniques to raise users' awareness of environmental issues including mental mapping, photography, community profiling, community planning forums, photo surveys, reconnaissance trips, and others. The important principle is that the participants see the work as fun (Fig. 5.15) (Wates, 2000, p. 15).

Crime walks: A technique specific to exploring issues of crime and fear of crime is for mixed teams of local people and technical experts to go on a walking tour through the area. A route is carefully planned to include key local features and already known issues. The group makes notes, sketches, takes photographs and talks informally to people in their own setting. At the end of the walk the team is debriefed, and the notes and other materials put together into a form useful to the next stage of the environmental assessment and planning and design.

Stage 3: Define goals: The environmental assessment should be used in a positive way to help the community identify goals to be achieved. Goals are open-ended ideas coming out of the collective knowledge of the community, its skills, abilities and experience. These are:

- What do we wish to keep?
- What should be added that does not exist?
- What should be removed?
- What do we not have that is needed?

A goal statement should not specify how it will be met. This comes later when strategies are identified for accomplishing goals. Statements should

Figure 5.15 Participation in Italy (Turin) is fun.

begin with an action word such as "develop, provide, maintain, reduce, continue, increase, or upgrade" (Sanoff, 2000, p. 41).

Stage 4. Strategy selection: This provides a direction for the goals to achieve a specific result. This is usually undertaken through group workshops of not more than 12 members. Several workshops take place if more people wish to participate. Participants select their own priorities, which are displayed for all to see prior to discussion until an agreement is reached on what is important for the community as a whole.

Stage 5: Assemble information: Next, participants share information and identify additional information required. Site visits take place to look at similar problems and how they have been solved. This includes interviews with experts, slide presentations and a review of technical reports, journals and books. Training is invaluable to all activities and attendance at courses can considerably help this stage.

Stage 6. Define the key problems: Once the information is collected and discussed, the task is to identify common ground – first by small groups and then by everyone. Projects to achieve it are identified, which must be manageable within the time and resource constraints. Methods to define a problem can include, as well as verbal descriptions, the use of diagrams, flow charts and models, which can help participants understand the problems better. Large, complex problems can be subdivided into smaller manageable parts and assigned to various task groups that will report their findings to the larger group. Consensus on a problem statement can be reached by having each participant state and re-state the problem in his or her own words, thus ensuring that all participants understand all elements of the problem. This process can help develop a collective vision in which all participants can state their wishes for the future of their neighbourhood.

Stage 7. Generate the vision: The next step is to create ideal futures – visions developed in small groups and acted out on everyone. This process has to be positive, keeping criticism and discussion until after brainstorming has been completed. This step must encourage alternative solutions, which are prioritised by participants from most to least desired, or advantages and disadvantages can be identified for each option.

Where possible, an initiating committee representing the whole community should plan the participatory events. These are people who come forward through care for the future of their community. They are frequently referred to as the "stakeholders". It is important to develop a positive approach for each stage right from the beginning. People can participate far more effectively if information is presented visually rather than in words. Graphics, maps, illustrations, cartoons, drawings, photo montages and models should be used wherever possible. The process itself should be visible by using flipcharts, Post-it notes, coloured dots and banners. Everything must be open and meaningful and information must be shared and evaluated with the community. A social event at the beginning to enable people to get to know each other, and a community "celebration" at the end, are means of acknowledging the work of all the participants. This can also help with announcing the project to local councillors, the press, etc.

Participation expands the role of the planner and architect to include, in addition to being an advocate for the principles of good design and planning, that of instructor and facilitator of the education and decision-making process. This means allocating time from project development to the early stages of development. Most important to the success of participation is the involvement of a community development worker to help engage the community. This is the most evident factor of success in the case studies that follow.

Participation in practice

Whilst many of the projects described earlier in the book were subject to resident participation, those that follow have important messages about the process that make them worthy of special note. In particular, designing out crime and fear of crime was a high priority.

Tudor Road renewal, Belfast

The Tudor Road renewal area lies between Crumlin Road and Shankhill Road, North Belfast, in one of the areas of Northern Ireland most affected by the political difficulties of the last 50 years. Built in the early twentieth century, its housing is small with only two bedrooms, and not up to present day standards. The Northern Ireland Housing Executive (NIHE) has operated a rolling redevelopment programme in the area for the last 20 years and the proposals for this location are to build 790 new houses and 30 shops.

Design approach: Residents are fully involved in determining the design approach, which is based on defensible space and quality urban design, both strongly influenced by the need to create a safe and secure environment. A major aim is to design new housing to an urban density along the lines of the Urban Task Force recommendations using traditional forms of streets. This is achieved by creating a clear hierarchy of vehicular/pedestrian circulation and a matrix of housing blocks – "squares" – with optimal supervision of all streetscapes.

At the beginning the residents did not want the demolition of their housing. Some moved out and the environment deteriorated, causing problems of vandalism. Now people like the new housing that is being built and have changed their minds. However, when shown town houses, apartments and other higher density housing forms being built in regeneration areas in London, an instant dislike was expressed. Most people favoured three-bedroom, two-storey housing with gardens, which they felt catered for the needs of elderly and young people without children as well as families. They were keen on the lifetime homes concept but considered the three-bedroom house offered flexibility because of its size and was therefore more sustainable. They also had a preference for semi-detached forms of housing, but the NIHE would only permit this for private development in the area.

Permeability: The roads in the area form a three-tier hierarchy whereby the two main arterial roads, Crumlin and Shanklin, link with Agnes Street and Tennent Street to form an overall boundary grid (Fig. 5.16). The local roads within that area form a smaller permeable grid, and through movement between the arterial roads are discouraged except at low speed. To achieve this, streets are designed to 20 mph maximum by the use of junctions, bends and occasional vertical speed restrictions to existing streets (Fig. 5.17). The housing areas either front onto these traditional streets or on to shared surface courts, which provide a safe environment for children. These are through roads designed in a "Z" or "L" shape to create two or three short spaces that appear closed off at one end. Entrances are given a gateway treatment (Fig. 5.18). Where it is necessary to provide rear access paths, they are short and secured with gates, preventing general access for which residents have keys. A preferable arrangement is the "pend" solution giving rear access through a terrace preferably serving only two dwellings.

Mixed tenure: Small groups of private and housing association development are integrated into the rented housing, but every effort is made in design terms to ensure that they are perceived as part of the neighbourhood and are not stigmatised. In her publication, *Building Balanced Communities*, Anna Minton praises the policy of introducing home ownership into an area which has traditionally consisted solidly of social housing. It has "had an astonishing effect, turning round a previously blighted area into a thriving community. The specific content in the Shankhill Road is that the Protestant community there has a particularly strong stake in maintaining the area and, given the incentives offered (housing for sale at construction cost price), many of the better off have jumped at the chance to buy into the community" (Fig. 5.19) (Minton, 2002a).

Layout and housing form: An urban block form of terraces links the new housing into its surroundings. The housing is modelled to provide vistas and to mould spaces. Taller development on corners and at the ends of streets frame or close off vistas, and views to significant open areas are framed with taller corner units. Rear gardens are back to back and there are no end gables without windows. Planting is mainly in the form of street trees rather than shrub planting.

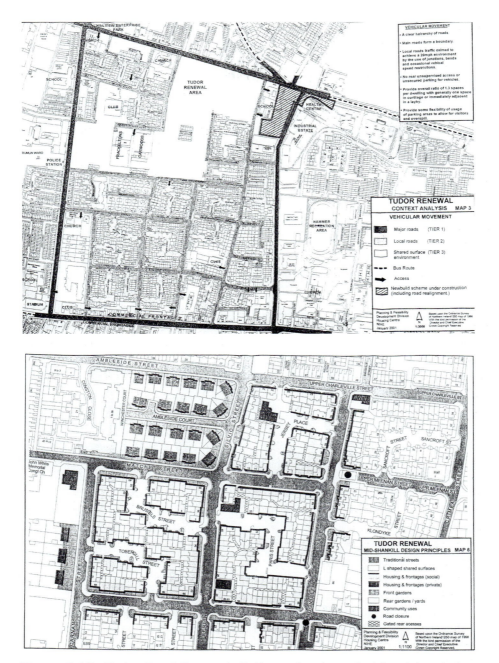

Figure 5.16 Tudor Road Renewal, Belfast: planning principles (above), layout design (below).

Figure 5.17   Tudor Road, Belfast. Front door and entrance to passageway to rear gardens.

Car parking is provided on an overall ratio of 1.3 spaces per dwelling, with generally one space within the curtilage or immediately adjacent in a lay-by. Unsecured car parking is generally avoided. Meaningful open space is provided into the heart of the development with the agreement of the residents. Planting that forms and enhances space is provided but it is of a size that does not provide hiding places or shelter to those who would abuse the area through antisocial behaviour. All other spaces are incorporated within private gardens.

Figure 5.18 Tudor Road renewal: gateway into one of the shared pedestrian/ vehicular areas.

Resident participation is conducted through the committee of the Tudor Residents' Association, which is selected by local people at a public meeting every year. The Association has very clear objectives to be achieved through participation:

- To protect the long-established community through engaging it in the redevelopment process.
- To influence the decisions affecting the design of the new housing.
- To protect individual and group interests in the new development.

Community involvement has succeeded because it has been supported by the NIHE, with whom there is a regular dialogue. The NIHE provides funding

Figure 5.19 Tudor Road renewal: semi-detached private housing. Corner house positioned to offer wide natural surveillance.

for a community development worker, Gary Hughes, whose involvement with residents is not restricted. Also the NIHE provides premises for the Tudor Residents' Association, free of charge, in one of their houses.

Regeneration in Turin and Milan

Milan and Turin are two of Italy's largest cities with populations of 2 and 1.2 million respectively. They have similar housing problems to Britain with high levels of crime, vandalism and antisocial behaviour, but added is the presence of the Mafia, which frequently takes over ownership of properties unlet for any length of time. Resident participation is seen as vital to regeneration.

Studies undertaken by Dr Massimo Bricocoli from the Politechnico di Milano, Instituto di Architettura Venezia, and his colleagues, have helped tenants in the two cities cope with the improvement of their housing as part of a community development project. Regeneration in Italy is less focused on social issues than in Britain, but as estates are generally smaller there is greater integration of social levels within an area and less social polarisation in schools.

Local policing is an important part of the regeneration strategies set within a structure of four levels of policing in Italy: military, police, carabinieri and Vigili Urbani (neighbourhood police). The participation of uniformed local policing came from bottom-up pressure of people who were critical that the police "never get out of their cars so never saw what was really happening". Many of the offenders were known within the community but people did nothing for fear of reprisal. Now the police have a local office in estates and are frequently seen cycling or walking around the estates (Fig. 5.20). Women play an equal part in policing. Everyone goes to them for help, particularly to settle neighbourhood disputes, and their presence has helped

Figure 5.20 Regeneration in Turin: local policeman and community development worker discuss the problems of the day.

to reduce fear of crime. It has required a lot of trust and good communication – not merely reporting problems – to bring about changes of attitude. The reward is a more open environment that everyone can enjoy.

Crime walks. Dr Bricocoli used simple techniques to assess fear of crime amongst residents. He and his researchers walked with them along their daily routes to find points of conflict. They recorded what happened in the morning, the afternoon, in the evening and at night. The essential criterion according to Dr Bricocoli is to listen – be a "Listening Pole – something like a lightning conductor". This helps people overcome their shyness. For the process to work, people had to talk together in small groups. "The key is to show respect for the residents – everyone has an opinion, which is valuable", says Dr Bricocoli. The exercise took a considerable amount of time and did not always produce a result, but was well worth the effort in terms of building community spirit. Dr Bricocoli had to positively encourage people to think about the issues, but key concerns were similar to those that could have come up in a British survey: more local policing, better street lighting, improved fencing, provision of a concierge service and better use of the open space around the blocks.

Project in Milan

The project in Milan was located about two miles from the city centre. The 1930s housing was planned around a series of hard-paved courts between a grid of perimeter roads. Improvements were made to the housing and its environment but Dr Bricocoli was concerned that, despite resident participation, the architects were proceeding with little regard to community and security. The courts were being divided across the middle, cutting them into two halves, and storage was located in basement areas into which the residents feared to go (Fig. 5.21).

Projects in Turin

In Turin Dr Bricocoli undertook his study in two estates in the north of the city. The regeneration projects were funded by the Regional Government as part of a national housing improvement programme called "PRU" (Programma Recupero Urbana). The project at the Quartiere di Via Sospello was built between 1919 and 1939 and comprises a series of small courtyards of five-storey walk-up apartments within a city block situated between two main roads. The spaces between the blocks were linked and it was possible to drive and walk through the spaces at random, which created a high perception of crime particularly amongst elderly people, who were even afraid of young people playing football. Non-residents perceived the courts as public spaces. Drug dealing was a huge problem, particularly around the

Figure 5.21 Milan housing court divided into two parts by railings: staircases to the basement stores are at the front of the picture.

kindergarten from where there is easy access to many escape routes. When the scheme was first built there were six concierges employed on the estate who collected the rent and oversaw entry by visitors. These were long gone (Fig. 5.22).

The regeneration plans involved improving the dwellings, sometimes joining two together to create one larger one. Lifts were provided to give better access to upper floors. Environmental improvements included dividing the space in the courts so that cars were confined to the outer areas leaving the centre free as a garden. Footpaths were to be provided with seating for elderly people to sit and talk (Fig. 5.23).

Techniques for engaging the community included parties and dancing – mainly Latin American, which apparently appeals to all ages in Italy. There was no estate committee. For the purposes of participation in the regeneration, residents came together on a staircase basis. This worked satisfactorily but with some difficulty, as everyone had to be involved in making decisions. Resident participation was managed through an office at the entrance to the estate which acted is an important source of information gathering and communication. A local worker from the estate, recruited for her communication skills, regularly staffed the office. An architect was also employed to provide an informative link between builders and residents. This also helped integrate building plans and social action and offered a

Figure 5.22 Quartiere di Via Sospello, Turin: lack of definition between public and private space.

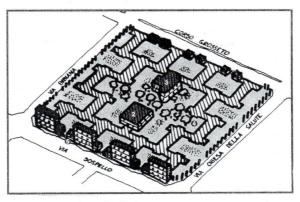

Quartiere di via Sospello, Turin
Environmental proposals

1. Communal gardens
created in inner courtyards.

2. Existing swimming pool
converted into a day centre
with a health centre for elderly
people and a new
physiotherapy pool.

3. The former kindergarden
converted to a play centre for
children under 10
accompanied by an adult.

4. New street lighting
throughout, including in
passageways and areas set
back in which people feel
unsafe to walk at night.

5. Gated entrances with
street lighting to car parking
areas in the perimeter
courtyards.

Figure 5.23 Quartiere di Via Sospello: regeneration principles.

measure of professional guidance to residents in bidding their ideas into the programme.

Quartiere di Via Fiesole: The second project in Turin is high-rise/ high-density, social rented development built in 1975, comprising two long blocks of seven-storey housing and 16 towers. There are no through roads and none of the housing has street frontage. It suffers a stigma from immigrants squatting illegally in some apartments. The housing suffered from physical deterioration and the large amount of open space around the housing caused serious security and social problems. There is very little overlooking of public areas or defensible space around the dwellings and car parking is poorly organised. The two long blocks are single aspect facing away from the parking areas on the entrance side (Fig. 5.24). There is a school on the site with some sports activity but no community links. The community centre was a kindergarten but this is not used except for one end where there is a restaurant. There are no focal points on the estate so people have made their own in the main open space area with barrels covered in graffiti art (Fig. 5.25).

There are real problems after dark. Young men congregate under covered areas and women fear to come out. Noise is a problem. People making complaints are revenged by their cars being burnt out but no one says anything. Drug dealing is a real problem with people congregating under canopies linking the tower blocks.

Engaging the residents: The architect liaison officer initially researched the strengths and weaknesses of the community and produced a list of "loves and hates". Loves primarily related to people. Hates were dog

Figure 5.24　Quartiere di Via Fiesole: 7 storey terraces afford little overlooking of car parking and open space.

Figure 5.25 Quartiere di Via Fiesole: barrels covered in graffiti art provide a focal point for the estate.

dirt, badly lit streets and spaces at night, cars making a noise at night and loud music at night. The local police gave considerable help throughout the process. They were involved in meetings with the community to establish common rules. When people complained about metal rubbish merchants, the local police sorted out the problem.

This interaction between residents and the authorities on the estates led to the sharing of information and thoughts on how the quality of life could be improved. The idea of collaboration had previously been unheard of. As a result of the newfound relationship it has been possible to make drastic changes.

Regeneration proposals (Fig. 5.26) include traffic calming, relating car parking more closely to dwellings, and creating a central piazza in which people can meet. New crossings over the main boulevard (Corso

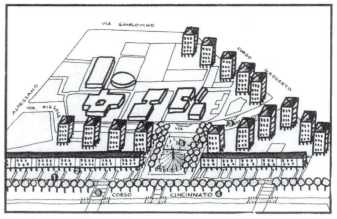

Quartiere di via Fiesole, Turin.
Overall proposals

1.   Defensible space created
by enclosing space beneath
and around housing blocks
including: 2. Resident parking
in an enclosed area close to
housing blocks.

3.   Traffic calming measures
on Via Fiesole.

4.   Elderly people's meeting
place on Corso Cincinatto to
link neighbourhoods

5.   Park and shelter for
social activity.

6.   Extra crossing points on
Corso Cincinatto to link area
with surroundings

Figure 5.26   Quartiere di Via Fiesole: regeneration principles.

Cincinnato) will link the estate into its surroundings. The residents in the centre of the boulevard requested a small café/meeting place so that they could enjoy the comings and goings along and across the street. A number of residents have taken control of and converted into gardens small leftover spaces along the internal roadway (Fig. 5.27).

A sense of community has been established and there is now pride in the areas. Many environmental changes have been made to great effect. Space now has a clear role and it is not left to become neglected or abandoned (*Journal of the Design Out Crime Association*, 2001, p. 10).

Gated communities in the USA and Britain

The American concept of "gated communities" is making startling inroads into Britain. Almost 90 per cent of people in the USA think that crime is

Figure 5.27 Leftover space in the roadway at Quartiere di Via Fiesole has been taken over by residents as private gardens.

getting worse and this fear is given as the main reason for at least 12 per cent choosing to live in gated communities (Minton, 2002a, p. 5). In the USA there are now some 20,000 gated communities complete with their own police forces and other services, providing homes for around 8 million people. About a third are "luxury" developments for people who have opted out of the public system. The concept has spread around the world and is particularly popular in Far Eastern countries (Fig. 5.28).

The epitome of a gated community in the USA is the "lifestyle development" based around communities or golf and country leisure developments and elite and prestige developments. However, "security zones" where fear of crime and outsiders are the primary motivation are by far the fastest growing types. Anna Minton writes:

> *"the fear of crime and the emphasis on private security is clearly reflected in quite staggering statistics – In the USA, three times more people now work in private security – from equipment manufacturers to armoured car drivers – than in official law enforcement, and private security outspends public law enforcement by 73 per cent."*

Figure 5.28 Gated housing in Beijing.

The problem with gated communities in the USA is that they contribute to the social divide, which is increasing at an alarming rate. At the other end of the social/economic scale around 15 per cent of the population are trapped in ghettos with little hope of ever moving out (Minton, 2002a, p. 7). Gated communities are not part of the New Urbanism and Smart Growth codes in the USA. These see permeability and merging new development with the surroundings as an essential planning requirement to reduce crime and fear of crime. In this respect there is a common sharing of values with current British approaches to planning and design.

Gated private roads have existed on a very small scale almost without notice for many years in Britain (Figs. 5.29 and 5.30). What is alarming now about gated communities is that they are becoming more exclusive and popular, not with security-conscious elderly people, but with the young. The combination of a village feel within a high-shared security perimeter wall or fence, gates and state-of-the-art surveillance and security, has crept into the wealthy suburbs of almost every British city. Such refuges are increasingly attractive hotspots in the property market commanding high sale prices.

The overriding problem with gated communities is that the "gated mindset tends to opt out of wider society, particularly when shops, gyms and private services such as rubbish collection are included in the deal" (Minton, 2002b). People become detached from mainstream society, not only physically but also politically. In the USA there is even a growing trend to opt out of local government. This voluntary exclusion is mirrored by the involuntary isolation from society of socially excluded people living in the ghettos. Also schools, hospitals and other public facilities become increasingly marginalized. In addition, a consequence of such fortressing is higher levels of fear. Fear of crime is merely displaced to outside the walls where people feel more threatened. The outside world with its dangers inevitably becomes a threat as people must enter the gated community and residents must go out to work, shop and carry out their normal lives. This is superbly illustrated below in the following scenario of life in a gated society in the year 2020 by the UK government's Foresight crime prevention panel in its publication, *Just Around the Corner* (Foresight, 2002).

Brightlands: The Gated Society

This is an extract from *Just Around the Corner*, a narrative of a socially exclusive world with the impact of crime being central. It is extreme and designed to stimulate thought.

Meg wakes up to the sound of the alarm. It is the Brightlands perimeter siren. Her partner does not stir – they moved in together because that was the only way they could afford to move to Brightlands – "the walled estate where people

281

Figure 5.29 Gated road in Blackheath, London, which is symbolically closed once a day.

care". They were lucky to get in given the approval criteria of the neighbours. Both work from home . . . neither want to use the poor public transport with its high level of violence to get to work. Drivers don't relax until they re-enter a walled area – either another estate or the business park. Road users are often tense and aggressive. All public space is potentially more hostile than before. People prefer the isolation offered by their personal technology systems and increasingly resent being disturbed, or even spoken to in public. Personal radar systems and security devices are relied upon for protection.

All this means people in walled estates don't venture out much. They had hoped that moving to Brightlands would mean they could socialise with others inside. But they have only been there a few months and don't really know

Figure 5.30 Span housing at the Hall, Blackheath, with private roads. Architect: Eric Lyons.

anyone yet – despite the promotional material and interviews people are still wary of newcomers. Walled communities such as Brightlands are increasingly targets for young criminals, partly through resentment, partly as a challenge. Crime between residents is almost non-existent due to the screening process and heavy patrols. But Meg wonders sometime whether the patrols are her protectors or her warders.

The story concludes with a mugging outside the walled estate but Meg is rescued by pressing her alarm, which triggers a patrol to rescue her. She lives in a state of perfect security ever after (Foresight, 2002).

There is considerable debate about whether gating reduces crime, but the majority of mainstream commentators conclude that is has little impact on real criminals. The main benefit to the residents is that they feel safer even if they are not – they feel their gates and walls keep out crime. However, experience in the USA suggests that gated communities become targets for ever more determined criminals, and that the growth of gated communities has not reduced crime (Wainwright, 2002, p. 11).

Gating on a small scale is now an accepted principle in Britain (Fig. 5.31). The principle is embodied in the regeneration of public sector estates and high-rise blocks of council flats (Fig. 4.5). Improvements include the provision of door entry phones, security fences to create semi-private space around the base of the flats, a concierge service on the ground floor and even meeting facilities when the blocks are converted into sheltered housing for elderly people. However, the main difference to the large, private gated housing developments is one of scale. The residents relate with each other for their immediate needs but they join the wider community when carrying out their lives beyond their homes. A good example of this is at Cromer Street in the centre of London.

Gated community: Cromer Street, London

Cromer Street, situated across Euston Road from King's Cross and St Pancras Stations, is an extremely successful example of Estate Action making a significant change. It is successful because the regeneration was designed in the context of the surrounding built environment (Fig. 5.32) and it was supported by extensive community involvement through the King's Cross Community Development Project.

The area around the two railway stations as a whole suffers acutely from an image of deprivation. It has a large ethnic population and high levels of social exclusion, prostitution and drug taking. Crime and fear of crime is rife, stopping many, especially older people and women, from going out at night. Cromer Street is a community of over 1,000 council and housing association properties containing a mixture of pre-1919 "railway" tenement housing of fine architectural quality and substantial 1970s high-rise slab blocks. Both suffered poor heating and thermal insulation, a lack of safe places for children to play and underused or misused storage areas such as laundry rooms and basements. The problem for security was one of location in an area of such public activity. King's Cross is one of the few areas in Britain that has such good public transport connections which makes it an attractive place to commit a large range of crimes. The local police Crime Prevention Design Advisers, Terry Cocks and Calvin Beckford, have a wealth of information on the environmental features of the area that encourage crime (Fig. 5.33).

Since 1996 the Cromer Street area has been subject to a £46 million King's Cross Estate Action Project. The designs for the regeneration were prepared by a number of architects in order to create variety. The post-1950s

Figure 5.31 Green Dragon Court, Camden. CGHP Architects.

Figure 5.32 King's Cross Estate Action Area: environmental improvement plans. Architects: Tibbalds Monro Ltd.

housing was overclad to reduce energy costs, which creates a colourful image without shouting out as something different; nor does it portray an image of social rented housing. The brick tenement housing has been carefully and sensitively restored and freshly cleaned brickwork emphasises the architectural qualities.

Figure 5.33 King's Cross Estate Action Area: an environmentally improved back alleyway is still a potential danger area.

Design principles: Secured by Design principles were adopted throughout the project and defensible space principles are very evident. The area between the blocks is landscaped, fenced and gated, although gates are left open during the day. Car parking is also gated, and users really do lock the gates after putting away their car. Considerable attention was given to increasing security by providing a concierge-controlled access or new door-entry systems and improved lighting. The residents were asked for their commitment to the controlled entry before it was implemented, "without which it would all have been a complete waste of time" (Dillon, 2003) (Fig. 5.34).

Figure 5.34 King's Cross Estate Action Area: new entrances and gates have transformed the perception of safety amongst residents.

The environmental improvements were built on the quality of the existing urban structure of streets and squares. Permeability is maintained throughout and a 20 mph speed zone was introduced with speed tables and pinch points. Pedestrian/cycle routes were introduced and pavements were renewed (Fig. 5.35). Street lighting is designed to suit location with different

Figure 5.35 King's Cross Estate Action Area: environmental improvements add to the quality of the existing urban structure of roads.

columns and fittings dependent upon location. The three urban squares, Regent, Argyle and Bamber Green, have been upgraded to relate to their local environment. Generally all have been given higher railings, gated entrances, new seating and extensive planting (Fig. 5.36).

Throughout the sequence of open spaces the fencing and gates are substantial but not overpowering. High quality robust design is clearly evident, as is effective management and maintenance that includes 24-hour call-out service for repairs to the entry system.

Management of the project: A local office was established and the community was fully engaged in planning the regeneration proposals. A Community Steering Group consisted of representatives of the blocks

Figure 5.36 King's Cross Estate Action Area: the existing squares have become places for active play and leisure pursuits.

and the local Bangladeshi community was fully involved. The project included training initiatives for people to develop their employment prospects. Some were employed directly in the regeneration work, both in its management and construction. The area office still remains although the building work finished a couple of years ago. It is now the focus of the Community Trust.

Crime reduction: Crime within the housing has virtually disappeared but Melissa Dillon, the Head of Capital Investments for Camden Borough Council, admits it has been somewhat dispersed to other parts of the area (Dillon, 2003).

Neighbourhood management and maintenance

Neighbourhood management

An essential factor in reducing crime is the quality of management and maintenance of the built environment (Fig. 5.37 and Fig. 5.38). The apparent decay suggested by poorly maintained housing and environment can have a significant influence on crime levels and the fear of crime. Recent research by Dr Paul Cozens, Dr David Hillier and Gwyn Prescott, at the University of Glamorgan in Wales, has attempted to probe this area. Their research found that houses were perceived to be less prone to crime, and generated lower levels of fear of crime, than flats. Semi-detached housing was more prone to crime whilst high-rise flats generated most fear. Terraces were viewed as possessing good surveillance potential due in part to bay windows (Fig. 3.22). However, the research indicated that physical design only partially explained these perceptions. Important also was the level of maintenance and repair of the property.

Figure 5.37 Poorly maintained planting along the highway cuts off any chance of natural surveillance.

Figure 5.38 Shrub planting kept at waist-high level at Sudbury Court sheltered housing for elderly people: Whittlesey, Peterborough. Architects: Matthew Robotham & Quinn.

Well-maintained versions of each design were seen as safer, suggesting that image is crucial. Poorly managed and vacant properties are associated to a greater extent with crime and fear of crime. Further, communities can become disillusioned if properties are allowed to fall into disrepair (Cozens et al., 2003, p. 24).

Regular on-the-spot management of social housing can therefore make a real difference to crime reduction in a neighbourhood. It must be coordinated and continuous. Broken windows must be replaced immediately, litter and graffiti removed quickly and repairs carried out to match the original materials. It is vital that the public realm does not lose its character through neglect, thus alienating people and giving encouragement to potential offenders because they feel no one cares. At Broadwater Farm in London, the employment of "super-caretakers" has made a considerable contribution to reducing the causes of crime. Their responsibilities include cleaning communal areas and reporting damage, abandoned cars, etc. They provide a supportive presence for elderly people and disabled residents. The Estate's services manager is available in the neighbourhood office every morning. The result of this improved management is that complaints are rare and the estate is a much better place in which to live.

In The Netherlands, the approach is even more radical. They frequently approach management and maintenance from a "third-way" community direction in which local people are paid to look after their estates. They become involved with all aspects of the estate's life, keeping the place tidy and, most importantly, providing a security presence to cut crime (Hetherington, 1999).

Neighbourhood wardens

Neigbourhood wardens are perhaps one of the most important features of the government's strategy in Britain to reduce crime in residential areas and tackle antisocial behaviour. They are not intended to replace the police and can and do work successfully alongside them, providing an alternative function. In many areas neighbourhood wardens have expanded their role beyond patrolling the neighbourhood and combating antisocial behaviour to arranging things for young people to do, cleaning up the environment and making the area a better place in which live. Measures include removing graffiti from public places, reporting vandalism and fly-posting, co-ordinating the removal of abandoned cars and rubbish, and collecting discarded needles. By working with the local people they can identify issues which affect the community and help people find solutions. On the Great Thornton Estate in Hull, the Community Warden scheme contributed to a drop in crime overall of 45 per cent with a drop of 51 per cent in burglary (Social Exclusion Unit, 2001).

Neighbourhood Watch

Neighbourhood Watch has the responsibility of bringing local communities in Britain together with the police, schools, youth clubs and so on to work together to reduce crime in an area. According to Alene Branton – Chief Executive of the Humberside Association of Neighbourhood Watch Groups – it is about "bringing village life into urban areas".

Well-run schemes provide the police with extra "eyes and ears" and can provide a focus for group involvement in a whole range of activities associated with the built environment. A Neighbourhood Watch group could contain as few as 12 dwellings and ideally the maximum number is 250, although some are larger. Most groups are small and are fully engaged. The members make the decisions including process, budget and its source. For Neighbourhood Watch to be effective, communities must have lobbying powers and be able to seek grants for physical and environmental improvements. Typical of what can be achieved is in Hull where the Hessle Road group has secured £1.2 million from the Alleygate Fund in the City's Single Regeneration Budget to pay for gates at the entrances to rear footpaths and for lighting.

Conclusion: the need for joined-up action

This book has considered policy and practice in crime prevention through environmental design from the British perspective and from the policies of other countries and cities around the world. It has not found a universal solution. What is clear, though, is the need for a planning and design approach that relates crime prevention with all the other requirements of a housing design brief to create sustainable communities. This needs a joined-up approach to a whole range of policies – planning, housing, social and economic development, health, transport and employment.

Many governments now support this kind of joined-up thinking. In Britain, Local Strategic Partnerships have been established for this purpose. Community Safety Partnerships are also developing broad strategies to combat crime, fear of crime and antisocial behaviour in their area. What is needed to make it happen on the ground is for these policies to be translated holistically into action at community level. Neighbourhood Management is one way of finding neighbourhood solutions to neighbourhood problems, but these schemes must have the capability and the funding to be effective. In the past, government's response has been to introduce special funding initiatives into disadvantaged areas and to make partnership a condition of that funding. But the amount of money available in Britain through special programmes is still a drop in the ocean in comparison with overall need. Furthermore, funding is frequently time-limited, which places a huge burden on communities. What is needed is for mainstream public sector budgets to be sufficient, flexible and deployed through communities to make crime reduction through environmental design a mainstream activity.

Planning and urban design are clearly part of the agenda. The quality of publications on the design of the built environment coming from government circles is most encouraging. It is also encouraging that the European Parliament is taking a serious interest in the subject. In the USA, New Urbanism and Smart Growth are challenging the American suburban dream. Architects and planners have a vital role to play, but only if they become more concerned with the real needs of the people they serve than with the aesthetic demands of their professional colleagues.

Appendix

CEN (2002) Committee for European Standardisation. Prevention of Crime – Urban Planning and Design, Part 2: Urban Design and Crime Reduction; Part 3: Dwellings. CEN/TC325 (in progress)

Part 2: Urban Planning

The text of the Prestandard for Urban Planning is divided into three parts:

- The introduction, which poses three questions: where, what and who?
- Design guidelines to help the user of the standard.
- A process flow chart that explains the process step by step.

Introduction questions: where, what and who?

The approach starts with answering three questions:

- Where? – the location and classification of the area.
- What? – the identification of the crime problems occurring in this area or the problems that might in future occur in this new area.

- Who? – the identification of the stakeholders involved in defining the problem and implementing the measures to prevent and reduce the crime problem.

When these three questions have been answered, two important issues remain to be solved:

- What guidelines can be given for CPTED strategies, measures and actions, which are necessary and feasible to make an area more safe and secure? The Prestandard identifies several guidelines on what measures and actions can be taken.
- How will these CPTED standards, measures and actions be implemented and executed? What will the co-operation process look like in which all stakeholders participate?

Where? Classification of the area

- In the case of a new area only a plan exists. New environment of crime and fear of crime can therefore only be assessed by using theories or by using experiences and lessons from other neighbourhoods/projects closely resembling the plan for the new environment; such a crime analysis (ex ante) shall be called a "crime assessment".
- Existing environments: characteristics of crime and fear of crime can be analysed in real situations by way of, e.g., registered crime figures, surveys, safety audits, recording experiences and opinions of residents, people visiting/using the area, professionals (police officers, shopkeepers, etc.), observatory interviews with victims and/or offenders, etc.; such a crime analysis (ex post) in an existing area shall be called a "crime review".

What? Identification of possible crime problems

Having identified the area, the possible crime problems need considering. The Prestandard observes that women and elderly people are the most fearful of street danger particularly after dark. However, frightening or fearful places are not necessarily places where actual crimes occur. The main factors that may characterise an "unsafe location" are defined:

- Locations characterised by fear-generated features (zones of prostitution, drug abuse, certain types of entertainment)
- Neglected or badly maintained locations suffering from problematic urban design features (lack of surveillance, visibility, orientation)

The next step is to target likely crime and the fear of crime in the existing or proposed development and determine what action might be possible, necessary and feasible.

Strategies for urban planning and design

Urban planning and design includes not only the preparation of physical proposals, but planning "before the design" and "management after the design is realised".

Urban planning strategies include:

- Respecting existing social and physical structures
- Creating liveliness (blending functions and attractive street layout)
- Mixed status (blending socio-economic groups, avoiding isolation and segregation)
- Urban density (creating sense of neighbourliness, avoiding waste land and desolate areas)

Urban design strategies include:

- Visibility (overview, lines of site between, e.g., dwellings and public space, lighting, etc.)
- Accessibility (orientation, space to move, alternative routes, limiting access for non-authorised people)
- Territoriality (human scale, clear public/ private zoning, compartmentalism)
- Attractiveness (colour, material, lighting, noise, smell, street furniture)
- Robustness (doors, windows, street furniture)

These strategies aim at creating the conditions for social control and sense of ownership, as well as regulating the accessibility of areas and buildings in such a way that the individual can keep control over the situation, and that trespassers are discouraged from entering the area.

Management strategies

These include:

- Target hardening/removal
- Maintenance
- Surveillance (patrolling, camera monitoring)
- Rules (for conduct of the public in public spaces)
- Providing infrastructure for particular groups (youth, homeless, drug addicts)
- Communication (of preventative messages and rules of conduct for the public)

Practically no urban area is completely self-regulating; most urban areas need a certain level of professional surveillance and maintenance. These strategies aim at supporting and encouraging the natural surveillance and sense of ownership by residents and visitors. They do not aim to take this task away from residents.

Effective management strategies can help offset issues that cannot be resolved by design and vice versa. This is very important in existing areas where the possibility of implementing planning and design strategies may be limited.

Who? Process

The central idea of the standard is that a group of stakeholders (e.g., local politicians (where appropriate), architects and planners, developers, police (crime prevention design advisers) community/social workers, schools and local residents etc.) should look together at a plan (say for the redevelopment of a dockland area) and discuss the crime risks and likely strategies. Items to discuss will be chosen according to criteria such as spatial issues, time, budget, local preferences, etc. The working group will make its definitive recommendations to a responsible body (usually the local planning authority in Britain) to take the final decision.

A flow chart is presented showing essential steps in a process aimed at preventing crime and fear of crime.

The working group will follow a procedure including the following steps:

- Step 1: **Analyse;** analyse the present or future crime preventative and fear-reducing performance of the environment.
- Step 2: **Objectives;** the working group should define more precisely the objectives being pursued and the time by which they should be attained (project plan, milestones).
  Step 3: **Plan**; the working group should draft a plan containing:
  1) A proposal of what is likely to happen in the near future if no measures are taken to prevent crime and fear of crime;
  2) Strategies probably most effective to reach the safety and security objectives formulated in step 2;
  3) Measures and actions to be taken including costs and anticipated effects. The working group should present the plan to the responsible body of authorities and all stakeholders.
- Step 4: **Decision** by (local or regional) authorities.
- Step 5: **Action and implementation.**
- Step 6: **Checking and corrective action**; in case crime problems and/or fear of crime occur at an unacceptable level, authorities decide upon corrective action, such as taking additional crime prevention measures or further refurbishment of the area.

Design recommendations

It gives design recommendations in the context of housing and its neighbourhood:

- Respect the social and physical structure of the location for development.
- Create mixed-use residential areas with offices, workshops and shops, as well as green space and footpath networks which invite the use of space as children's playground.
- Do not build large-scale isolated and segregated low-income housing. A careful mix of socio-economic groups within a district reduces the risk crime and fear of crime.
- Integrate residential areas into the urban system and build at urban densities (10–30 dwellings per acre or 25–70 dwellings per hectare) to create a sense of neighbourliness.
- Good surveillance of public spaces and public paths from the windows and good street lighting is important. Ground-floor shops are especially important.
- Plan to limit traffic through a neighbourhood (without building 'gated communities' or 'fortresses') and avoid the total seclusion of people from the outside.
- Build on a human scale (not high-rise blocks) and create a sense of ownership of public spaces by residents.
- Ensure attractive landscaping, architecture, street furniture and pavements.
- Good maintenance is important. Motivate residents to become engaged with the professional maintenance organisations through establishing a neighbourhood management system and a certain degree of self-government of the area.
- Regular surveillance from police and security services, in particular by officers who are familiar with the neighbourhood, is important. Preferably this should be conducted on foot (not by car).
- Set out clear rules for the use of public spaces – either by the proprietor of a block or by the association of homeowners.
- Make provision for juvenile groups (e.g. a youth centre) as well as provisions for drug addicts and homeless people. This reduces the presence of fear-causing groups in public spaces.
- Layout, architecture and signage should make people feel welcome in the area.
- Avoid rear access as well as cul-de-sac layouts. There should be a clear difference between public roads and semi-private entrance roads to dwellings and apartments.
- Maintenance strategies, established by residents, work most effectively when they are linked to clear rules for the use of public space. Good communication with youth groups is vital. Meeting places must be provided for youth.
- Good surveillance is essential. This can be provided by police or security services, but also by a concierge/janitor or by block guards, eventually (in the case of a housing estate) supported by CCTV which allows sur-

veillance of entrances, lifts, stairways, parking areas and garages, and bicycle stores.

■ Parking garages should be accessible only to residents (key card system); parking areas in the open air are less attractive for car theft when provided with a barrier.

■ Individual car parking directly in front of houses or clustering parking facilities in very small lots increases the sense of ownership and control, thereby reducing the risk for car crime.

Part 3: Dwellings

The European Prestandard 14383 – Part 3: Dwellings, includes the following recommendations for the design of residential neighbourhoods and housing:

Risk management: Before an effective strategy can be developed, it is important to identify and understand the risk factors involved. It is essential to give high priority to local factors. A diagnostic survey of crime in the immediate neighbourhood should be carried out to identify the type of crime reported, when incidents occurred and who the victims were. It is also important to identify factors that may influence the opportunity for crime in a particular area but which may not necessarily be obvious.

Image: The image of the neighbourhood is very significant. First impressions gained by potential offenders will have the greatest influence on their decision to offend or not. A well cared for residential area will be a deterrent as residents who take a pride in their property are also more likely to be vigilant and protective.

Territoriality: It is important to create perceived zones of territorial influence and a sense of ownership by the use of defensible space concepts. These include classifying space into four different categories – public, semi-public, semi-private (front gardens), private – using real or symbolic barriers. Examples of real barriers are hedges and walls and symbolic barriers include signboards, vegetation and changes of surface material.

Design and layout of public space: Roads and footpaths should be designed with clear sightlines, good lighting and an absence of places for potential offenders to lurk. Where an access road leads from public to semi-public spaces, the transition should be marked with surface texturing. Pedestian foortpaths should be well lit and open to surveillance from as many directions as possible. There should be a 2 m gap between any path and adjacent vegetation and this should be maintained to a maximum height of 1 m. Dwellings should be grouped so that neighbours can give maximum natural surveillance of vulnerable entry points. Where walls are susceptible to graffiti, provision of graffiti surface protection for walls should be considered at an early stage.

Design for the layout of semi-public space: Semi-public open spaces are areas that are more public than private and for which there may be few opportunities for limiting access. Footpath systems, resident parking, garage courts, enclosed play areas and entrances to multiple dwelling complexes are all examples of semi-public space. Visitors' car parking should be located as close as possible to dwellings so that the residents can see them. Pedestrian footpaths linking ends of culs-de-sac should be avoided. Alleyways to the rear of dwellings should be avoided. Unsupervised, separate footpaths running through housing areas are seen as public space and should be avoided as they provide escape routes for offenders, access routes for burglars, more opportunity for assault and increase fear of crime.

Design and layout for semi-private space: Semi-private space includes such areas as front gardens, paths or steps to main entrance doors, and hard standing for vehicles. A minimum distance of around 3 m and effective landscaping should be used to delineate this type of area from public space in a manner that combines privacy to dwellings with just enough mutual surveillance to provide significant social control over potential crime.

Defensible private space: Simple elements such as walls, hedges, railings, gates, etc., should be used to create a clear barrier. To improve security, consideration should be given to combining different physical and/or electrical elements, e.g., walls surmounted with non-climbable coping stones, angled bricks and anti-intrusion sensors connected to a central alarm system.

Layout: Whenever possible access to the public area adjacent to individual dwellings should be visible from the entrance of a dwelling to imply control and surveillance by the residents. One method of enhancing collective security is by grouping houses in such a way that as many dwellings as possible face a relatively limited length of street. Another method is by, for example, changing the character of space from public to semi-public by altering the colour of the road surface to create the impression of a threshold.

Garages: These should function as storage place for bicycles, motorcycles and gardening tools as well as for vehicles. Garages should be located close to dwellings, preferably with their access door facing the street and at least a car length from the street.

Fencing: To delineate the perimeter of an individual dwelling, consideration should be given to the use of hedges or walls, railings, or timber, wire mesh or precast concrete fencing approximately 2 m high at the side and rear of the property. As potential offenders can climb over a 2 m wall or fence with little difficulty, consideration should be given to adding a lattice trellis to increase the height without impacting adversely on the environment.

Management: The Prestandard emphasises that success or failure will depend upon residents themselves and the manner in which dwellings and environment are maintained. It recommends the importance of residents being included in the decision-making process.

External lighting: Lighting should be designed in such a way as to avoid shadow areas and ensure an average luminance sufficient for the risk level at the particular location. Lighting should be uniform across the area. The lighting of the targeted area by movement detectors should be considered if it is decided that this is more appropriate than having a continuous light. There is growing evidence that a continuous low light level is more effective than floodlighting that is tripped by various detection devices.

Schools/Youth facilities

Prestandard 2 (Urban Design) also gives recommendations for the design of other prominent neighbourhood buildings.

- School routes along lively streets reduce the fear of crime; to reduce the level of nuisance to the environment, youth facilities are best located near a busy road and preferably also near a bus stop.
- Schools should be located in a populated urban area (not in isolated areas or in a park). However, there must be sufficient distance from nearby housing to prevent disturbance of the residents by noise and nuisance.
- A compact school design (not sprawled developments) and landscaping with grass and trees (no shrubs) is preferable; special attention should be given to parking areas, entrance zones and playgrounds.
- Fencing off the school area or youth facility should be done in such a way that it is not detrimental to their attractiveness nor prevents their use outside school hours. Access to a school should be limited to as few points as possible, preferably only one.
- Surveillance of school routes and school areas can reduce the fear of crime; a janitor/caretaker is effective, especially when living in or near the school. At the entrance to the building there should be a clearly defined reception area with staff (caretaker) present.
- Provisions should be made for drug addicts and homeless people in the neighbourhood to prevent these groups hanging around in the school area.
- There should be clear rules for the use of playgrounds and behaviour in the surrounding neighbourhood.
- Future users (local youth groups) and residents of the surrounding areas should be involved in the design of youth facilities.
- Integrating parking facilities within the premises gives protection to the vehicles without disturbing the neighbouring community.

Bibliography/ References

Adams, E., and Kinoshita, I. (2000). *Machi-work: Education for Participation*. Fudosha.

Aldous, A. (1992). *Urban Villages*. (Foreword by HRH The Prince of Wales). Urban Village Group.

Alexander, C., Ishikawa, S., Silverstein, M., with Jacobson, M., Fiksdahl-King, I., and Angel, S. (1977). *A Pattern Language*. Oxford University Press.

Alexander, C. (1987). *A New Theory of Urban Design*. Oxford University Press.

The Architects' Journal (1973). October.

The Architects' Journal (1976). 14 August, pp. 533–552.

The Architects' Journal (1976). 22 September, p. 366.

The Architectural Review (1992). *Process and Product*, March 1992, Volume CXC, Number 1141, pp.25–29.

The Architectural Review (1997). *Outrage*. July 1997, Volume CII, Number 1205, p. 213.

The Architecture Foundation (2000). *Creative Spaces/A Toolkit for Participatory Urban Design*. The Architecture Foundation.

Arkitektur dk (2002). *Bo01 Malmo Park Projects*. 1.2002, Number 46, pp. 12–19.

Armitage, R. (1999). *An Evaluation of Secured by Design Housing Schemes Throughout the West Yorkshire Area*. The Applied Criminology Group, The University of Huddersfield.

Armitage, R. (2000). *An Evaluation of Secured by Design Housing Within West Yorkshire*. Home Office Briefing Note 7/00.

Arnstein, S. R. (1969). A Ladder of Citizen Participation. *Journal of the American Institute of Planners*. Volume 35, Number 4, July 1969, pp. 216–224.

Association of Chief Police Officers (1999). *Secured by Design Standards*. ACPO.

Barclay, G. C., and Taveres, C. (1988). *International Comparisons of Criminal Justice Statistics*. HOSB, Home Office.

Barker, P. (1993). "Street violence for export", *The Guardian*, 4 December p. 25.

Barr, R., and Professor Pease, K. (1990). Crime Placement, Displacement and Deflection. In *Crime and Justice: A Review of Research* (M. Tonry and N. Morris, eds.) Vol. 12. University of Chicago Press.

Beavon, D. J. K., Brantingham, P. L., and Brantingham, P. J. (1994a). The Influence of Street Networks on the Patterning of Property Offences. In *Crime Prevention Studies* (R. V. Clarke, ed.) Vol. 2. Criminal Justice Press.

Beavon, D. J. K., Brantingham, P. L., and Brantingham, P. J. (1994b). Cited in *Crime Prevention Studies* (R. V. Clarke, ed.) Vol. 2. Criminal Justice Press.

Beckford, C., and Cogan, P. (2000). *The Alleygater's Guide to Gating Alleys*. New Scotland Yard. Metropolitan Police.

Beinhart, S., Anderson, B., Lee, S., and Utting, D. (2002). *Communities that Care: Youth at Risk? A National Survey of risk factors, protective factors and problem behaviour among young people in England, Scotland and Wales*. Communities that Care.

Bentley, I. et al. (1985). *Responsive Environments: A Manual for Designers*. Architectural Press Ltd (Reprinted 1987, 1992, 1993).

Birkbeck, D. (2002). *How to Home: Part 1, 7000 Words on Housing*. RIBA.

Bjorklund, E. (ed.) (1995). *Good Nordic Housing*. Nordic Council of Ministers.

Bone, S. (1989). *Safety and Security in Housing Design: A Guide for Action*. Institute of Housing and Royal Institute of British Architects.

Brand, S., and Price, R. (2000). *The Economic and Social Costs of Crime*. Home Office Research Study 217. Home Office Research, Development and Statistics Directorate.

Brantingham, P. J., and Brantingham, P. L. (1981). *Environmental Criminology*. Sage.

Brewerton, J., and David, D. (1997). *Designing Lifetime Homes*. Joseph Rowntree Foundation.

Buchanan, P. (1981). Patterns and Regeneration. *The Architectural Review*. December Volume CLXX, No. 1018, pp. 330–333.

Bullock, K., Moss, K., and Smith, J. (2000). *Anticipating the Legal Implications of s.17 of the Crime and Disorder Act 1998*. Home Office Briefing Note 11/00.

CABE/ODPM (2003). *The Value of Housing Design and Layout*. Thomas Telford.

Calthorpe, P. (1993). *The Next American Metropolis: Ecology, Community and the American Dream*. Princeton Architectural Press.

Camden Police (2003). *Secured by Design in the London Borough of Camden*. Camden Police.

Carvel, J. (2002). "Half of all pupils admit breaking the law" *The Guardian*, 8 April, pp. 1–15.

Castell, B. (Llewellyn Davies), and Levitt, D. (Levitt Bernstein Associates). (2002). *How does the built environment influence crime and what are the barriers to creating safe, sustainable places*. Paper presented to Breaking Down the Barriers Workshop, Blackburn.

CEN (2002). *Committee for European Standardisation. Prevention of Crime – Urban Planning and Design, Part 2: Urban Design and Crime Reduction; Part 3: Dwellings*. CEN/TC325 (in progress).

Chambers, J. (1985). *The English House*. Methuen London Ltd.

Chambers, R. (2002). *Participatory Workshops: A Sourcebook of 21 Sets of Ideas and Activities*. Earthscan Publications Ltd.

City of Toronto (2000). *Toronto Safe City Guide*. City of Toronto Council, Canada.

Clarke, R.V., (ed.) (1992). *Situational Crime Prevention: Successful Case Studies*, Harrow and Heston: Albany, New York.

Clarke, R. V. (ed.) (1997). *Situational Crime Prevention: Successful Case Studies*, Second Edition. Harrow and Heston: Albany, New York.

Clarke, R. V. and Homel, R. (1997). A Revised Classification of Situational Crime Prevention Techniques, in Lab S.P. (ed.), *Crime Prevention at a Crossroads*, Anderson: Cincinnati, Ohio, pp. 17–27.

Clarke, R. V., and Mayhew, P. (1980). *Designing Out Crime*. HMSO, London.

Coleman, A. (1985). *Utopia on Trial: Vision and Reality in Planned Housing*. Hilary Shipman.

Coleman, A. (1990). *Utopia on Trial*, Revised Edition. Hilary Shipman.

Coleman, C., and Moynihan, J. (1996). *Understanding Crime Data: Haunted by the Dark Figure*. Open University Press.

Colquhoun, I. (1995). *Urban Regeneration*. B. T. Batsford.

Colquhoun, I. (1999). *The RIBA Book of 20th Century British Housing*. Architectural Press (Butterworth-Heinemann).

Colquhoun, I., and Fauset, P. G. (1991a). *Housing Design in Practice*. Longman UK.

Colquhoun, I., and Fauset, P. G. (1991b). *Housing Design: An International Perspective*. B. T. Batsford.

Commission for Architecture and the Built Environment (CABE) (2002). *Our Street: Learning to See*, Third Edition. CABE, London.

Commission for Architecture and the Built Environment (CABE) in Partnership with the Department of the Environment, Transport and the Regions (DETR) (2001). *The Value of Urban Design: Executive Summary and the Value of Urban Design*. Full Report. Thomas Telford Ltd.

Commission for Architecture and the Built Environment (CABE) & Office of the Deputy Prime Minister (ODPM) in Association with Design for Homes (2003). *The Value of Housing Design and Layout*. Thames Telford.

Community Development (2001). *Strategic Framework for Community Development*. Standing Conference.

Conservation and Design Service, Development Department, City of Nottingham (1998). *Community Safety in Residential Areas*.

County Surveyors Society (1999). *Code of Good Practice for Street Lighting*. Institution of Lighting Engineers.

Cowan, R. (1992). From Hospital to Housing. *The Architects' Journal*, 15 July 1992, Volume 196, Number 3, pp. 20–23.

Cowan, R. (1997). *The Connected City*. Urban Initiatives.

Cozens, P., Hillier, D., and Prescott, G. (2003). Safety is in the Upkeep. *Regeneration and Renewal* 7 February 2003, p. 4.

Crime Prevention Panel (2002). *Turning the Corner*. Foresight.

Crouch, S., Shaftoe, H., and Fleming, R. (1999). *Design for Secured Residential Environments*. Longman.

Crowe, T. D. (1991). *Crime Prevention Through Environmental Design*. Butterworth-Heinemann.

Crowe, T. (1997). Crime Prevention Through Environmental Design Strategies and Applications, in *Effective Physical Security* (L. J. Fennelly, ed.), Second Edition. Butterworth-Heinemann.

Crowe, T. (2000). *Crime Prevention Through Environmental Design*, Second Edition. Butterworth-Heinemann.

Cullen, G. (1961). *Townscape*. The Architectural Press.

Davey, C. L., Cooper, R. and Press, M. (2001a). *Design Against Crime Case Studies*. The Design Policy Partnership. Salford University/Sheffield Hallam University.

Davey, C. L., Cooper, R., and Press, M. (2001b). *Parrs Wood School: Design Against Crime Case Studies*. The Design Policy Partnership. Salford University/Sheffield Hallam University.

Davis, C. (1988). Maiden Amendments. *The Architectural Review*. November 1988, Volume CLXXXIV, Number 1101, pp. 74–78.

Department of the Environment (DOE) & Department of Transport (DOT) (1977). Design Bulletin 32, *Residential Roads and Footpaths – Layout Considerations*. HMSO.

Department of the Environment (DOE) (1992). Design Bulletin 32, *Residential Roads and Footpaths – Layout Considerations*, Second Edition. HMSO.

Department of the Environment (DOE) (1993). *Crime Prevention on Housing Estates*. HMSO.

Department of the Environment (DOE) (1994a). *Planning Out Crime*. Circular 5/94. HMSO.

Department of the Environment (DOE) (1994b). *Quality in Town and Country*, A Discussion Document, Department of the Environment.

Department of the Environment (DOE), *Planning Out Crime*, Circular 5/94. (Circular 16/94 Welsh Office).

Department of the Environment (DOE now DTLR), *Planning Policy Guidance Notes*, London.

    PPG1: *General Policy and Principles*

    PPG3: *Housing*

    PPG7: *The Countryside: Environmental Quality and Economic and Social Development*

    PPG12: *Development Plans and Regional Guidance*

    PPG13: *Transport*

    PPG15: *Planning and the Historic Environment*

    PPG17: *Planning for Open Space, Sport and Recreation*.

Department of the Environment, Transport and the Regions (DETR) (1988). *Crime and Disorder Act*, Circular 1998. HMSO.

Department of the Environment, Transport and the Regions (DETR) (1998a). *Planning for the Communities of the Future*. DETR.

Department of the Environment, Transport and the Regions (DETR) (1998b). *Places, Streets and Movements: A Companion Guide to Design Bulletin 32: Residential Roads and Footpaths*. DETR.

Department of the Environment, Transport and the Regions (DETR) (1998c). *Planning for Sustainable Development: Towards Better Practice*. HMSO.

Department of the Environment, Transport and the Regions (DETR) (1998d). *The Use of Density in Urban Planning*. DETR.

Department of the Environment, Transport and the Regions (DETR) (1999a). *Revision of Planning Policy Guidance Note 3: Housing*. DETR.

Department of the Environment, Transport and the Regions (DETR) (1999b). *Towards an Urban Renaissance*. Urban Task Force. Final Report. E. & F.N. Spon.

Department of the Environment, Transport and the Regions (DETR) (1999c). *A Better Quality of Life – A Strategy for Sustainable Development in the United Kingdom*. HMSO.

Department of the Environment, Transport and the Regions (DETR) (2000a). *Planning Policy Guidance Note 3: Housing*. DETR.

Department of the Environment, Transport and the Regions (DETR) (2000b). *Our Towns and Cities: The Future: Delivering an Urban Renaissance*, Cm 4911. HMSO.

Department of the Environment, Transport and the Regions and Commission for Architecture in the Built Environment (2000). *By Design, Urban Design in the Planning System: Towards Better Practice*. Thomas Telford Publishing.

Department of Transport, Local Government and the Regions and Commission for Architecture in the Built Environment (DTLR/CABE) (2001). *By Design: Better Places to Live: A Companion Guide to PPG3*. Thomas Telford.

Dijk, A. G. van., and Soomeren, P. van. (1980). *Vandalism in Amsterdam*. Univesiteit Van Amsterdam.

Dillon, M. (2003). Paper to *Improving Safety Through Design: The Liveability Agenda Conference*.

DOCA, Journal of the Designing Out Crime Association (2001). Winter.

Edwards, B., with Hyett, P. (2001). *Rough Guide to Sustainability*. RIBA Publications.

English Partnerships and The Housing Corporation (2000). *Urban Design Compendium*. English Partnerships.

Essex County Council Planning Department (1973). *A Design Guide for Residential Areas*. Essex County Council.

Essex County Council and Essex Planning Officers' Association (1997). *The Essex Design Guide for Residential and Mixed Use Areas*. Essex County Council.

Felson, M., and Clarke, R. V. (1998). *Opportunity makes the Thief: Practical Theory for Crime Prevention*. Police Research Series Paper 98. Home Office Research, Development and Statistics Directorate.

Fennelly, L. J. (ed.) Applications, in *Effective Physical Security*, pp. 35–88, Second Edition. Butterworth-Heinemann.

Foresight Crime Prevention Panel (2002). *Just Around the Corner*. Home Office (www.foresight.gov.uk).

Genre, C. (2002). *Basic Tips on Lighting for CPTED*. International CPTED Association (ICA) Newsletter, February 2002, Volume 5, Issue 1, pp. 3–4.

Gill, T. (2001). Putting Children First. *The Architects' Journal*., Volume 214, Number 11, pp. 38–39.

Government's Crime Reduction Strategy (1990). Home Office Communication Directorate.

Gronlund, B. (2000). *Towards the Humane City for the 21st Century*. Paper presented at the Radberg Seminar, Stockholm.

The Guinness Trust (1996). *Planning and Architecture Guide*. The Guinness Trust.

The Guinness Trust (undated). *Landscape and Design Guide*. The Guinness Trust.

H. M. Government (1999). *A Better Quality of Life, A Strategy for Sustainable Development for the UK*. The Stationery Office.

Hall, P. (1988). *Cities of Tomorrow: An Intellectual History of Urban Planning and Design in the Twentieth Century*. Blackwell.

Hall, P., and Ward, C. (1998). *Sociable Cities*. John Wiley.

Hampshire, R., and Wilkinson, M. (1999). *Youth Shelters and Sports Systems: A Good Practice Guide*. Architectural Liaison: Thames Valley Police.

Harris, R., and Larkham, P. (1999). *Changing Suburbs: Foundation, Form and Function*. E. & F.N. Spon.

Hetherington, P. (1999). "The Dynamic Duo", *The Guardian*, 23 June, pp. 4–5.

Hesselman, T. (2001). *The Dutch Police Labelled Secured Housing® – Politiekeurmerk Veileg Wonen*. Paper presented to the E-DOCA International Conference on Safety and Crime Prevention by Urban Design, Barcelona (The Netherlands National Police Institute).

Hillier, W. (1996). *Space is the Machine*. Cambridge University Press.

Home Office. *Crime Prevention News*, Quarterly.

Home Office (1998). Human Rights Act, Crown Copyright.

Home Office (1998). The Crime and Disorder Act, Crown Copyright.

Home Office (1999). *Government Crime Reduction Strategy*. HMSO.

Home Office Crime Reduction College (2003). *Crime Reduction Basics – Tackling Crime and Anti-Social Behaviour in the Community*. Home Office.

The Housing Corporation. (1998). *Scheme Development Standards*, Third Edition. August 1998.

House Builders Federation (1996). *Families Matter*. HBF.

Housing Development Directorate, Department of the Environment (1981). (HDD) Occasional Paper 1/81. *Reducing Vandalism on Public Housing Estates*. HMSO.

Hulme City Challenge (1994a). *Hulme – A Guide to Development*, Hulme City Challenge.

Hulme Regeneration Ltd (1994b). *Rebuilding the City: A Guide to Development in Hulme*. Hulme Regeneration Ltd.

ICA (2002). *International CPTED Association Newsletter*, February, Volume 5, Issue 1, pp. 1 and 7.

The Institute of Highway Incorporated Engineers (2002). *Home Zone Design Guidelines*. The Institute of Incorporated Engineers.

Jackson, A. (1973). *Semi-Detached London*. Wild Swan.

Jacobs, J. (1961). *The Death and Life of Great American Cities*. Jonathan Cape (Latest edition – Pimlico 2000).

Jeffrey, C. R. (1969). Crime Prevention and Control Through Environmental Engineering. *Criminologica*, 7, 35–58.

Jeffrey, C. R. (1971). *Crime Prevention Through Environmental Design*. Sage Publications.

Jeffrey, C. R. (1977). *Crime Prevention Through Environmental Design*, Second Edition. Sage Publications.

Jeffrey, C. R. (1999). *CPTED: Past, Present and Future*. A Position Paper prepared for the International CPTED Association Conference. September. Ontario, Canada.

Jenks, M., Burton, E., and Williams, K. (1996). *The Compact City, A Sustainable Urban Form?* E. & F.N. Spon.

Johnson, S., and Loxley, C. (2001) *Installing Alley-Gates: Practical Lessons from Burglary Prevention Projects*. Home Office Briefing Note 2/01.

Joseph Rowntree Foundation (1995). *Made to Last: Creating Sustainable Neighbourhoods and Estate Regeneration*. Joseph Rowntree Foundation.

Joseph Rowntree Foundation (1997). *The Safety and the Security Implications of Housing over Shops*. Findings – Housing Research 203.

Journal of the Design Out Crime Association (2001). Winter 2001, p. 10.

Kaplinski, S. (PRP Architects) (2002). *Urban Environment Today*, 24 January, p. 14.

Karn, V., and Sheridan, L. (1998). *Housing Quality: A Practical Guide for Tenants and their Representatives*. Joseph Rowntree Foundation.

Katz, P. (1994). *The New Urbanism: Towards an Architecture of the Community*. McGraw-Hill.

Kelly, P. (1999). The Marquess Estate, *Building Homes*, May, pp. 13–15.

Kershaw, C., Budd, T., Kinshott, G., Mattinson, J., Mayhew, P., and Myhill, A. (2000). *The 2000 British Crime Survey*. Home Office Statistical Bulletin 18/00. Home Office.

Kershaw et al. (2001). *British Crime Survey 2000/01*.

Knights, R., and Pascoe, T. (2000a). *Burglaries Reduced by Cost Effective Target Hardening*. DETR Contract Number cc1675. Building Research Establishment.

Knights, R., and Pascoe, T. (2000b). *Target Hardening: A Cost Effective Solution to Domestic Burglary*. BRE.

Knights, R., Pascoe, T., and Henchley, A. (2002). *Sustainability and Crime*. BRE. *Layout of New Houses*. The Popular Housing Forum.

Knights, R., Pascoe, T., and Henchley, A. (2003). *Sustainability and Crime: Managing and Recognising the Drivers of Crime and Security*. Building Research Establishment (BRE).

Llewellyn-Davies, English Partnerships, The Housing Corporation (2000). *Urban Design Compendium*.

London Planning Advisory Committee (1998). *Sustainable Residential Quality: New Approaches to Urban Living*. LPAC.

Lynch, K. (1960). *The Image of the City*. MIT Press.

Lynch, K. (1981). *A Theory of Good City Form*. MIT Press.

Lynch, K. (1984). *Good City Form*. MIT Press.

Lynch, K. (1990). *The Image of the City*. MIT Press.

Martin, G., and Watkinson, J. (2003). *Rebalancing Communities: Introducing Mixed Incomes into Existing Rented Housing Estates*. Joseph Rowntree Foundation.

Ministry of Health (1949). *Housing Manual*. HMSO.

Minton, A. (2002a). *Building Balanced Communities, the US and UK Compared*. RICS Leading Edge Series, RICS, London.

Minton, A. (2002b). "Utopia Street". *Guardian Society*. 27 March, pp. 10–11.

Moorcock-Ably, K. (2001). "Go Play in the Traffic." *The Architects' Journal*, 27 September, Volume 214, Number 11, pp. 38–39.

Moss, K., and Pease, K. (1999). Crime and Disorder Act 1998: Section 17, "A Wolf in Sheep's Clothing"? *Crime Prevention and Community Safety: An International Journal*, 1, 4, 15–19. Perpetuity Press.

Moss, K. (2001). Crime Prevention v Planning: Section 17 of the Crime and Disorder Act 1988. Is it a Material Consideration? *Crime Prevention and Community Safety: An International Journal*, pp. 43–48. Perpetuity Press.

Moughton, C. (1992). *Urban Design, Street and Square*. Butterworth Architecture.

Muir, H. (2003). "Community that saw off the BNP". *The Guardian*, 27 May, p. 9.

Muthesius, S. (1982). *The English Terraced House*. Yale University Press.

National House Building Council (1988). *Guidance on How the Security of New Homes Can be Improved*. NHBC.

National Housing Federation (1998a). *Car Parking and Social Housing*. National Housing Federation.

National Housing Federation (1998b). *Standards and Quality in Development: A Good Practice Guide*. National Housing Federation.

New Forest District Council (2000). *Supplementary Planning Guidance, Design for Community Safety*.

Newman, O. (1971). *Architectural Design for Crime Prevention*. National Institute of Law Enforcement and Criminal Justice, Law Enforcement Assistance Administration.

Newman, O. (1973a). *Defensible Space: Crime Prevention Through Urban Design*. Macmillan.

Newman, O. (1973b). *Defensible Space: People and Design in the Violent City*. Architectural Press.

Newman, O. (1976). *Design Guidelines for Creating Defensible Space*. National Institute of Law Enforcement and Criminal Justice.

Newman, O. (1981). *Community of Interest*. Anchor Press/Doubleday.

Newman, O. (1996). *Creating Defensible Space*. U.S. Department of Housing and Urban Development, Office of Policy Development and Research.

Nottingham City Council, Conservation of Design Service (1998). *Design Guide: Community Safety in Residential Areas*. Nottingham City Council.

Office of the Deputy Prime Minister (ODPM) (2002a). *Living Places: Cleaner, Safer, Greener*. HMSO.

Office of the Deputy Prime Minister (ODPM) (2002b). *Paving the Way – How we can Achieve Clean, Safe and Attractive Streets*. Thomas Telford.

Oliver, P., Davis, L., and Bentley, I. (1981). *Dunroamin: The Suburban Semi and its Enemies*. Barrie & Jenkins Ltd.

Osborne, S., and Shaftoe, H. (1995). *Successes and Failures in Neighbourhood Crime Prevention*. Safe Neighbourhood Unit, Joseph Rowntree Foundation, Housing Research 149.

Page, D. (1993). *Building for Communities*. Joseph Rowntree Foundation.

Painter, K., and Farrington, D. P. (1997a). The Crime Reducing Effect of Improved Street Lighting: The Dudley Project. In *Situational Crime Prevention: Successful Case Studies* (R. V. Clarke, ed.) Second Edition. Harrow and Heston.

Painter, K., and Farrington, D. P. (1997b). The Dudley Experiment. In *Situational Crime Prevention: Successful Case Studies* (R. V. Clarke, ed.) Second Edition. Harrow and Heston.

Painter, K., and Farrington, D. P. (1999). Street Lighting and Crime: Diffusion of Benefits in the Stoke-on-Trent Project. In *Surveillance of Public Space: CCTV, Street Lighting and Crime Prevention* (K. Painter and N. Tilley, eds.). Criminal Justice Press.

Painter, K. (2003). Ray of Hope. *Regeneration and Renewal*. 24 January 2003, p. 23.

Parker, J. (2001). Reducing crime through Urban Design. *The Journal of the Designing Out Crime Association*, Winter 2001, pp. 16–18.

Parker, B., and Unwin, R. (1901). *The Art of Building a Home – A Collection of Lectures and Illustrations*. Longman, Green and Company.

Pascoe, T. (1992). *Secured by Design – A Crime Prevention Philosophy*. Cranford Institute of Technology, M.Sc. Thesis.

Pascoe, T. (1993a). *Domestic Burglaries: The Burglar's View*. BRE Information Paper 19/93, Building Research Establishment.

Pascoe, T. (1993b). *Domestic Burglaries: The Police View*. BRE Information Paper 20/93, Building Research Establishment.

Pascoe, T. (1999). *Evaluation of Secured by Design in Public Sector Housing*. Building Research Establishment & Department of the Environment, Transport and the Regions.

Pease, K. (1999). *Lighting and Crime*. The Institution of Lighting Engineers.

Power, A. (2000). Social Exclusion. *Royal Society of Arts Journal*, Number 5493, pp. 46–51.

Poyner, B. (1983). *Design against Crime: Beyond Defensible Space*. Butterworth.

Poyner, B., and Webb, B. (1991). *Crime Free Housing*. Butterworth Architecture, pp. 9–21.

PRP Architects (2002). *High Density Housing in Europe, Lesson for London*. East Thames Housing Group, p. 13.

Rapoport, A. (1969). *House Form and Culture*. Prentice-Hall.

Rapoport, A. (1977). *A Human Aspect of Urban Form*. Pergamon Press.

Ravetz, A. (1980). *Remaking Cities*. Croom-Helman.

Rouse, J. (Commission for Architecture and the Built Environment) (2003). *The Importance of Design in Creating Safe Communities*. Paper presented at the Conference "Improving Safety by Design", London.

The Royal Dutch Touring Club (ANWB). (1980). *Woonerf.*

Rudlin, D., and Falk, N. (1995). *21st Century Homes: Building to last*. URBED.

Rudlin, D., and Falk, N. (1999). *Building the 21st Century Home, The Sustainable Urban Neighbourhood*. Architectural Press.

Safe City Committee, Healthy City Office (Whitzman et al.) (1997). *Toronto Safer City Guidelines*. Toronto Community Services, Toronto City Council.

Sanoff, H. (2000). *Community Participation Methods in Design and Planning*. John Wiley & Sons Inc.

Saville, G. (1997). *Displacement: A Problem for CPTED Practitioners*. Paper presented at the second Annual International CPTED Conference, December, Orlando, USA.

Saville, G., and Cleveland, G. (undated). *2nd Generation CPTED: An Antidote to the Social Y2K Virus of Urban Design* (www.ica@cpted.net).

Scarman Centre National CCTV Evaluation Team (2003). *National Evaluation of CCTV; early findings of scheme implementation – effective practice guide*, Home Office Statistical Bulletin 5/03.

Schneider, R. H., and Kitchen, T. (2002). *Planning for Crime Prevention: A Transatlantic Perspective*. Routledge.

Sherlock, H. (1991). *Cities Are Good For Us*. Paladin.

Simmons, J., et al. (2002). *British Crime Survey 2001/2002*.

Social Exclusion Unit (1998). *Bringing Britain Together: A National Strategy for Neighbourhood Renewal*, Cm 4045. HMSO.

Social Exclusion Unit (2000). *National Strategy for Neighbourhood Renewal: A Framework for Consultation*. HMSO.

Social Exclusion Unit (2001). *A New Commitment to Neighbourhood Renewal: National Strategy Action Plan*. HMSO.

Soomeren, P. van. (2001). *Crime Prevention Through Environmental Design: (CPTED) and Designing Out Crime (DOC)*. Paper presented to E-DOCA Conference, Barcelona.

Spring, M. (1998). Whatever Happened to the Millennium Village of the 1970s? *Building*, 6 November 1998.

Steering Group Experiments (1998). Public Housing (SEV) Service Centre. Safe Living (Veilig Wonen), The Police Label Secured Housing® New Estates. *Politiekeurmerk Veilig Wonen® Nieubouw*.

Stollard, P. (ed.) (1991). *Crime Prevention Through Housing Design*.

Stones, A. (1989). Towns, Villages or Just Housing Estates? *Urban Design Quarterly*, January 1989.

Straw, J. (Home Secretary) (2001). *Crime Prevention News*, April/June, p. 8.

Stubbs, D. (Thames Valley Police) (2002). Culs-de-sac and Link Footpaths: Academic Research Foundation. *The Journal of the Designing Out Crime Association* (DOCA). Summer 2002, pp. 11–19.

Summerskill, B. (2001). New Homes Crisis Hits UK Families, *The Observer*, 28 April, p. 1.

Taylor, M. (2000). *Top Down Meets Bottom Up: Neighbourhood Management*. Joseph Rowntree Foundation.

Tilley, N., Pease, K., Hough, M., and Brown, R. (1999). *Burglary Prevention: Early Lessons from the Crime Reduction Programme*. PRCU Research Paper 1. Home Office Research, Development and Statistics Directorate.

Town, S. (1996). *West Yorkshire Police Recommended Standards*. Unpublished paper for West Yorkshire Police.

Town, S. (2001). *Designing Out Crime: Building Safer Communities*. Unpublished paper for West Yorkshire Police.

Unwin, R. (1909). *Town Planning in Practice*. T. Fisher Unwin.

Urban Design Group (2000). *The Community Planning Handbook*. Earthscan.

Urban Renewal Unit/ODPM (2001/02). *Places, People, Prospects*. Neighbourhood Renewal Unit – Annual Review 2001/02.

Urban Task Force (1999). *Towards an Urban Renaissance*. E. & F.N. Spon.

Urban Task Force (2000). *Paying for an Urban Renaissance*. Urban Task Force.

Urban Villages Forum and English Partnerships (1998). *Making Places, A Guide to Good Practice in Undertaking Mixed Development Schemes*. English Partnerships.

Urban Villages Forum (1995). *The Economics of Urban Villages*. Urban Villages Forum.

URBED (1997). The Model Sustainable Urban Neighbourhood. *Sun Dial*, Issue 4, pp. 2–3.

URBED (1998). *Tomorrow: A Peaceful Path to Urban Reform*. Friends of the Earth.

URBED (1999). *New Life for Smaller Towns, A Handbook for Action*. Action for Market Towns.

URBED, MORI, and University of Bristol (1999). *But Would You Live There? Shaping Attitudes to Urban Living*. Urban Task Force.

Wainwright, M. (2002). "Gated Estates Attract the Young", *The Guardian*, 28 November, p. 11.

Wadham, C., and Associates (1998). *Holly Street 1998, Upwardly Mobile*, commissioned by the Hackney Council Comprehensive Estates Initiative.

Wallop, M. (1999). *Breaking the Cycle of Burglaries – The Haarlem Approach*. Paper to the Workshop on European Crime Prevention Initiatives, 22nd Symposium on the International Society of Crime Prevention Practitioners, Pennsylvania, USA.

Ward, D. (2001). "Streets Ahead", *Guardian Society*, 1 August, p. 4.

Warren, F., and Stollard, P. (1988). *Safe as Houses*. Institute of Advanced Architectural Studies. University of York. Working Paper.

Wates, N. (2000). *The Community Planning Handbook*. Earthscan Publications Ltd.

Webb, L. (2003). *The Royds – Bradford*. Paper presented at the Conference, Improving Safety by Design, London.

Webster T. (2003). *A Ray of Hope*. Paper presented to the Improving Safety Through Design Conference, April, London.

Williams, G., and Wood, R. (2001). *Planning and Crime Prevention: Final Report*. Small Scale Research Study to the DETR, Manchester University.

Wines, J. (2000). *Green Architecture*. Taschen.

Wood, E. (1961). *Housing Design: A Social Theory*. Citizens, Housing and Planning Council Inc.

Zelinka, A. (2002a). *How possible is it to create safer, more liveable communities through planning and design*. Paper presented to the Smart Growth Conference, USA.

Zelinka, A. (2002b). *Smart Growth is Crime Prevention*. Paper presented to New Partners for Smart Growth Conference, USA.

www.apc.cpted.org
www.bre.co.uk
www.cabe.org.uk
www.cabinet-office.gov.uk
www.cpted.net
www.crimecheck.co.uk
www.crimereduction.gov.uk
www.crimereduction.gov.uk/active communities27.htm

www.crimereduction.gov.uk/securebydesign12.htm
www.designagainstcrime.org.uk
www.designcouncil.org.uk
www.designforhomes.org
www.detr.gov.uk
www.doca.org.uk
www.dtlr.gov.uk
www.e-doca.net
www.foresight.gov.uk
www.housingcorp.gov.uk
www.homeoffice.gov.uk
www.homeoffice.gov.uk/perg/psdb
www.met.police.uk/camden
www.politiekeurmerk.nl
www.research.linst.ac.uk/dac
www.rudi.net/
www.securedbydesign.com
www.scottish.police.uk
www.spacesyntax.com/housing
www.suzylamplugh.org
www.teachernet.gov.uk/extendedschools
www.wales.gov.uk/crimereduction
www.wales.gov/index/housing

International CPTED Association,
ICA: 439 Queen Alexandra Way SE, Calgary, Alberta, T2J 3P2, Canada. Email: ica@cpted.net Website: www.cpted.net
E – DOCA; European Designing Out Crime Association, CI – DSP – van Dijk, van Soomeren en Partners, van Diemenstraat 374, 1013 CR Amsterdam, The Netherlands.
Email: mail@e-doca.net. Website: www.e-doca.net
UK Chapter: General Secretary: Terry Cocks, Designing Out Crime Association, P.O. Box 355, Staines, Middlesex TW18 4WX, UK. Email: gensec@doca.org.uk; Website: www.doca.org.uk
Asia/Pacific Chapter: International CPTED; Association Asia/Pacific Chapter Inc., P.O. Box 222, Browns Plains, Queensland, 4118 Australia. Email: info@apc.cpted.org Website: www.apc.cpted.org

Index

Ackroyd, Jane, 151
Aldgate Estate, City of London, 27, *28*
Alexander, Christopher, 64–68,
    167–168, 212
Alleygater's Guide, 192
Antisocial behaviour, 16–17
Antisocial behaviour orders, 16, 259
Architectural Liaison Officers (Crime
    Prevention Design Advisers), 198,
    204
Armitage, Dr R, 209
Arnstein, S, 260–261
Australia, *92, 97, 101, 102, 103,*

Bank Top, Blackburn, UK, 8, 9, 202, *9,*
    202, 203
Baxter, Alan, Associates, 133
Beckford, Calvin, 192, 284
Beddington Zero Energy Houses, 239,
    240
Bennett Street Housing, Manchester,
    UK, 48, *53, 54*
Bevan, Aneurin, 238
Brantingham, Patricia and Paul, 43–44,
    56
Bricocoli, Massimo, 270–272
Brief, 76
Brightlands, 281–283
British Crime Survey, 2002, 3–4, 7, 8, 16
Bruntland Report, 238
Buchanan, Peter, 33
Building Image, 40–42, 167

Building Research Establishment,
    (BRE), 56
Byker, Newcastle upon Tyne, UK,
    33–36, *33, 34*

Canada:
    Toronto Safer City Guidelines,
        187–188, 230–233, *232*
Car parking, 48, 67, 129–130, 206, 209,
    266, 268, *130, 131*
CCTV, 169, 184, 189–191, *191*
Child density, 110–112
Children's play, 38, 172, 173–175,
    171–179,
Circular 5/94, *Planning out Crime*, 198
Citizenship, 22
Civic pride, 12
Clarke, Ronald V, 5, 51, 54–55, 56,
    61–63
Cleveland, Gerry, 61–63
Cocks, Terry, 284
Coleman, Alice, 45–51
Commission for Architecture and the
    Built Environment, (CABE) 22,
    200
Community, 237–238
Community:
    Balanced, 239–242
    Definition, 237–238
    Density and sustainability, 247
    Gated, 279
        Brightlands, 281–283

Cromer Street, London, UK, 284–290, *286–287*
of interest, 42
Hulme, Manchester, UK, 241, 242–243, *243–246*
Joined up action, 294
Neighbourhood:
  Management and maintenance, 291–293
  Wardens, 293
  Watch, 293–294
Participation, 122, 171, 260–265
Pattern language, 64–68, 167–168, 212
Safety Action Zones, 258–260
Sustainability, 61, 237–238
Trust, 155
Communities Count, North East/ North Lincolnshire, 25
Community development worker, 274
Community Safety Partnerships, 199, 258, 294
Community Safety Zones, 258–260
Cowan, Robert, 125, *126*
Court layouts, 117–118, *123*
Crawford Square, Pittsburgh, USA, 162–165, *163–165*
Crease Strickland Parkins, Architects, 86–89, 104, 114, 123, 124, 132, 154
Creative Partnerships, 22
Crime:
  Anti–social behaviour, 16–17
  Audit of:
    Banktop, Blackburn, UK, 8, 9, 202
    Bradford, UK, 8
  British Crime Survey 2002, 3–4, 7
  Causes of:
    Social, 8–12
    Economic, 10–11
  CCTV, 169, 184, 189–192, *191*
  CGHP Architects, *285*
  Cost of, 4
  Crime and Disorder Act 1998, 24
  Crime Pattern Analysis, 77, 297
  Cultural aspects, 12, 112
  Design, and, 26–27

  Displacement of, 6–7, 7
  Economic causes, 10
  Fear of, 7–8
  Gating alleys, 192–195, 266, *193, 194, 268*
  Household variations, 4
  International comparison, rates of, 2–3
  Levels of in Britain, 3–4
  Living over the shop, 247–248
  Nature of, 1–2
  Opportunity of, 5–6
  Prevention Design Advisers, 204
  Quality of life and, 24–26
  Regional variations, 4
  Rural, 24
  Situational Crime Prevention, 51, 54–55
  Social causes, 8–12
  Space Syntax Theory, 70–73
  Young people and, 17–22, 38
Crime and Disorder Act, 1998, 24, 198–99
Crime Pattern Analysis, 77, 297
Crime Prevention through Environmental Design, (CPTED) 37, 55–57, 230, 254, 257
  Second Generation (CPTED) 38, 61–63
Crime Walks, 263, 272
Cromer Street, London, 286–290, *286–290*
Crowe, Timothy, D, 56
Crown Street, Glasgow, UK, 155–158, *156, 157*
Cullen, Gordon, 84
Culs–de–sac, 117–122, 229, *118 –121*
Culture:
  Density and, 112
  Twenty–four hour, 12
Cycleways, 152–155,

Darbourne and Darke, 27, 30
Darke, Geoffrey, 27
Decline of urban areas, 8–11

Defensible Space:
  Newman, Oscar, 39–42, *40*
  Principles of, 37, 39–42
  Theory of, 5
Demographics, 11–12
Denmark
  Egebjerggard, Copenhagen, 249–252, *252–254*
  Sibeliusparken, 57–61, *58–61*
  Urban renewal, Copenhagen, 248, *236, 250*
Density 94–112, 226–227
  Child, 110–111
  Culture and 112
  And sustainability, 247–255
Design:
  Access and permeability, 51, 117–128, 158, 266
  Aldgate Estate, Mansell Road, London, UK, 27, *28*
  Bank Top, Blackburn, UK, 8, 202, *9*
  Bennett Street, Manchester, UK, 48, *53, 54*
  Brief, 76
  Building image, 40–42, 167
  Car parking, 48, 67, 129–130, 209, 266, *130, 131*
  CCTV, 169, 184, 189–192, *191*
  Child density, 110–112
  Children's play 173–178, *174–179*
  Court design, 117–118, 121–122, *123, 124*
  Crime and, 26–27
  Crime pattern analysis, 77, 297
  Culs de sac, 117–122, 118–121, 229
  Density and:
    Crime, 98–108
    Culture, 12, 112
    Saleability, 108–109
  Density, form and tenure, 94–109
  Design brief, 76
  Entrances into housing areas/ gateways, 91, 266, *92–96, 269*
  Footpaths and Cycleways, 152–155, *153, 154*
  Gating alleys, 192–195, *193, 194, 268*

Graffiti, designing out, 112, 177, 185–186, 251
Holly Street, London, UK, 133–139, 185, *137, 138*
Home Zones, 139–149, *147, 149*
Juxtaposition of housing and other facilities, 42
Landscaping, 176, 178, 205, *180,*
Legibility, 233
Lighting: 186–189, 205, 209, 303, *187, Cover*
  Design Process, 188–189
  Requirements, 186–187
  Minimum Standards, 187–188
Marquess Road, London, UK, 27–33, 241, *29–32*
Methleys, Leeds, UK, 148–149, *149*
Middleton Hills, Madison, U.S.A. 165–167, *166–167*
New Urbanist Movement, 101, 158–162, 281
  Charter, 158–162
Old Royal Free Square, London, UK, 140, 149–142, *150–152*
Open space, 167–172, *170–172*
Orientation, 87–88, 112
Parks and playgrounds, 38, 173–179, *170–172, 175–179*
Parr's Wood High School, Didsbury, Manchester, UK, 181, *184*
Pattern Language, 64–68, 167–168, 212
Permeability, 51, 122–128, 158, 266, *125–126, 128*
Planning and design process, 75
Principles of (Alice Coleman), 47–48
Roads and footpaths, 67, 115–155, 205
Royds, Bradford, UK, 210, 213, 241, *211–213*
Scale and proportion, 80–83, *85*
Schools, 67, 179–183, 239, 303, 181, *182–184,*
Shutters, 185
Site survey and analysis, 76–77
Smart Growth, 158, 162

Space Syntax Theory, 70–73
Spatial design, 78–93
Stainer Street, Northmoor, Manchester, UK, 146–148, *147*
Street design, 139–146, 160–162
Structure, 86–87
Sustainability, 238–247
Territory, 40–41
Urban Village, 155–158
User requirements, 77–78
Vandalism, designing out, 185–186, 233
Variable Design Features (Alice Coleman), 45–47
Walls and fences, 91–93, *97–107*
Woonerfs, 139, 233, *140–142*
Design for Homes, 108
Design Guidance 197
  Allegater's Guide, 192, *193*
  Circular 5/94, *Planning out Crime*, 198
  Community Safety Partnership, 199, 294
  Crime and Disorder Act 1998, 24, 198–199
  Crime Prevention Through Environmental Design (CPTED), 37, 55–57
    Second Generation (CPTED), 61–63
  Design Bulletin 32, *Residential Roads and Footpaths*, 120
  Department of the Environment, Circular 5/94, *Planning out Crime*, 198
  Dutch Police Labelling, 212–220
  Essex Design Guide, 112, 120–122, 127, 169, 181, 222–227, *120–121, 223–225, 227–229*
  European Prestandard prENV14383: Prevention of Crime, 197, 233–235, 296–303
  Good Practice Guidance in planning out crime, 200–202
  Government Guidance in planning out crime, 200–202
  Local Authority Guidance, 220–230

Nottingham City Council Guide, 169–170, 227–230, *172*
Planning Policy Guidelines, 199–200
  Note No 3, *Housing*, 109, 129, 197–199
  Note No 17, *Planning for Open Space, Sport and Recreation*, 168–169, 200
Police Guidance – *Secured by Design*, 197, 198, 202–209, 287, *207, 208*
Toronto Safer City Guidelines, 170–171, 230–231, *232*
Towards a European Standard, 233–235, 296–303
  Urban planning, 234, 296–301
  Dwellings, 235, 301–303
Design Improvement Controlled Experiment, (DICE), 48–51, *50–54*
Designing Out Crime Associations:
  UK, (DOCA), 56
  European, (E–DOCA), 56
  International, Crime Prevention Through Environmental Design Association (ICA), 56
DICE projects, 48–51
Doorstep (Grimsby) 22, *23*
Dunster, Bill, Architects, 239
Dutch Police Labelling, 212–220
  Principles, 212–213
  Standards, 214
  Urban Planning, 215
  Public Areas, 215–216
  Layout, 216–217
  Success, 217
  De Paerel, Hoorn, 217–220, *218–221*

East London Housing Association, 158
Education in the built environment, 20–22
Edwards, Brian, 247
Egebjerggand, Denmark, 249–253, *252, 254*
Entrances into housing areas/gateways, 91, 266, *92–96, 269*
Erskine, Ralph, 35

Essex Design Guide, 112, 120–122, 169, 222–227, 120, 122, *222*
  2nd Edition, 112, 127, 181, 222–227, *223–225*, *228*, *229*
  Police views of the guide, 224–226
  Developers' and Architects' views, 227
European Prestandard, prENV 14383, 197, 233–235
  Why standardisation is necessary, 233
  Purpose of the standard, 234
  Urban Planning and Crime Reduction, 234–235
  Dwellings, 235

Felson, Marcus, 5
Finland:
  Pikku–Huopalahti, Helsinki, 68, *69–71*
Footpaths, 152–155, *153–154*
Foresight 2002, 11–12, 281–283

Garages, 302
Garden Cities, 117
Gated alleys, 192–195, *193*, *194*, *268*
  In Haarlem, The Netherlands, 192, 195
Gated Communities, 279–281
  Brightlands, 281–283
  Cromer Street, London, UK, 284–290, *286–290*
  In the USA, 279–281
Gated private roads, 281
Gipsyville, Hull, UK, 246
Glasgow, UK, Crown Street, 155–158, 241, *156*, *157*
Globalisation, 12
Good Nordic Housing, 248–249
Good Practice Guidance in Planning out Crime, 200–202
Gracie, Vernon, 35
Graffiti, designing out, 112, 185–186, 251
Great Notley, Essex, UK, 227, *228*, *229*
Gronlund, Professor Bo, 56–57
Guinness Trust, 122, 171, 242

Haarlem, gating alleys, 192, 195
Hillier, Bill, 70–73
Holly Street Regeneration, London, UK, 133–139, *137*, *138*
Homes for Change, Hulme, 242, *245*, *246*
Home Zones, 139
  The Methleys, Chapel Allerton, Leeds, 148–149, *149*
  Stainer Street, Northmoor, Manchester, 146–148, *147*
HOPE VI Programme (USA), 239
Housing:
  Accessibility, 117–128
  Alexander, Christopher, 64–68, 167–168, 212, 259
  Antisocial behaviour, 16–17
  Building image, 40–42, 167
  Child density, 110–111
  Coleman, Alice, 45–51,
  Corporation, 15, 204
  De Paerel, Hoorn, 217–220, *218–220*
  Density:
    Crime and, 98–108
    Culture and, 112, 12
    Saleability, 108109
    Density, Form and Tenure, PPG3, 94–109
  Design:
    Crime and, 26–27
    Denmark: Copenhagen, urban renewal, 249, *236*, *250*
      Egebjerggard, 249–253, *252*, *254*
    Guidance New Housing, 197–236
    Housing and neighbourhood Planning, 75
      Crime pattern analysis, 77
      Principles of, 75
      Site survey and analysis, 76–77
      Spatial design, 78–94
      The brief, 76
      User requirements, 77–78
  Elderly people, housing for, 112–115, 231, *114–115*
  Great Notley, Essex, UK, 227, *228*, *229*

Holly Street, London, UK, 133–139, *137–138*
Hulme, Manchester, UK, 242–243, *243–246*
Investment, lack of, 15
Jacobs, Jane, 38–39, *36*
Joseph Rowntree Foundation, 18, 243–247
Layout design, 88–90, 302, 303
Marquess Road, London, UK, 27–33, 72, *29–32*
Mediation service, 16
Methleys, Leeds, UK, 148–149, *149*
Neighbourhood nuisance, 16
Newman, Oscar, 26, 39–42, *40*
Old Royal Free Square, London, UK, 149–152, *150–152*
Permeability, 122–128, *125, 126, 128*
Planning and Design Process, 75
Policy, 13–17
Poundbury, UK, 82, 130–133, *133–136*
Royds Regeneration, Bradford, UK, 210–212, *211–213*
Scale and proportion, 80–84, *85, 133–134*
Selling social housing, 243–246
Space Syntax Theory, 70–73
Stainer Street, Northmoor, Manchester, UK, 146–148, *147*
Sustainable housing, 248–249
Sustainability, 237–258
Sweden, Malmo, BoO1 Housing, 253–255, *255–257*
Tenure, 15–16
Vandalism, 185–186
Housing Corporation, 15, 204
HRH. Prince Charles, 130, 155
Hulme Redevelopment, Manchester, UK, 242–243, *243–246*
Human Rights Act, 2000

Individuality and independence, 12
Image, 40–42, 167 301
Investment, lack of, 15
Italy:

Milan, 270–272, *273*
Turin, 270–279, *263, 271, 274–279*

Jacobs, Jane, 33–39, 56, *36*
Japan, 3, 83, 212, *83, 96*
Jeffrey, C.R., 55
Joseph Rowntree Foundation, 18, 243–247
Julius, Professor John, 15

Kelly, R., 27
Kings Cross Estate Action Project, 284–290, *286–290*
Kitchen, Professor E, 8, 56

Landscaping, 176–178, 205
Layout of public space, 88–90, 301, 302
Legibility, 233
Leisure, 200
Levitt, Bernstein Architects, 8, 135, 137, 203, 204
Lighting, 186–189, 187, 303, *187, cover*
  Benefits of good lighting, 186
  Canadian experience, 177–188
  Design Process, 188–189
  Requirements, 186–187
Living over the shop, 247–248
Local Strategic Partnerships, 13, 24, 294
London, UK:
  Aldgate Estate, 27, *28*
  Bexley, Slade Green, 258–260, *176, 177, 179, 259*
  Cromer Street, 284–290, *286–290*
  Green Dragon Court, Camden, *285*
  Holly Street, 133–139, *137, 138*
  Marquess Road, 27–33, *29–32*
  Mozart Estate, Westminster, 48, *52*
  Old Royal Free Square, 149–142, *150–152*
  Ranwell Road Estate, Tower Hamlets, 48, *50, 51*
  West Silvertown Urban Village, 149–152, *150–152*

Manchester City Council, 146

Manchester Methodist Housing
    Association, 146
Malpass, J., 57
Marquess Road Estate, Islington,
    London, 27–33, 72, *29–32*
Mayhew, Patricia, 56
Methleys, Leeds, UK, 148–149, *149*
Minton, Anna, 239–241, 279, 281
Monbijougaton Street Housing,
    Malmo, Sweden, 253, *100*
Munday, Barry, PRP Architects, 30

Neighbourhood:
    Joined up action, 294
    Management and maintenance, 291
    Nuisance, 16–17
    Planning and Housing Design, 75
        The brief, 76
        Site survey and analysis, 76–77
        Crime pattern analysis, 77
        User requirements, 77–78
        Spatial design, 78–94
    Renewal, 255–260
    Sustainability, 238
    Wardens, 293
    Watch, 293
Netherlands,
    De Paerel, Hoorn, 217–220, *218–221*
    Haarlem, gating alleys, 192, 195
    Police Labelling, 197, 212–220
    Woonerfs, 139, 140–142
New Deal for Communities, 13,
    257–258
New Earswick, 243–246
New Urbanism, 101, 158, 160–162, 281
Newman, Oscar, 26, 39–42, 56
Northern Ireland, UK:
    Tudor Road renewal, Belfast,
    265–270, *267–270*
Northmoor Home Zone, Manchester,
    UK, 146–148, *147*
Nottingham City Council Guide,
    169–170, 197, 227–230, *172*

Office of the Deputy Prime Minister,
    (ODPM), 115, 220–221

Old Royal Free Square, London, UK,
    140, 149–152, *150–152*
Open space, 167–173, *170–173*
Orientation, 87–88, 112

Painter, Dr K, 186, 189
Parker, Dr J., 77, 186, 190
Parr's Wood High School, Didsbury,
    Manchester, UK, 181, *184*
Participation: 122, 171, 260–265
    Denmark:
        Egebjerggard, 251
    Engaging young people, 19–22, *20,
    21*
    Italy:
        Milan, 270–272
        Turin, 270, 274, 276–277, *263*
    Neighbourhood renewal, 255–260
    New Deal for Communities, 13,
        257–258
    Principles of participation, 260–262
        Levels of, 261
        Purpose of, 261
        Stages of, 262–265
    Tudor Road Renewal, Belfast, UK,
        269–270, *267–270*
Pascoe, Tim, 56, Foreword
Pattern Language, 64–68, 167–168, 212
Peabody Trust, 239
Pease, Ken, 6, 186
Permeability, 51, 117, 122–128, 266
Pikku–Huopalahti, Helsinki, 68, 69–71
Planning Policy Guidance Notes
    (PPG's), 199–200
    PPG3; *Housing*, 97–98, 109, 129, 199
    PPG17: *Planning for Open Space, Sport
    and Leisure*, 168–169, 200
Play, 38, 172, 173–178, *174–179*
Play Areas, 38, 173, 175–179
Police Labelling, Netherlands, 197,
    212–220
Policing, local, 271–272
Pollard Thomas and Edwards, 150,
    frontispiece
Saville, Greg, 61–63

Poundbury, UK, 82, 130–133, 155, *133–136*
Poyner, Barry, 56, 181
Protection from Harassment Act 1997, 16
PRP, Architects, 30, 97, 180

Quality of life, 24–26

Radburn, USA, 117
Radburn housing layouts, 118–119
Ranwell Road Estate, Tower Hamlets, 48, *50, 51*
Rational choice theory, 5, 55
Rational and Routine Activity Theories, 55
Risk Management, 301
Roads and footpaths, 115–155, 205
    Culs–de–sac, 117–122, *118–121*
    Cycleways, 152–155
    Footpaths, 152–155, *153, 154*
    Home Zones, 139–151
    Permeability, 122–128
    Street design, 139
    Tracking, 128–129, *129*
    Woonerfs, 139, 140–142
The Royds, Bradford, 210–212, 241, *211–213*
Rouse, John, (CABE), 200
Routine activities theory, 5, 55
Rudlin, D. and Falk, N. L., 238
Rural crime, 24

Safety Action Zones (Community), 258–260
Saville, Greg, 61–63
Scale and Proportion, 80–84, 85, 133–134
Scheme Development Standards, (Housing Corporation), 204
Schneider Richard, H. and Kitchen, E., 8, 56, 243
Schools, 179–183, 239, 303, *82–184*
    Magnet 239
    Extended, 181
    Shopfront, 67

Secured by Design, 4, 202–210
    Block boundaries, 209
    Car parking, 209
    Cost, 210
    Formal surveillance, 206
    Lighting, 209
    Multi-storey dwellings, 206
    Natural surveillance, 41, 201, 204, 207
    New housing, 205–206
    Public areas, 206–207
    Refurbishment, 206
    Sheltered housing, 206
Selling Council Housing, 243–246
Shopping, local and facilities, 183–185
Shutters, 185
Sibeliusparken, Denmark, 57–61, *58–62*
Simmons et al, 3–4, 7, 8, 16,
Situational Crime Prevention, 51–55
Slade Green, Bexley, London, UK, 258–260, *176, 177, 259*
Smart Growth, 144, 158, 162, 281
Social and economic causes of, 13
Social Exclusion, 13, 256
    Balanced Communities, 112
    Exclusion Unit, 256
Society, changes in, 11–12
Soomeren Paul van, 44, 233
Southern Housing Group, 32
Space Syntax Theory, 70–73
Sport, 168
St Andrew Street, Beverley, *87–89*
Stainer Street, Manchester, UK, 146–148, *147*
Straw, Jack, Home Secretary, 24
Street Design, 139–146, 160–162
Street Lighting, 186–189
Stubbs, D., 127–128
Sustainable Housing, 248–249
Surveillance:
    Natural, 41, 201, 204, 207
    CCTV, 169, 184, 189–192, 207, *191*
    Defensible Space, 5, 37, 39–42, *40*
Sustainable Development, 238

Sustainability:
   Alexander, Christopher, 64–68,
     167–168, 212
   Community and Sustainability,
     237–238
   Community Safety Action Zones
     (CSAZ), 258–260
   Density and Mixed Use, 247
   Housing, 248–249
     Denmark, Egebjerggard, 249–253,
       252–254
     Sweden, Malmo, 253–255, *255–257*
   Participation, 260
     Principles, 260–262
     Practice in, 265–279, 263
     Stages of, 262–265
   Regeneration, 120
     Neighbourhood Renewal, 255–260
     New Deal for Communities, 13,
       257–258
Sweden:
   Bo01, Malmo, 253–255, *255–257*
   Monbijougaten Street housing, 253,
     100

Taylor, David, 133
Territoriality, 301
Thatcher, Margaret, 45
Toronto, Canada, 170–171, 187–188,
   197, 230–233, *232*
Tracking, 128–129, 133, *129*
Tudor Road Renewal, Belfast,
   Northern Ireland, UK, 265–270,
   267–270
Twenty–four hour culture, 12

United Kingdom,
   Belfast, Tudor Road Renewal,
     265–270, *267–270*
   Beverley, East Yorkshire, St Andrew
     Street, *87–89*
   Blackburn, Bank Top, 8, 42–43, 202,
     9, 203, 204
   Bradford, 8
     The Royds, 210–212, 241, *211–213*

Dorchester, Dorset, Poundbury, 82,
   162–165, *163, 164*
Essex, Great Notley, 227, *228, 229*
Glasgow, Crown Street, 155–158,
   156–157
Hull, Gypsyville, 246
Leeds, Methleys, 148–149, *149*
London:
   Aldgate Estate, 27, *28*
   Bexley, Slade Green, 258–260, *176,*
     177, 259
   Cromer Street, 284–290, *286–290*
   Green Dragon Court, Camden,
     285
   Holly Street, 133–139, *137, 138*
   Marquess Road, Islington, 27–33,
     72, *29–32*
   Mozart Estate, Westminster, 48,
     50
   Old Royal Free Square, 140,
     149–152, *150–152*
   Ranwell Road Estate, Tower
     Hamlets, 48, *51*
Manchester:
   Bennett Street, 48, *53, 54*
   Hulme Redevelopment, 242–243,
     243–246
   Northmoor, Stainer Street,
     146–148, *147*
   Parr's Wood High School, 181,
     184
Newcastle upon Tyne, Byker, 33–35,
   33, 34
Urban planning and crime reduction,
   215
Urban Renewal, Copenhagen, 249, *250*
   236
Urban Task Force, 247
Urban Villages, 155–158
USA,
   Middleton Hills, Madison, 165–167,
     166, 167
   New Urbanism, 101, 158, 160–162,
     281
   Pittsburgh, Crawford Square,
     162–165, *163,164*

Radburn Housing, 117
Regeneration of inner city
  neighbourhoods, 14–15
Smart Growth, 144, 158, 162, 281

Vandalism, designing out, 185–186, 232

Waldhor, Ivo, 253
Walls and fences, 91–93, *97–107*
Webb, Seeger Moorhouse, 210
West Silvertown Urban Village,
  London, UK, 158, 159–161
Wood, Elizabeth, 38
Woonerfs, 139, 140–142, 233
  In Germany, 139, 143, 144
Wright, Frank L., 167

Young people
  Anti–social behaviour, 16–17
  Crime and, 17–19

Education in the built environment,
  20–22
Engaging of, 19–20
European Standard, (Appendix),
  School Youth Facilities, 303
Joseph Rowntree Foundation, survey,
  18–19
Neighbourhood nuisance, 16–17
Participation, 260–265
Schools/Youth Facilities, 303
Tudor Road Project, Belfast, UK,
  265–270, 267–270
Youthbuild, 22, *23*
Youth clubs, 19, 67
Youth crime, 17–19
Youth shelters, 19, 174, 259, *179*
Wood, Elizabeth, 38
Youth facilities 119, 303
Youth shelters, 19, 174, 259, *179*

Zelinka, A., 17, 99–101, 162, 165